Inside Government and Parliament

How do they work?

by
Sandra Royle

2

First edition, 2013

Published by Fresh03 Publications
193A St Davids Road North
Lytham St Annes
FY8 2JS

ISBN 978-0-9926011-6-4

Designed and typeset by Fresh03 Publications

The author and publisher are grateful to the following for permission to reproduce copyright material in this book: © Crown copyright.

Re-used under the terms of the Open Government Licence 1.0
http://www.nationalarchives.gov.uk/doc/open-government-licence/open-government-licence.htm

Every effort has been made to contact the copyright holders and we apologise if any have been overlooked. Should copyright have been unwittingly infringed in this book, the owners should contact the publishers, who will make corrections at reprint

Contents

FOREWORD

Inside Government and Parliament

People sometimes confuse Parliament and government. Both have important powers, but each is responsible for different areas of our democracy.

Government: running the country

The government is in charge of managing the country and deciding how our taxes are spent. Different government departments run different things. For example, there is a department in charge of health and another in charge of transport.

Led by the Prime Minister, the UK government is formed by the political party (or coalition of parties) with the greatest representation in the House of Commons. The Prime Minister selects a team of MPs and members of the House of Lords to help run the country.

He or she doesn't select every member of the Commons or Lords to join the government. All the other MPs and members of the House of Lords carry out the work of Parliament.

Parliament: lawmaking ... and more

Parliament doesn't get into the business of running the country, but it is responsible for approving and changing the country's laws. Most new laws presented to Parliament are suggested by the government. To pass a new law both the House of Commons and the House of Lords must agree it is a good idea.

Members of Parliament are also responsible for keeping an eye on the work of the government, to make sure it's doing a good job. For example, members of both the Commons and the Lords will look at how the government is spending the money it receives from people when they pay tax.

How government works

In the UK, the Prime Minister leads the government with the support of the cabinet and ministers. You can find out *who runs government* and *how government is run*, as well as learning about the *history of government.*

Who runs government?

The Prime Minister

The Prime Minister is head of the UK government. He is ultimately responsible for all policy and decisions. He:
- oversees the operation of the Civil Service and government agencies
- appoints members of the government
- is the principal government figure in the House of Commons

The Prime Minister is David Cameron MP and he is based at Number 10 Downing Street in London.

Prime Minister's Office, 10 Downing Street

Meet the Prime Minister

David Cameron became Prime Minister after the General Election in May 2010. He was elected Leader of the Conservative Party in December 2005.

Biography

David Cameron became Prime Minister in May 2010, leading a Conservative and Liberal Democrat coalition government. He has been the Conservative MP for Witney in West Oxfordshire since 2001.

Education

David studied at Eton College before graduating from Oxford University with a first class degree in politics, philosophy and economics.

Political career

Before being elected as an MP, David worked for the Conservative Party Research Department and then as a special adviser in government, first to the Chancellor of the Exchequer and then to the Home Secretary.

In Parliament he held a number of positions on the Opposition Front Bench, including Shadow Deputy Leader of the House of Commons, Front Bench Spokesman for Local Government Finance, and Head of Policy Co-ordination in the run-up to the 2005 General Election. He was also a member of the influential House of Commons Home Affairs Select Committee from 2001 to 2003.

He was appointed Shadow Secretary of State for Education and Skills after the 2005 General Election and, on a mandate to change and modernise the Party, he was elected Leader of the Conservative Party in December 2005.

In 2010 the Conservative Party and Liberal Democrats formed a coalition government. David became Prime Minister, making him the youngest Prime Minister in 198 years.

Career outside politics

David spent 7 years at Carlton Communications where he served on the management board.

Personal life

David is married to Samantha. They have 3 children and live in London and West Oxfordshire. Sadly, their eldest child, Ivan, who suffered from cerebral palsy and severe epilepsy, died in February 2009.

The Prime Minister is head of the UK government and is ultimately responsible for the policy and decisions of the government.

As head of the UK government the Prime Minister also:

- oversees the operation of the Civil Service and government agencies
- appoints members of the government
- is the principal government figure in the House of Commons

Minister for the Civil Service

The Minister for the Civil Service is responsible for regulating the Civil Service.

The Civil Service (Management Functions) Act of 1992 allows the Minister for the Civil Service to delegate power to other ministers and devolved administrations.

This role was created in 1968 and is always held by the Prime Minister.

First Lord of the Treasury

The First Lord of the Treasury is one of the Lords Commissioners of the Treasury. This role is usually held by the Prime Minister.

Since the 17th century, the Lords Commissioners of the Treasury have collectively carried out duties that were previously held by the Lord High Treasurer (head of Her Majesty's Treasury).

The Lords Commissioners of the Treasury also include:

- the Second Lord of the Treasury - the Chancellor of the Exchequer, who has most of the functional financial responsibilities

Junior Lords Commissioners of the Treasury - other members of the government, usually government whips in the House of Commons

10 Downing Street is the official residence of the First Lord of the Treasury, and not of the Prime Minister.

The coalition

David Cameron leads a Conservative / Liberal Democrat coalition. He chairs Cabinet, which meets in 10 Downing Street.

Behind the black door

275 years of history is behind the famous black door of 10 Downing Street. Learn about past events and take a tour through the office and official home of the Prime Minister.

History

10 Downing Street

10 Downing Street, the locale of British Prime ministers since 1735, vies with the White House as being the most important political building anywhere in the world in the modern era. Behind its black door have been taken the most important decisions affecting Britain for the last 275 years.

In the 20th century alone, the First and Second World Wars were directed from within it, as were the key decisions about the end of the empire, the building of the British nuclear bomb, the handling of economic crises from the Great Depression in 1929 to the great recession of today, and the building up of the welfare state.

Some of the most famous political figures of modern history have lived and worked in Number 10, including Robert Walpole, Pitt the Younger, Benjamin Disraeli, William Gladstone, David Lloyd George, Winston Churchill and Margaret Thatcher.

Number 10 have 3 overlapping functions. It is the official residence of the British Prime Minister: it is their office, and it is also the place where the Prime Minister entertains guests from Her Majesty The Queen to presidents of the United States and other world leaders. The Prime Minister hosts countless receptions and events for a whole range of British and overseas guests, with charitable receptions high up the list.

The building is much larger than it appears from its frontage. The hall with the chequered floor immediately behind the front door lets on to a warren of rooms and staircases. The house in Downing Street was joined to a more spacious and elegant building behind it in the late 18th century. Number 10 has also spread itself out to the left of the front door, and has taken over much of 12 Downing Street, which is accessed by a corridor that runs through 11 Downing Street – the official residence of the Chancellor of the Exchequer.

Origins and early inhabitants

The area around Downing Street was home to ancient Roman, Anglo-Saxon and Norman settlements, and was already a prestigious centre of government 1,000 years ago.

The Romans first came to Britain under the command of Julius Caesar in 55 BC. Making their capital at Londinium downriver, the Romans chose Thorney Island – a marshy piece of land lying between two branches of the river Tyburn that flowed from Hampstead Heath to the Thames – as the site for their early settlement.

These Roman settlements, and those of the Anglo-Saxons and Normans, who supplanted them, were not very successful. The area was prone to plague and its inhabitants were very poor. A charter granted by the Mercian King Offa in the year 785 refers to "the terrible place called Thorney Island". It took royal patronage to give the area prestige. King Canute (reigned 1017 to 1035) built a palace in the area, and Edward the Confessor (reigned 1042 to 1066) and William the Conqueror (reigned 1066 to 1087) maintained a royal presence there. The position of Westminster (as the area became known) as the centre of government and the church was solidified following the construction of the great abbey nearby, on William's orders.

The earliest building known to have stood on the site of Downing Street was the Axe brewery owned by the Abbey of Abingdon in the Middle Ages. By the early 1500s, it had fallen into disuse.

Henry VIII (reigned 1509 to 1547) developed Westminster's importance further by building an extravagant royal residence there.

Whitehall Palace was created when Henry VIII confiscated York House from Cardinal Wolsey in 1530 and extended the complex. Today's Downing Street is located on the edge of the Palace site.

The huge residence included tennis courts, a tiltyard for jousting, a bowling green, and a cockpit for bird fights. Stretching from St James's Park to the Thames, it was the official residence of Tudor and Stuart monarchs until it was destroyed by fire in 1698. It made the surrounding real estate some of the most important and valuable in London – and the natural home of power.

The first domestic house known to have been built on the site of Number 10 was a large building leased to Sir Thomas Knyvet in 1581 by Queen Elizabeth I (reigned 1558 to 1603). He was one of the Queen's favourites and was an MP for Thetford as well as a justice of the peace for Westminster. His claim to fame was the arrest of Guy Fawkes for his role in the gunpowder plot of 1605. He was knighted in 1604 by Elizabeth's successor, King James I (reigned 1603 to 1625), and the house was extended.

After the death of Sir Knyvet and his wife, the house passed to their niece, Elizabeth Hampden, who continued to live there for the next 40 years.

The middle of the 17th century was a period of political upheaval and Mrs Hampden's family was right in the middle of it. Her son, John Hampden, was one of the MPs who opposed King Charles I (reigned 1625 to 1649), and Oliver Cromwell, the Lord Protector, was Mrs Hampden's nephew.

Hampden House, as it was then known, gave Mrs Hampden a prime view of the tumultuous events during the Civil War and the Commonwealth and the early years of the Restoration.

The execution of Charles I in 1649 took place on a scaffold in front of Banqueting House in Whitehall, within earshot of the house. Mrs Hampden was still living there when King Charles II (reigned in Scotland from 1649 to 1685) was restored to the English throne in 1660.

The Parliamentary Commissioners, who took over Crown lands during the time of the Commonwealth, described the house in 1650:

"Built part of Bricke and part with Tymber and Flemish qalle and covered with Tyle, consistinge of a Large and spacious hall, wainscoted round, well lighted, and Paved with brick Pavements, two parls wherof one is Wainscoted round from the seelinge to ye floor, one Buttery, one seller, one Large kitchen well paved with stone and well fitted and Joynted and well fitted with dresser boards…

And above stayres in the first story one large and spacious dyneinge Roome, Wainscoted round from the seelinge to the floore, well flored, Lighted and seeled, and fitted with a faire Chimney with a foote pace of paynted Tyle in the same. Also 6 more Roomes and 3 Closetts in the same flore all well lighted and seeled. And in the second story 4 garretts…"

The emergence of Downing Street

George Downing gave his name to the most famous street in the world. It is unfortunate that he was such an unpleasant man. Able as a diplomat and a government administrator, he was miserly and at times brutal.

However, George Downing was responsible for the street, its name and the building we know today. A former diplomat at The Hague serving the Commonwealth, he changed allegiance with finesse. He traded enough secrets to gain a royal pardon in March 1660 and, by the Restoration in May 1660, to be rewarded with a knighthood.

Interested in power and money, he saw an opportunity to make his fortune in property. He had already gained the Crown interest in the land around Hampden House, but could not take possession as it was under lease to Knyvet's descendants. In 1682 he secured the leases to the property and employed Sir Christopher Wren to design the houses.

Between 1682 and 1684, existing properties were pulled down and in their place a cul-de-sac of 15 to 20 terraced houses was built along the north side of the new street, Downing Street. In order to maximise profit, the houses were cheaply built, with poor foundations for the boggy ground. Instead of neat brick façades, they had mortar lines drawn on to give the appearance of evenly spaced bricks. In the 20th Century, Prime Minister Winston Churchill wrote that Number 10 was:

Shaky and lightly built by the profiteering contractor whose name they bear.

A rather important neighbour complained, however. The new houses were built directly behind a large and impressive house overlooking Horse Guards. Its occupier, the Countess of Lichfield, daughter of Charles II, was less than pleased with the emergence of the unwelcome terrace behind. She complained to her father, who wrote back with advice:

I think that it is a very reasonable thing that other houses should not look into your house without permission, and this note will be sufficient for Mr Surveyor to build up your wall as high as you please

The original numbering of the Downing Street houses was completely different from what we see today. The sequence of numbers was haphazard, and the houses tended to be known by the name or title of their occupants. The current Number 10 started out life as Number 5, and were not renumbered until 1779.

The Downing Street house had several distinguished residents. The Countess of Yarmouth lived at Number 10 between 1688 and 1689, and was followed by Lord Lansdowne from 1692 to 1696 and the Earl of Grantham from 1699 to 1703. The last private resident of Downing's terrace was one Mr Chicken. Little is known about him except that he moved out in the early 1730s.

King George II presented both the house on Downing Street and the house overlooking Horse Guards to Sir Robert Walpole, who held the title First Lord of the Treasury and effectively served as the first Prime Minister. Walpole refused the property as a personal gift. Instead, he asked the king to make it available as an official residence to him and to future First Lords of the Treasury – starting the tradition that continues today. The brass letterbox on the black front door is still engraved with this title.

Walpole took up residence on 22 September 1735, once the townhouse on Downing Street and the house overlooking Horse Guards had been joined together and completely refurbished. Walpole employed architect William Kent – who had already worked on Walpole's Norfolk home, Houghton Hall – to undertake the work.

Kent carried out extensive work on the 2 houses, connecting them on 2 storeys. The main entrance now faced onto Downing Street rather than towards Horse Guards and the Downing Street building became a passageway to the main house. At the back of the house, where the Walpoles lived, Kent created grand new rooms suitable for receiving important guests, and built an unusual, 3-sided staircase. It is still one of the most impressive features of the building.

Walpole used the ground floor for business, taking the largest room, on the north-west side of the house, as his study. This is now the Cabinet Room. Upstairs on the first floor, the Walpoles lived in the rooms facing onto Horse Guards Parade. Lady Walpole used today's White Drawing Room as her sitting room, and the present day Terracotta Room served as their dining room. The Walpoles were soon entertaining important guests in their smart house, including George II's wife Queen Caroline, politicians, writers and soldiers. Number 10 became – as it continues to be today – a place for politics and entertainment.

Pelham to Pitt

When Walpole left Downing Street in 1742, it was over 20 years before another First Lord of the Treasury moved in. His successors saw the house as a perk of the job, and Prime Ministers Henry Pelham (1743 to 1754) and the Duke of Newcastle (1757 to 1762) preferred to live in their own residences.

In 1763 George Grenville (1763 to 1765) took up residence but was sacked by King George III in 1765 for imposing stamp duty on the American colonies. The next Prime Minister to move into Downing Street was Lord North (1770 to 1782). He was very fond of the house and often entertained there. Visitors included the writer Samuel Johnson and Thomas Hansard, founder of the parliamentary reporting system that is still in use today. One guest, Clive of India, was so popular that furniture was made for him, which is still present today in the first floor anteroom and Terracotta Room.

During one memorable dinner party held by Lord North on 7 June 1780, civil unrest broke out in the street outside when angry Protestants unhappy with North's policy towards Roman Catholics rioted all over London, in what became known as the Gordon Riots. The Grenadier Guards held off a large mob, a situation that might have ended with bloodshed had North not gone outside to warn the protestors of the dangers of being shot, following which the crowd dispersed. North's dinner guests climbed to the top of the house to view the fires burning all over London.

Major improvements were made to the house during North's time, including the addition of many distinctive features: the black and white chequerboard floor in the entrance hall, the lamp above the front door and the famous lion's head door knocker.

Following the loss of the American colonies North resigned and was followed by the Duke of Portland, who was Prime Minister for only 9 months in 1782.

Fall and rise of Number 10

At the turn of the 19th century, Downing Street had fallen on hard times. Although Number 10 continued to serve as the Prime Minister's office, it was not favoured as a home. Most Prime ministers preferred to live in their own townhouses.

But by the 1820s, Downing Street had emerged as the centre of government. Prime Minister Viscount Goderich employed the brilliant, quirky architect Sir John Soane, designer of the Bank of England, to make the house more suitable for its high-profile role. Soane created the wood-panelled State Dining Room and the Small Dining Room for elegant entertaining.

But this wasn't good enough for his successor, Lord Wellington, who only moved in while his own lavish home, Apsley House, was being refurbished. Later leaders such as Lord Melbourne and Viscount Palmerston used Number 10 only as an office and for Cabinet meetings. In 1828, Number 11 became the Chancellor of the Exchequer's official residence, but the surrounding area was becoming seedier, with brothels and gin parlours multiplying. Things became so bad that by 1839 there were plans to demolish Number 10 and the other buildings on the north side of Downing Street to make way for a remodelled Whitehall.

Security also became an issue. In 1842, Edward Drummond, secretary to Prime Minister Robert Peel (1841-1846), was murdered in Whitehall on his way back to his home in Downing Street by an assassin who mistook him for Peel. The prestige of Downing Street was reduced even further by the building of the magnificent new Foreign Office building at the end of the 1860s. George Gilbert Scott's creation, with a huge open court and elaborate staterooms, dwarfed Number 10 opposite. It even had its own Cabinet Room in which the Cabinet sometimes met, rather than at Number 10.

By the time Benjamin Disraeli became Prime Minister, the house was in poor shape. The living quarters had not been used for 30 years and Disraeli described it as "dingy and decaying". It was time for modernisation.

The late 19th and early 20th century saw 10 Downing Street transformed from a humble terraced house into a grand residence with modern facilities – a home and office fit for the most powerful politician in the country. Disraeli persuaded the state to pay for renovation to the entrance halls and public rooms, though he paid for the refurbishment of the private rooms himself. His own first floor bedroom and dressing rooms were improved, and a bath with hot and cold water in the First Lord's Dressing Room was installed for the sum of £150.3s.6d.

When William Gladstone moved into the house for the first time in 1880, he insisted on redecorating, spending £1,555.5s.0d – an enormous sum for the time – on furniture. During his occupancy in 1884, electric lighting was fitted and the first telephones were installed.

The Marquess of Salisbury, who succeeded Gladstone on one occasion, was the last Prime Minister not to live at Number 10. Salisbury never liked the Cabinet Room, describing it as a "cramped close room". Preferring to work in the larger Cabinet Room in the Foreign Office and live in Arlington Street, he offered Number 10 to his nephew, Arthur Balfour, who would later become Prime Minister himself. Balfour was the first inhabitant of Number 10 to bring a motor car to Downing Street.

Over the years, more and more changes and improvements were made to the house. When Prime Minister Ramsay MacDonald first entered the house, he wanted Number 10 to regain some of the grandeur it had during the times of Walpole and Pitt. Missing a proper library (or at least, one containing more than just Hansard reports), MacDonald set about creating one. He started the Prime Minister's Library, originally housed in the Cabinet Room. The custom of the Prime Minister and other ministers donating books to the library continues to this day. Central heating was installed in 1937 and work began to convert the labyrinth of rooms in the attic, which had formerly been used by servants, into a flat for the Prime Minister.

Number 10 at war

World War One

In 1912, Herbert Henry Asquith found himself at odds with Ulster and the Tory opposition following renewed attempts to introduce Irish Home Rule. This unrest and fierce opposition would continue, and civil war in Ireland was only averted with the outbreak of the First World War in August 1914.

The Cabinet Room at Number 10 was the nerve centre of Britain's war effort. Asquith's Cabinet included future Prime Ministers David Lloyd George and Winston Churchill, in their posts as Chancellor and First Lord of the Admiralty respectively. Asquith had been forced to take on the additional role of Secretary of State for War following the resignation of the incumbent in March 1914, but quickly appointed Lord Kitchener following the outbreak of war.

On 16 April 1915, Number 10 was the site of a meeting between General Haig, Commander-in-Chief of British forces in France, and the Cabinet to go over the detail of the planned Somme offensive, later known as the Battle of the Somme.

During a Cabinet split on 25 May 1915 (caused by public outcry at allegations the army had been under-supplied with shells and the failed offensive in the Dardanelles, for which Kitchener and Churchill respectively were blamed), Kitchener was stripped of his control over munitions and strategy, and Churchill lost his post as First Lord of the Admiralty. As a result of the split, Asquith formed a coalition government with the opposition Conservatives, whose leader was future Prime Minister, Andrew Bonar Law.

Asquith remained leader of the coalition until his resignation on 5 December 1916. After Andrew Bonar Law refused to form a government, David Lloyd George became leader of the coalition and Prime Minister on 7 December 1916.

Under Prime Minister Lloyd George the number of staff at Number 10 expanded and offices spilled out into the garden to cope with the demands of the administration of the war.

Lloyd George immediately formed his 'War Cabinet', whose members included Lord Curzon, Bonar Law and Arthur Henderson. In the first 235 days of its existence, the War Cabinet met 200 times.

This cabinet took total responsibility for the war, and on 3 occasions it sat as the Imperial War Cabinet when Prime ministers from the Dominions attended. It provided vigour previously lacking from the war effort.

Highly able young men were appointed to collect and collate data and to bypass slow moving government departments. These men were nicknamed the 'Garden Suburb' because they lived in huts at the end of gardens near to Downing Street. They were not liked by die-hard civil servants, which they continually bypassed. However, the men from the Garden Suburb gave Lloyd George the one thing Asquith seemingly never had – up-to-date, meaningful statistics. Their work was invaluable, providing the War Cabinet with data on merchant ships sunk and UK farm production, issues essential to address if the country was not to be starved into defeat.

When armistice was finally declared on 11 November 1918, crowds thronged Downing Street chanting 'LG'. Lloyd George made an appearance at one of the first floor windows to acknowledge them.

World War Two – Chamberlain

During the 1930s the world's eyes rested on Europe. With rising tensions between Germany and Czechoslovakia, the Prime ministers of France and Britain did what they could in an attempt to avoid another war. On 12 September 1938, thousands gathered at Downing Street to listen to Hitler's speech on the final night of the Nuremberg Rally convinced Britain stood on the brink of war.

As tension mounted further in Europe, Prime Minister Neville Chamberlain made several attempts to appease the situation, and Number 10 became the focus of international attention. On the morning of 29 September 1938, Chamberlain travelled to Germany for the final time as Prime Minister to hold talks with the French Prime Minister Édouard Daladier, Hitler, and Mussolini.

The Munich Agreement was signed and war – for now – had been averted. Before leaving for England, Chamberlain held a private meeting with Hitler where he obtained his signature on the famous "Peace in our Time" document, which declared that any future disputes between Britain and Germany would be settled peacefully.

Upon Chamberlain's return to Heston Airfield, he was mobbed by large crowds and gave the resounding "Peace in Our Time" speech, waving aloft the document signed by Hitler.

When he returned to Downing Street following a meeting with George VI, the Prime Minister found Downing Street and Number 10 itself packed with people. Chamberlain gave the speech a second time, from a first floor window of Number 10:

My good friends, this is the second time there has come back from Germany to Downing Street peace with honour. I believe it is peace for our time. We thank you from the bottom of our hearts. Now I recommend you go home, and sleep quietly in your beds.

But over the following 12 months tension did not lift, and on 3 September 1939, Chamberlain broadcast to the nation from the Cabinet Room at Number 10, announcing that the country was now at war with Germany. Chamberlain resigned as Prime Minister on 10 May 1940 and advised King George VI to ask Winston Churchill to form a government.

When Winston Churchill replaced Chamberlain as Prime Minister, he and his wife moved into Downing Street's second-floor flat, where Churchill did much of his work.

He often dictated speeches, memos and letters to his secretary while lying propped up in bed in the morning or late in the evening, cigar in hand.

By October 1940, the intense bombing period known as the Blitz began. On 14 October, a huge bomb fell on Treasury Green near Downing Street, damaging the Number 10 kitchen and state rooms, and killing three Civil Servants doing Home Guard duty. Churchill was dining in the Garden Rooms when the air raid began. As he recalled in his memoir Their Finest Hour (1949):

We were dining in the garden-room of Number 10 when the usual night raid began. The steel shutters had been closed. Several loud explosions occurred around us at no great distance, and presently a bomb fell, perhaps a hundred yards away, on the Horse Guards Parade, making a great deal of noise.

Suddenly I had a provincial impulse. The kitchen in Number 10 Downing Street is lofty and spacious, and looks out through a large plate-glass window about 25 feet high. The butler and parlour maid continued to serve the dinner with complete detachment, but I became acutely aware of this big window. I got up abruptly, went into the kitchen, told the butler to put the dinner on the hot plate in the dining-room, and ordered the cook and the other servants into the shelter, such as it was.

I had been seated again at the table only about 3 minutes when a really loud crash, close at hand, and a violent shock showed that the house had been struck. My detective came into the room and said much damage had been done. The kitchen, the pantry and the offices on the Treasury were shattered.

Keeping Downing Street safe became the priority of the Prime Minister and the War Cabinet. Steel reinforcement was added to the Garden Rooms, and heavy metal shutters were fixed over windows as protection from bombing raids. The Garden Rooms included a small dining room, bedroom and a meeting area, which were used by Churchill throughout the war. In reality, though, the steel reinforcement would not have protected him against a direct hit.

In October 1939, the Cabinet had moved out of Number 10 and into secret underground war rooms in the basement of the Office of Works opposite the Foreign Office, today's Churchill War Rooms.

Following near misses by bombs, in 1940, Churchill and his wife moved out of Downing Street and into the Number 10 Annex above the war rooms. Furniture and valuables were removed from Number 10 and only the Garden Rooms, Cabinet Room and Private Secretaries' office remained in use.

Churchill disliked living in the Annex and, despite it being almost empty, he continued to use Number 10 for working and eating.

A reinforced shelter was constructed under the house for up to 6 people, for use by those working in the house. Even George VI sought shelter there when he dined with Churchill in the Garden Rooms. Although bombs caused further damage to Number 10, there were no direct hits to the house, allowing Churchill to continue to work and eat there right up until the end of the war.

As soon as war was over, Churchill and his wife moved back to Number 10, where he made his Victory in Europe (VE) Day broadcast, which was delivered from the Cabinet Room at 3pm on 8 May 1945.

Falklands Conflict – Margaret Thatcher

On 19 March 1982, the Argentinian flag was raised by a group of scrap metal merchants on the island of South Georgia, a British overseas territory and dependant of the Falkland Islands. There had been a lengthy dispute between Argentina and the United Kingdom over the sovereignty of the Islands and this action was seen as a precursor to the Argentinian invasion, which would follow.

Argentine General Leopoldo Galtieri ordered the invasion of the Falklands to be brought forward to 2 April 1982, pre-empting any reinforcement of the United Kingdom's military presence in the area. Margaret Thatcher responded by sending a naval task force to recapture the islands, which set sail from Portsmouth on 5 April following a meeting of the Cabinet and the granting of a UN Resolution.

The Prime Minister stayed up all night in the Downing Street flat for the entire Falklands conflict. Margaret Thatcher's personal assistant, Cynthia Crawford, who moved into the flat at Number 10 to keep the Prime Minister Company during the all-night vigils, recalls the 74 days of the conflict inside Number 10:

She did not once change into her night-clothes in the flat for the duration of the war. We would sit in the flat listening to the BBC World Service for news of the task force. She couldn't sleep because she wanted to be ready in case anything happened.

She wanted to be able to go to any briefings with the naval commanders at any time without the fuss and bother of having to get dressed. She also wanted to know everything that was happening, every single detail, so she could keep on top of events. She had to know how the soldiers, sailors and airmen were getting on.

She was so worried about them. It was awful when we heard any reports of our ships being hit. Her determination and powers of endurance were unbelievable. Denis was in the room next door. The 2 of us would sit in armchairs either side of a two-bar electric fire, listening to the radio.

Crawford recalls the Prime Minister leaving Downing Street at 8am each morning to attend military briefings for an update of events during the night and to discuss the next part of the campaign:

I would take advantage of that and jump into bed at the flat so I could get some sleep. I'd tell the Downing Street switchboard to wake me when she was on her way back so I could be ready for work. We don't all have her energy.

The conflict ended with Argentinian surrender on 14 June 1982. Margaret Thatcher looked back on this period:

When I became Prime Minister I never thought that I would have to order British troops into combat and I do not think I have ever lived so tensely or intensely as during the whole of that time.

Margaret Thatcher – The Downing Street Years.

Restoration and modernisation

By the 1950s, the material state of 10 Downing Street had reached crisis point. Bomb damage had worsened existing structural problems: the building was suffering from subsidence, sloping walls, and twisting doorframes and an enormous annual repair bill.

The Ministry of Works carried out a survey in 1954 into the state of the structure. The report bounced from Winston Churchill (1951 to 1955) to Anthony Eden (1955 to 1957) to Harold Macmillan (1957 to 1963) as one Prime Minister followed the other. Finally, a committee set up by Macmillan concluded that drastic action was required before the building fell or burnt down.

The committee put forward a range of options, including the complete demolition of Number 10, 11 and 12 and their replacement with a new building. That idea was rejected and it was decided that Number 12 should be rebuilt, and Numbers 10 and 11 should be strengthened and their historic features preserved.

The architect Raymond Erith was selected to supervise the work, which was expected to take 2 years and cost £500,000. It ended up taking a year longer than planned and costing double the original estimate. The foundations proved to be so rotten that concrete underpinning was required on a massive scale.

Number 10 was completely gutted. Walls, floors and even the columns in the Cabinet Room and Pillared Room proved to be rotten and had to be replaced. New features were added too, including a room facing onto Downing Street and a veranda at Number 11 for the Chancellor.

It was also discovered that the familiar exterior façade was not black at all, but yellow. The blackened colour was a product of two centuries of severe pollution. To keep the familiar appearance, the newly cleaned yellow bricks were painted black to match their previous colour. Erith's work was completed in 1963, but not long afterwards, dry rot became apparent and further repairs had to be undertaken.

Margaret Thatcher (1979 to 1990) appointed architect Quinlan Terry to refurbish the state drawing rooms at the end of the 1980s. Two of the rooms, the White Drawing Room and Terracotta Room, gained ornate plasterwork ceilings. In the White Drawing Room, this included adding the national emblems of England, Northern Ireland, Scotland and Wales.

All the building work of the past few decades could have been ruined when a terrorist bomb exploded in 1991. An IRA mortar bomb was fired from a white transit van in Whitehall and exploded in the garden of Number 10, only a few metres away from where Prime Minister John Major (1990 to 1997) was chairing a Cabinet meeting to discuss the Gulf War.

Although no one was killed, it left a crater in the Number 10 gardens and blew in the windows of neighbouring houses. John Major and some of his staff moved into Admiralty Arch while damage caused by the bomb was repaired.

By 2006, it was clear that the Downing Street complex was no longer able to support the business of the Prime Minister's Office reliably. Independent surveys established that the building was no longer weather-tight, the heating system was failing, and the information and communications technology (ICT) network was at the limits of its operation. Power outages and water leaks were frequent occurrences and impacted significantly on the day-to-day operation of the Prime Minister's Office.

In addition to deterioration through age, pressures on the buildings had increased dramatically over recent years, through an increase in occupancy (stable at around 50 for many years) to around 170. In 2006, Prime Minister Tony Blair (1997 to 2007) authorised a new programme of improvements, with the building remaining operational throughout. Work was launched to address structural failure, renew the infrastructure, improve access and enhance the building's sustainability.

Structural issues were among the first to be tackled, and a phased exterior repair project was launched to address failing lead guttering, cracking brickwork and other structural issues. The distinctive black colourwash was also renewed, as it had faded away in many areas to reveal the yellow brickwork beneath. During the course of the works it was discovered that the façade of 11 Downing Street was unstable, and had to be secured using 225 stainless steel pins. All work was carried out in consultation with English Heritage.

Other projects have been undertaken to renew the building's ageing infrastructure and to replace many of the building's key services, including heating, fire protection and electrical power distribution. Sustainability is a key feature of the programme and a 10% reduction in carbon emissions was achieved during 2011. Rainwater harvesting was introduced in 2009, providing a sustainable source of water for the garden. Accessibility for disabled visitors has been significantly improved through the introduction of ramps and modernisation of lifts. Many of the public areas of the building have also been restored, including the front entrance hall, the state and small dining rooms and the study.

An ongoing programme is in place to upgrade facilities to modern standards, and to ensure the preservation of this historic building for years to come.

A place of entertainment

Every week, Number 10 is the venue for official functions including meetings, receptions, lunches and dinners.

It is not only heads of state and official dignitaries who visit – functions are held for people from all areas of UK society, including notable achievers, public service employees and charity workers.

Receptions tend to be informal gatherings. Lunches and dinners are more formal events. The Small Dining Room will sit a maximum of 12, and the State Dining Room up to 65 around a large, U-shaped table. The dining table is laid with items from the state silver collection: a range of modern silverware pieces commissioned by the Silver Trust to promote modern British craftsmanship.

Installations at Number 10 timeline

Since 10 Downing Street became the official residence of the premier, the building has performed the dual role of both residence and place of work for Britain's Prime Ministers.

Number 10 has been upgraded – including new technology – throughout its history, to ensure both an acceptable standard of living for its residents and to keep the Prime Minister at the heart of decision making within government. Often, the prompt for new technology or an upgrade was the arrival of a new Prime Minister.

Here are some of the more notable developments across 3 centuries of history, from the arrival of hot running water to the first tweet:

Timeline

1877 – hot and cold running water installed. The living quarters were renovated for Benjamin Disraeli – including a bath.

1894 – installation of electric lighting and first telephones. Following Disraeli's departure William Gladstone redecorated the building and oversaw the installations.

1902 – first motorcar driven onto Downing Street. Arthur Balfour brought the first car and since then, Prime Ministers have looked to select British marques for their official car, with a procession of Wolseleys, Humbers, Rovers, Daimlers and Jaguars sweeping successive Prime Ministers into – and out of – Downing Street.

1937 – first central heating.

1963 – electrical and telephone systems were replaced. 1963 was a major period of renovation for the building.

1982 – the first direct hotline between No10 and Washington was established during Margaret Thatcher's first term of office.

1982 – first 'micro-computer' and microfilm reader installed.

1983 – wider rollout of computers machines for Number 10 staff following a review of the building's needs.

1990s – first videoconference. John Major used the technology from his study.

1996 – desktop PCs installed at all workstations.

1996 – the launch of the first No10 website.

1998 – Internet access became mainstreamed across Number 10 staff desktops.

2002 – dedicated video conferencing suite was installed. This followed the events of 9/11 and allowed the Prime Minister and his team to be in face to face contact with counterparts around the world in an instant.

2005 – a new e-mail account allowed the public to contact the Prime Minister directly.

2008 – Number 10's very own online TV station – Number10 TV

2008 – Number 10's first tweet – and there have been over 3,000 since.

Larry the cat, Chief Mouser to the Cabinet Office

15 February 2013 marked 2 years of residence at Downing Street for Larry, Chief Mouser – the first cat at Number 10 to be bestowed the title officially.

Larry was recruited from Battersea Dogs & Cats Home on recommendation for his mousing skills. He joined the Number 10 household and has made a significant impact.

He has captured the hearts of the Great British public and the press teams often camped outside the front door. In turn the nation sends him gifts and treats daily.

Larry spends his days greeting guests to the house, inspecting security defences and testing antique furniture for napping quality. His day-to-day responsibilities also include contemplating a solution to the mouse occupancy of the house. Larry says this is still 'in tactical planning stage'.

The Deputy Prime Minister's Office

Office of the Leader of the House of Commons

We provide support to the Leader of the House of Commons, who is responsible for planning and supervising the government's legislative programme (including the Queen's speech), and managing government business within the House of Commons while also upholding the rights and interests of the backbench members of the House. OLHC is a ministerial department of the Cabinet Office

What we do

We are responsible for:

- delivering the government's legislative programme
- managing business in the House of Commons
- reform of the House of Commons, including co-ordinating e-petitions across government and parliament
- remaining issues relating to pay, pensions and expenses for MPs following the establishment of the Independent Parliamentary Standards Authority

Ministerial role
Deputy Prime Minister and Lord President of the Council

Responsibilities
The Deputy Prime Minister is the deputy head of the UK government, supporting the Prime Minister on the full range of government policy and initiatives.

Within government, the Deputy Prime Minister also has responsibility for:

- implementing the government's strategy to increase social mobility
- overseeing the government's drive to rebalance the economy
- leading the government's political and constitutional reform agenda
- chairing the Home Affairs Committee, co-chairing the Coalition Committee and deputy-chairing the National Security Council
- building strategic relationships in Europe and across the world

Current role holder:
The Rt. Hon Nick Clegg MP

Nick Clegg became Deputy Prime Minister and Lord President of the Privy Council in May 2010. He is the MP for Sheffield Hallam.

Biography
Nick Clegg became Deputy Prime Minister and Lord President of the Privy Council in May 2010. He is the MP for Sheffield Hallam.

Education
Nick did his undergraduate degree at the University of Cambridge and holds postgraduate qualifications from the University of Minnesota and the College of Europe in Bruges.

Political career
Nick was elected MEP for the East Midlands in 1999, and was Trade and Industry spokesman for the European Liberal Democrat and Reform group until he stood down in 2004.

He was elected as MP for Sheffield Hallam in 2005, and served as Liberal Democrat Spokesperson on Europe and Shadow Home Secretary before becoming Leader of the Liberal Democrats in 2007.

Career outside politics
Before being elected, Nick had spells in journalism, consultancy and university lecturing. He also worked for 5 years at the European Commission, where his role included managing aid projects in Central Asia and trade negotiations with China and Russia.

Personal life
Nick Clegg was born in Buckinghamshire in 1967. He is married to Miriam González Durántez. They have 3 sons.

Deputy Prime Minister and Lord President of the Council

The Deputy Prime Minister is the deputy head of the UK government, supporting the Prime Minister on the full range of government policy and initiatives.

Within government, the Deputy Prime Minister also has responsibility for:

- implementing the government's strategy to increase social mobility
- overseeing the government's drive to rebalance the economy
- leading the government's political and constitutional reform agenda
- chairing the Home Affairs Committee, co-chairing the Coalition Committee and deputy-chairing the National Security Council
- building strategic relationships in Europe and across the world

The Cabinet

The Cabinet is made up of the senior members of government. Every Tuesday during Parliament, members of the Cabinet (Secretaries of State from all departments and some other ministers) meet to discuss what are the most important issues for the government.

Ministers = 1 Prime minister 21 Cabinet ministers 98 Other ministers = 120

Ministers are chosen by the Prime Minister from the members of the House of Commons and House of Lords. They are responsible for the actions, successes and failures of their departments.

The Rt. Hon David Cameron MP
Roles: Prime Minister, Minister for the Civil Service and First Lord of the Treasury

The Rt. Hon Nick Clegg MP
Roles: Deputy Prime Minister and Lord President of the Council

The Rt. Hon William Hague MP
Roles: First Secretary of State and Secretary of State for Foreign and Commonwealth Affairs

The Secretary of State has overall responsibility for the work of the Foreign & Commonwealth Office, with particular focus on policy strategy, honours, Whitehall liaison and cyber-security

William Hague was appointed Secretary of State for Foreign and Commonwealth Affairs on 12 May 2010. He was elected to Parliament in 1989 and is the Conservative MP for Richmond (Yorks).

Education
William was educated at Wath-on-Dearne Comprehensive School and Magdalen College, Oxford where he studied philosophy, politics and economics and was President of the Oxford Union. He continued his studies at INSEAD Business School in France.

Political career
Joint Parliamentary under Secretary of State 1993 - 1994
Minister of State for Social Security and Disabled People 1994 - 1995
Secretary of State for Wales 1995 - 1997
Leader of the Conservative Party from 1997 - 2001
Shadow Foreign Secretary 2005 – 2010

Career outside politics

Before entering Parliament, William worked for Shell UK and then for management consultants McKinsey and Co. He has written 2 books. His first book, a biography of William Pitt the Younger, was published in September 2004 and won 'History Book of the Year' at the National Book Awards. His following book, a biography of William Wilberforce, was published in June 2007.

Personal life
William is married to Ffion.

The Rt. Hon George Osborne MP
Roles: Chancellor of the Exchequer

Chancellor of the Exchequer
The Chancellor of the Exchequer is the government's chief financial minister and as such is responsible for raising revenue through taxation or borrowing and for controlling public spending. He has overall responsibility for the work of the Treasury.

The Chancellor's responsibilities cover:

- fiscal policy (including the presenting of the annual Budget)
- monetary policy, setting inflation targets
- ministerial arrangements (in his role as Second Lord of the Treasury)

Biography
George Osborne became Chancellor of the Exchequer in May 2010. He has been the Conservative MP for Tatton, Cheshire since June 2001.

Education
He was born and educated in London, studying modern history at Oxford University.

Political career
George worked as Political Secretary to the Leader of the Opposition before being elected to Parliament. He entered Parliament as the youngest Conservative MP in the House of Commons.

After serving on the Public Accounts Committee and holding a number shadow ministerial posts, he was appointed to the position of Shadow Chancellor in 2005, aged 33, where he served opposite Chancellors Gordon Brown and Alistair Darling until 2010.

In 2005 he successfully ran David Cameron's campaign to become Leader of the Conservative Party. Following the 2010 Election he was part of the small Conservative negotiating team during the discussions that led to the formation of the Coalition Government. In May 2010 he became Chancellor of the Exchequer.

He was the youngest Chancellor to take office since Randolph Churchill in 1886.

The Rt. Hon Danny Alexander MP
Roles: Chief Secretary to the Treasury

Chief Secretary to the Treasury
The Chief Secretary is responsible for public expenditure including:

- spending reviews and strategic planning
- in-year spending control
- public sector pay and pensions
- Annually Managed Expenditure (AME) and welfare reform
- efficiency and value for money in public service
- procurement
- capital investment

Biography
Danny Alexander was appointed Chief Secretary to the Treasury in May 2010. He is the Liberal Democrat MP for Inverness, Nairn, Badenoch and Strathspey.

Education

Danny was educated at Lochaber High School, Fort William in the Scottish Highlands before studying philosophy, politics and economics at Oxford.

Political career

After university Danny worked as a press officer for the Scottish Liberal Democrats before spending four years at the European Movement and then four years as Director of Communications for the Britain in Europe campaign. In 2005 Danny was elected MP for the newly created seat of Inverness, Nairn, and Badenoch & Strathspey. He joined the Shadow Work and Pensions team in 2005 and in July 2007 he was appointed Shadow Secretary of State for Work and Pensions, holding the post until June 2008. He gave this up to concentrate on the roles of Chief of Staff to the party leader, Nick Clegg, and Chair of the Manifesto Group.

Danny played a key role in the negotiating team and in drawing up of the coalition document for the new government. Initially appointed as Secretary of State for Scotland, in May 2010 he became Chief Secretary to the Treasury and was appointed to the Privy Council.

Career outside politics

Danny worked as a press officer for the Scottish Liberal Democrats before spending 4 years at the European Movement, followed by 4 years as Director of Communications for the Britain in Europe campaign.

In 2003 he was appointed the Head of Communications for the recently formed Cairngorms National Park Authority.

Personal life

Danny is married with 2 daughters. His parliamentary responsibilities combined with having a young family do not afford a lot of time for hobbies but when they do he enjoys hill-walking, fishing, travel and sports of all kinds.

The Rt. Hon Theresa May MP
Roles: Secretary of State for the Home Department

Responsibilities

The Secretary of State has overall responsibility for all Home Office business, including:

- legislative programme
- expenditure issues
- security and terrorism

Current role holder:

The Rt. Hon Theresa May MP

Theresa May was appointed Home Secretary in May 2010. She is the Conservative MP for Maidenhead.

Education

Theresa had a varied education, spanning both the state and private sectors and attending both grammar school and comprehensive school. She studied geography at St Hugh's College, Oxford University.

Political career

Theresa has been involved in politics at all levels for many years, beginning by stuffing envelopes at her local Conservative association before going on to be a councillor in the London borough of Merton from 1986 to 1994. During her time at Merton, Theresa was Chair of Education from 1988 to 1990 and Deputy Group Leader and Housing Spokesperson from 1992 to 1994.

Theresa was elected MP for Maidenhead in May 1997, after which she held several shadow positions, including:

Shadow Secretary of State for Education and Employment 1999 to 2001
Shadow Secretary of State for Transport, Local Government and the Regions 2001 to 2002
Shadow Secretary of State for the Family 2004 to 2005
Shadow Secretary of State for Culture, Media and Sport 2005
Shadow Leader of the House of Commons 2005 to 2009
Parliamentary under Secretary of State for Women and Equalities 2010 to 2012

Career outside politics
After starting her career at the Bank of England, Theresa went on to the Association for Payment Clearing Services, firstly as Head of the European affairs unit from 1989 to 1996 and then as Senior Adviser on international affairs from 1996 to 1997.

The Rt. Hon Philip Hammond MP
Roles: Secretary of State for Defence

Responsibilities
The Secretary of State for Defence is the senior minister in charge of the department and gives strategic direction on:

- operations
- personnel
- delivery of the transformation programme
- defence policy, planning, programme and resource allocation
- international relations
- nuclear programme
- acquisition

Parliamentary business and communications

Current role holder:
The Rt. Hon Philip Hammond MP
Philip Hammond was appointed Secretary of State for Defence in 2011. He is the Conservative MP for Runnymede and Weybridge.

Education
Philip was born in Epping, Essex in 1955 and attended school in Brentwood before studying politics, philosophy and economics at University College, Oxford.

Political career
He was previously Secretary of State for Transport from May 2010, when he was appointed as a Privy Counsellor. Prior to this, he held a number of shadow portfolios. He was elected to Parliament in 1997.

Career outside politics
Philip had a business career in small and medium-sized companies in manufacturing, consultancy, property and construction, and oil and gas, both in the UK and abroad.

Personal life
He is married with 3 children and lives in Send, Surrey.

The Rt. Hon Dr Vince Cable MP
Roles: Secretary of State for Business, Innovation and Skills and President of the Board of Trade

Responsibilities
The Secretary of State is responsible for strategy and policy across the Department for Business, Innovation & Skills (BIS). The department's main policy areas are:

- business law
- consumer issues
- employment relations
- enterprise and business support
- trade policy
- higher education
- further education and skills
- science
- innovation

The Secretary of State also has the title of President of the Board of Trade, and:

- has overall responsibility for the BIS budget

- focuses on business and banking issues
- is the lead minister for reducing regulatory burdens across government

Current role holder:
The Rt. Hon Dr Vince Cable MP
Vince Cable was appointed Secretary of State for Business, Innovation and Skills in May 2010. He is the Liberal Democrat MP for Twickenham.

Education
Vince was educated at Nunthorpe Grammar School, York and Fitzwilliam College, Cambridge, where he studied natural science and economics and was President of the Union. He then studied for a PhD at Glasgow University.

Political career
He served in the Liberal Democrat Shadow Cabinet as Spokesman on Trade and Industry from 1999 to 2003, and Shadow Chancellor from 2003 to 2010. He was Deputy Leader of the Liberal Democrats from 2006 to 2010.

Career outside politics
After graduating, Vince worked as Treasury Finance Officer for the Kenyan Government between 1966 and 1968. From 1968 to 1974 he lectured in economics at Glasgow University. He then worked in a range of senior economic and foreign policy roles, before becoming Shell International's Chief Economist in 1995.

Personal life
Vince is married and has 3 children by his late wife.

The Rt. Hon Iain Duncan Smith MP
Roles: Secretary of State for Work and Pensions

Responsibilities
The Secretary of State has overall responsibility for the Department for Work and Pensions (DWP).

DWP is responsible for the administration of the state pension and working age benefits system, providing support to:

- people of working age
- employers
- pensioners
- families and children
- disabled people

Current role holder:
The Rt. Hon Iain Duncan Smith MP
Iain Duncan Smith was appointed Secretary of State for Work and Pensions in May 2010. He has been the Conservative MP for Chingford and Woodford Green since 1992.

Education
Iain was educated at Dunchurch College of Management, the Royal Military Academy in Sandhurst and the Universita per Stranieri in Perugia, Italy.

Political career
Iain was Shadow Secretary of State for Social Security from 1997 to 1999 and Shadow Secretary of State for Defence from 1999 to 2001. He was Leader of the Opposition from 2001 to 2003.

Career outside politics
After serving in the Scots Guards, Iain worked for General Electric. In 2004, he founded the Centre for Social Justice to help tackle poverty and remained Chairman of the organisation until taking up the post of Secretary of State.

The Rt. Hon Chris Grayling MP
Roles: Lord Chancellor and Secretary of State for Justice

Responsibilities
The Secretary of State has oversight of all of Ministry of Justice business and is responsible for making improvements to the criminal justice and prison system so that it better serves the public. Other responsibilities include:

- the resourcing of his Department
- overall strategy on criminal justice, penal policy and rehabilitation
- judicial policy, appointments and conduct
- other functions of the Lord Chancellor

EU and international

Current role holder:
The Rt. Hon Chris Grayling MP
Chris Grayling is the Secretary of State for Justice and Lord Chancellor. He has been the Conservative MP for Epsom and Ewell since 2001.

Education
Chris was educated at The Royal Grammar School, High Wycombe and Sidney Sussex College, Cambridge, where he studied history.

Career
In May 2010 he was appointed Minister of State at the Department for Work and Pensions. He has also held a number of shadow front bench posts, including Shadow Home Secretary and Shadow Secretary of State for Transport.

Personal life
Chris lives in the constituency with his wife and their 2 children.

The Rt. Hon Michael Gove MP
Roles: Secretary of State for Education

Responsibilities
The Secretary of State is responsible for the work of the Department for Education, including:

- early years
- adoption and child protection
- teachers' pay
- the school curriculum
- school improvement
- the establishment of academies and free schools

Current role holder:
The Rt. Hon Michael Gove MP
Michael Gove was appointed Secretary of State for Education in May 2010. He is the Conservative MP for Surrey Heath.

Education
Michael was educated at Robert Gordon's College, Aberdeen and Lady Margaret Hall, Oxford University.

Political career
Michael was Shadow Minister for Housing from 2005 to 2007 and Shadow Secretary of State for Children, Schools and Families from 2007 to 2010.

Career outside politics
Michael became a journalist after leaving university, working as a reporter for The Press and Journal in Aberdeen, a researcher and reporter at Scottish Television and a reporter for BBC Television. He was later Assistant Editor of The Times.

Personal life
Michael is married with 2 children.

The Rt. Hon Eric Pickles MP
Roles: Secretary of State for Communities and Local Government

Responsibilities
The Secretary of State is responsible for the overall strategic direction of the Department for Communities and Local Government (DCLG). Main areas of responsibility include:

- supporting local government
- communities and neighbourhoods
- local economic growth
- housing
- planning and building
- fire

Current role holder:
The Rt. Hon Eric Pickles MP
Eric Pickles was appointed Secretary of State for Communities and Local Government in May 2010. He is the Conservative MP for Brentwood and Ongar.

Education
Eric was educated at Greenhead Grammar School and Leeds Polytechnic.

Political career
Eric was Leader of Bradford City Council from 1988 to 1990. He held a number of positions while in opposition, including Shadow Secretary of State for Communities and Local Government from 2007 to 2009 and Chairman of the Conservative Party from 2009 to 2010.

Career outside politics
He worked as a consultant in employment practice and as Local Government Editor for Conservative Newsline before becoming an MP in 1992. He is a trustee of 2 local charities - Brentwood Foyer and Brentwood Theatre.

Personal life
Eric lives with his wife Irene in Brentwood, Essex.

The Rt. Hon Jeremy Hunt MP
Roles: Secretary of State for Health

Responsibilities
The Secretary of State has overall responsibility for the work of the Department of Health (DH). DH provides strategic leadership for public health, the NHS and social care in England, focused around 5 key priorities:

- older people
- mortality
- care
- dementia
- long-term conditions

Current role holder:
The Rt. Hon Jeremy Hunt MP
Jeremy Hunt was appointed Secretary of State for Health in September 2012. He was elected as MP for Southwest Surrey in May 2005.

Education
Jeremy was educated at Oxford University.

Political career
In May 2010 Jeremy was appointed Secretary of State for Culture, Olympics, Media and Sport. He was formerly Shadow Culture Secretary 2007 to 2010 and Shadow Minister for Disabled People 2005 to 2007.

Career outside politics
Before his election as an MP, Jeremy ran his own educational publishing business, Hotcourses. He also set up a charity to help AIDS orphans in Africa in which he continues to play an active role.

Personal life
He lives in Farnham and London with his wife, son and daughter.

The Rt. Hon Owen Paterson MP
Roles: Secretary of State for Environment, Food and Rural Affairs

Responsibilities
The Secretary of State has overall responsibility for the Department for Environment, Food and Rural Affairs. Responsibilities include:

EU and international relations:
* emergencies
* climate change

Common Agricultural Policy reform:
* biodiversity

Current role holder:
The Rt. Hon Owen Paterson MP
Owen Paterson was appointed Secretary of State for Environment, Food and Rural Affairs in September 2012. He is the Conservative MP for North Shropshire.

Education
Owen was educated at Radley College, Abingdon and Corpus Christi College, Cambridge where he studied history.

Political career
Owen held several posts while in opposition, including Shadow Minister for Transport from 2005 to 2007 and Shadow Secretary of State for Northern Ireland from 2007 to 2010. He was Secretary of State for Northern Ireland from May 2010 to September 2012.

Career outside politics
He joined the British Leather Company in 1979, becoming Sales Director in 1983 and Managing Director in 1993.

Personal life
Owen is married with 3 children.

The Rt. Hon Justine Greening MP
Roles: Secretary of State for International Development

Responsibilities
The Secretary of State leads the DFID ministerial team and sets the overall strategy and direction of the department. She has final authority over all DFID business.

Current role holder:
The Rt. Hon Justine Greening MP
Justine Greening was appointed Secretary of State for International Development on 4 September 2012. She is the Conservative MP for Putney, Roehampton and Southfields.

Education
Justine attended her local comprehensive school in Rotherham, South Yorkshire before going on to study economics at Southampton University. Justine has an MBA from the London Business School.

Career
Justine was a finance manager at Centrica plc before being elected as a Member of Parliament in May 2005. Following her election she was appointed as a Vice-Chairman of the Conservative Party, with responsibility for youth.

As well as being a member of the Work and Pensions Select Committee, in 2007 she became a Shadow Treasury Minister and in January 2009 became the Shadow Minister for London.

Justine was Economic Secretary to the Treasury from May 2010 to October 2011 and Secretary of State for Transport from October 2011 to September 2012.

The Rt. Hon Michael Moore MP
Roles: Secretary of State for Scotland

Responsibilities
The main role of the Scottish Secretary is to promote and protect the devolution settlement.

Other responsibilities include promoting partnership between the UK government and the Scottish government, and relations between the 2 Parliaments.

Current role holder:
The Rt. Hon Michael Moore MP
Michael Moore was appointed Secretary of State for Scotland in May 2010. He is the Liberal Democrat MP for Berwickshire, Roxburgh and Selkirk.

Education
Michael was educated at Jedburgh Grammar School and Edinburgh University, where he studied politics and modern history.

Political career
He previously served as Shadow Secretary for Scotland and Northern Ireland and Shadow Secretary of State for International Development.

Michael was elected as an MP in 1997 and has held a number of posts since, including:

Spokesperson for Scotland 1997 to 1999 and 2001
Spokesperson for Transport 1999 to 2001
Shadow Minister for Foreign Affairs 2001 to 2005
Shadow Secretary of State for Defence 2005 to 2006
Shadow Secretary of State for Foreign and Commonwealth Affairs 2006 to 2007
Shadow Secretary of State for Northern Ireland and Scotland 2008
Shadow Secretary of State for International Development 2007 to 2010
Career outside politics

After a year as a researcher for Archy Kirkwood MP, he joined Coopers & Lybrand where he qualified as a Scottish chartered accountant and became a manager in the corporate finance practice.

Personal life
Michael is married with a daughter. His interests include supporting local rugby teams, hill walking and films.

The Rt. Hon Edward Davey MP
Roles: Secretary of State for Energy and Climate Change

Responsibilities
The Secretary of State has overall responsibility for the business of the Department of Energy & Climate Change and its policies. Responsibilities include:

* department strategy and budgets
* energy market reform
* carbon price
* Annual Energy Statement
* energy security

National Security Council
Carbon Plan
Renewable Energy Strategy
2050 Pathways

Current role holder:
The Rt. Hon Edward Davey MP
Edward Davey was appointed Secretary of State for Energy & Climate Change in February 2012. He is the Liberal Democrat MP for Kingston and Surbiton.

Education
Edward was educated at Nottingham High School and Jesus College, Oxford, where he studied politics, philosophy and economics. He gained a MSc in economics from Birkbeck College, London University.

Political career
Edward served in the Liberal Democrat Shadow Cabinet in a number of posts including Shadow Chief Secretary to the Treasury from 2001 to 2002, Shadow Secretary of State for Education and Skills from 2005 to 2006 and Shadow Secretary of State for Foreign and Commonwealth Affairs between 2007 and 2010.

He was then Parliamentary Under Secretary of State for Employment Relations and Consumer Affairs at the Department for Business, Innovation & Skills from May 2010 to February 2012.

Career outside politics
After graduating Edward worked as an economics researcher for the Liberal Democrats in Parliament before joining Omega Partners, where he specialised in consultancy in the postal services sector.

Personal life
Edward is married and has a son.

The Rt. Hon Patrick McLoughlin MP
Roles: Secretary of State for Transport

Responsibilities
The Secretary of State has overall responsibility for the policies of the Department for Transport.

Responsibilities include:

- transport strategy, including economic growth and climate change
- spending review
- transport security
- high speed rail

Current role holder:
The Rt. Hon Patrick McLoughlin MP
Patrick McLoughlin was appointed Secretary of State for Transport in September 2012. He is the Conservative MP for Derbyshire Dales.

Education
Patrick studied at Staffordshire College of Agriculture.

Political career
Before becoming an MP in 1986, Patrick sat on Staffordshire County Council from 1981 to 1987 and Cannock Chase District Council between 1980 and 1987.

He has held a number of positions in government, including Parliamentary Under Secretary of State at the Department of Trade and Industry and Government Whip. In opposition, he served as Chief Whip from 2005 to 2010. He was appointed to the Privy Council in 2005.

He was appointed Chief Whip in the Coalition government in 2010.

Career outside politics
He worked for 5 years in agriculture, before becoming a coal miner at Littleton Colliery in Cannock.

Personal life
Patrick is married with 2 children.

The Rt. Hon Maria Miller MP
Roles: Secretary of State for Culture, Media and Sport and Minister for Women and Equalities

Responsibilities
The Secretary of State has overall responsibility for strategy and policy across the Department for Culture, Media and Sport.

The department's main policy areas are:

- arts and culture
- broadcasting
- creative industries
- cultural property, heritage and the historic environment
- gambling and racing
- libraries
- media ownership and mergers
- museums and galleries
- the National Lottery
- sport
- telecommunications and online
- tourism

Current role holder:
The Rt. Hon Maria Miller MP
Maria Miller was appointed as Secretary of State for Culture, Media and Sport in September 2012. She is the Conservative MP for Basingstoke.

Education
Maria was educated at Brynteg Comprehensive School, Bridgend and the London School of Economics. After graduating, she worked in marketing and as a company director at Grey Advertising Ltd and The Rowland Company.

Political career
She served as Shadow Minister for Education between 2005 and 2006, as Shadow Minister for Family Welfare between 2006 and 2007 and as Shadow Minister for Families from 2007 to 2010.

In May 2010 she was appointed Parliamentary under Secretary of State for Disabled People.

Personal life
Maria is married with 3 children.

The Rt. Hon Theresa Villiers MP
Roles: Secretary of State for Northern Ireland

Responsibilities
The Secretary of State has overall responsibility for the policies of the Northern Ireland Office.

Responsibilities include:

- overseeing the Northern Ireland devolution settlement
- representing Northern Ireland interests at UK government level and UK government interests in Northern Ireland
- national security
- human rights, elections
- legacy issues (including current ongoing public inquiries)

Current role holder:
The Rt. Hon Theresa Villiers MP
Theresa Villiers was appointed Secretary of State for Northern Ireland in September 2012. She is the Conservative MP for Chipping Barnet.

Education
Theresa went to Francis Holland School in London then studied law at the University of Bristol and Jesus College, Oxford.

Political career
Highlights include:

MP for Chipping Barnet 2003 to present

MEP for London 1999 to 2005
Shadow Chief Secretary to the Treasury 2005 to 2007
Shadow Secretary of State for Transport 2007 to 2010
Minister of State for Transport 2010 to 2012
Secretary of State for Northern Ireland September 2012 to present
Career outside politics
After university, Theresa worked as a barrister and as a lecturer in law at Kings College, London.

Personal life
Theresa was born in 1968 and grew up in St John's wood, north London. She lives in Arkley in Barnet.

The Rt. Hon David Jones MP
Roles: Secretary of State for Wales

Responsibilities
The Secretary of State is responsible for overall strategic direction of the Wales Office.

Responsibilities include:

- working with the Welsh Assembly
- constitutional issues and the Commission on Devolution in Wales
- major Acts of Parliament affecting Wales, including the Government of Wales Act
- assembly, parliamentary and local elections in Wales
- economic, financial and business issues in Wales
- foreign affairs, including interaction with the EU
- public appointments
- Welsh language issues, including the Welsh Language Scheme
- dealing with royal matters
- other policy areas affecting Wales, including the environment, energy and defence

Current role holder:
The Rt. Hon David Jones MP
David Jones was Parliamentary Under Secretary of State at the Wales Office from May 2010 to September 2012. He is the Conservative MP for Clwyd West.

Education
David was educated at Ruabon Grammar School and at University College, London where he studied law.

Political career
Following his election to Parliament in 2005, he held a seat on the Welsh Affairs Select Committee and was co-chairman of the Associate Parliamentary Sustainable Resource Group. He was Shadow Minister for Wales from 2006 to 2010.

Career outside politics
Before becoming an MP, David was Senior Partner in his own legal practice in Llandudno.

Personal Life
David is married with 2 children. A keen supporter of Liverpool Football Club, his interests include cars and travel.

Lord Hill of Oareford CBE
Roles: Leader of the House of Lords and Chancellor of the Duchy of Lancaster

Responsibilities
The Leader of the House of Lords is responsible for the organisation of government business in the House, providing assistance to all Lords and offering advice on procedure. The Leader also expresses the collective feelings of the House on formal occasions, such as motions of thanks or congratulations.

Current role holder:
Lord Hill of Oareford CBE
Lord Hill was appointed Leader of the House of Lords in January 2013. He is a Conservative member of the House of Lords.

Education
He was educated at Highgate School and Trinity College, Cambridge, where he studied history.

Career
Lord Hill worked as parliamentary Under Secretary of State for Schools from May 2010 to January 2013. He was an adviser in Whitehall in the 1980s and 1990s. He worked at 3 government departments - Employment, Trade and Industry and Health - before joining the Number 10 Policy Unit in 1991. He was Political Secretary and Head of the Prime Minister's Political Office from 1992 to 1994.

Personal life
Lord Hill is married with 3 children.

Also attends Cabinet

The Rt. Hon Kenneth Clarke QC MP
Roles: Minister without Portfolio

Responsibilities
Responsibilities include advising the Prime Minister on issues including economic strategy.

Current role holder:
The Rt. Hon Kenneth Clarke QC MP
Kenneth Clarke QC MP was appointed Minister without Portfolio in September 2012. He is the Conservative MP for Rushcliffe.

Education
He was educated at Nottingham High School and Gonville and Caius College, Cambridge.

Political career
Kenneth was Lord Chancellor and Secretary of State for Justice from May 2010 to September 2012. Other positions include:

Secretary of State for Health 1988 to 1990
Secretary of State for Education and Science 1990 to 1992
Home Secretary 1992 to 1993
Chancellor of the Exchequer 1993 to 1997
In opposition, he served as Shadow Secretary of State for Business, Innovation and Skills.

Career outside politics
A former barrister-at-law, Kenneth was called to the bar by Gray's Inn in 1963 and became a QC in 1980. He has practised on the Midland Circuit, based in Birmingham.

Personal life
Kenneth is married with 2 children.

The Rt. Hon Andrew Lansley CBE MP
Roles: Leader of the House of Commons and Lord Privy Seal

Responsibilities
The Leader of the House of Commons organises government business in the House of Commons and works closely with the government's Chief Whip.

Current role holder:
The Rt. Hon Andrew Lansley CBE MP
Andrew Lansley CBE MP was appointed Leader of the House of Commons in September 2012. He has been the Conservative MP for south Cambridgeshire since 1997.

Education
Andrew was educated at Brentwood School, Essex, and the University of Exeter, where he was President of the Guild for Students.

Political career
He served as Shadow Health Secretary from 2003 until the 2010 election. He then served as Secretary of State for Health until September 2012.

Career outside politics
Andrew began his career as a civil servant working at the Department of Trade and Industry. He was awarded a CBE for running the Conservative campaign for the 1992 general election.

Personal life
Andrew is married with 2 children. He also has 3 children from his first marriage.

The Rt. Hon Sir George Young Bt MP
Roles: Chief Whip and Parliamentary Secretary to the Treasury

Responsibilities
The Chief Whip is responsible for administering the whipping system that ensures that members of the party attend and vote in Parliament, as the party leadership desires.

Whips are MPs or Lords appointed by each party in Parliament to help organise their party's contribution to parliamentary business. One of their responsibilities is making sure the maximum number of their party member's vote, and vote the way their party wants.

Other whip duties
Whips frequently act as tellers (counting votes in divisions). They also manage the pairing system whereby Members of opposing parties both agree not to vote when other business (such as a select committee visit) prevents them from being present at Westminster.

Whips are also largely responsible (together with the Leader of the House in the Commons) for arranging the business of Parliament. In this role they are frequently referred to as 'the usual channels'.

Current role holder:
The Rt. Hon Sir George Young Bt MP
Sir George Young was appointed Chief Whip and Parliamentary Secretary to the Treasury in October 2012. He is the Conservative MP for Northwest Hampshire.

Education
Sir George was educated at Eton before attending Christ Church, Oxford where he studied politics, philosophy and economics.

Political career
Sir George was first elected to Parliament in 1974. His early ministerial career included time at the Departments for Health, Environment and Housing. He held several positions, including Minister for Housing, Inner Cities and Construction and Secretary of State for Transport.

He was Chairman of the Select Committee on Standards and Privileges between 2001 and 2009 before joining the Shadow Cabinet as Shadow Leader of the House of Commons. He was Leader of the House of Commons and Lord Privy Seal from May 2010 to September 2012.

Career outside politics
After university, he worked in the City for merchant bank Hill Samuel, and then for the National Economic Development Office from 1966 to 1967. He then spent 2 years at the University of Surrey, where he was awarded a MPhil. From 1969 to 1974 he was Economic Adviser to the Post Office Corporation.

Personal life
Sir George is married with 4 children.

The Rt. Hon Francis Maude MP
Roles: Minister for the Cabinet Office and Paymaster General

Responsibilities
The Minister for the Cabinet Office has overall responsibility for the policy and work of the department. Responsibilities include:

- public sector efficiency and reform

Civil Service issues

- industrial relations strategy in the public sector
- government transparency
- civil contingencies
- civil society
- cyber security

UK statistics

Current role holder:
The Rt. Hon Francis Maude MP
Francis Maude was appointed Minister for the Cabinet Office and Paymaster General in May 2010. He is the Conservative MP for Horsham, west Sussex.

Education
Francis studied at the University of Cambridge and The College of Law, specialising in criminal law.

Political career
He has held several government posts, including Minister of State at the Foreign and Commonwealth Office from 1989 to 1990 and Financial Secretary to the Treasury from 1990 to 1992.

While in opposition, he was Chairman of the Conservative Party from 2005 to 2007 and, among other roles, Shadow Foreign Secretary from 2000 to 2001 and Shadow Minister for the Cabinet Office from 2007 to 2010.

Career outside politics
After a career at the criminal bar between 1977 and 1985, he served as a councillor for the City of Westminster for 6 years. His other jobs outside politics have included being a non-executive director of ASDA Group, director at Salomon Brothers, and managing director of Morgan Stanley.

Personal life
Francis is married with 5 children.

The Rt. Hon Oliver Letwin MP
Roles: Minister for Government Policy

Responsibilities
The minister is responsible for:

- developing government policies with the Cabinet Office, as set out in the 'programme for government'
- implementing the departmental business plans

Current role holder:
The Rt. Hon Oliver Letwin MP
Oliver Letwin became Minister for Government Policy in the Cabinet Office in May 2010. He is the Conservative MP for west Dorset.

Education
Oliver studied at Eton College, then Trinity College, Cambridge. He has a PhD in philosophy from Cambridge.

Political career
After joining the Shadow Cabinet in 2000, he was Shadow Chief Secretary to the Treasury from 2000 to 2001, Shadow Home Secretary from 2001 to 2003, Shadow Chancellor of the Exchequer from 2003 to 2005, Shadow Environment Secretary in 2005 and Chairman of the Policy Review from 2005 to 2010.

Career outside politics
He taught philosophy at the University of Cambridge. He has also worked as a civil servant in Margaret Thatcher's policy unit and as a bank director.

Personal life
Oliver is married with 2 children.

The Rt. Hon David Laws MP
Roles: Minister of State for Cabinet Office and Minister of State for Schools

Responsibilities
As Minister of State, Cabinet Office, he supports effective Coalition Government working and policy development, with a particular focus on domestic policy.

He leads on delivery of the Programme for Government and departmental Business Plans.

Current role holder:
The Rt. Hon David Laws MP
David Laws became Minister of State for Schools in the Department for Education and Minister of State in the Cabinet Office in September 2012. He is also the Liberal Democrat MP for Yeovil.

Education
David studied economics at King's College, Cambridge.

Political career
David was elected MP for Yeovil in 2001.

He served on the Treasury Select Committee until becoming the Liberal Democrats' Shadow Chief Secretary, Shadow Work and Pensions Secretary, and finally Shadow Education Secretary.

David helped negotiate the Coalition agreement with the Conservative Party before briefly serving as Chief Secretary to the Treasury, where he oversaw the Coalition public spending plans.

Career outside politics
From 1987 to 1992, David worked as a vice president at JP Morgan before leaving to join Barclays as a managing director. He left the City in 1994 to become economics adviser to the Liberal Democrats.

The Rt. Hon Baroness Warsi
Roles: Minister of State for Faith and Communities and Senior Minister of State

Responsibilities
The minister works with religious and community leaders to promote faith, religious tolerance and stronger communities within the UK.

Current role holder:
The Rt. Hon Baroness Warsi
Baroness Warsi was appointed Senior Minister of State at the Foreign & Commonwealth Office and Minister for Faith and Communities at the Department for Communities and Local Government in September 2012. She was previously Chairman of the Conservative Party and Minister without Portfolio.

She is a Conservative member of the House of Lords.

Education
Baroness Warsi attended Birkdale High School and Dewsbury College before studying law at the University of Leeds, gaining an LLB. She later attended the College of Law, York, to complete her legal practice training.

Political career
She became Conservative Party Vice Chairman for Cities and Diversity and was appointed to the House of Lords in 2007, becoming Shadow Minister for Communities and Social Action in the Shadow Cabinet. In May 2010 she was appointed Minister without Portfolio.

Career outside politics
Baroness Warsi trained with the Crown Prosecution Service and the Home Office Immigration Department before setting up her own specialist legal practice.

She has also been a racial justice campaigner for many years and was instrumental in the launch of Operation Black Vote, a not-for-profit national organisation that works towards greater racial justice and equality throughout the UK.

Personal life
Baroness Warsi is a keen cook and a fan of cricket and home improvement programmes. She lives in Wakefield with her husband Iftikhar and their 5 children.

The Rt. Hon David Willetts MP
Roles: Minister of State for Universities and Science

Responsibilities
The minister is responsible for universities and science in the Department for Business, Innovation and Skills. Responsibilities include:

- higher education (including the Higher Education Funding Council for England and Student Loans Company)
- science and research (including research councils)
- life sciences
- innovation
- technology and the arts - National Endowment for Science, Technology and the Arts (NESTA)

UK Space Agency

Current role holder:
The Rt. Hon David Willetts MP
David Willetts was appointed Minister for Universities and Science in May 2010. He is the Conservative MP for Havant in Hampshire.

Education
David was educated at King Edward's School, Birmingham and Christ Church, Oxford, where he studied philosophy, politics and economics.

Career in politics
David began his career in Parliament as the MP for Havant in 1992. He served as Paymaster General and then in the Shadow Cabinet in a range of roles, including Shadow Secretary of State for Trade and Industry, Shadow Secretary for Education and Skills, and Shadow Secretary for Innovation, Universities and Skills. He has also worked at HM Treasury and in the Number 10 Policy Unit.

Career outside politics
David was a visiting fellow at Nuffield College, Oxford, is a governor of the Ditchley Foundation and a member of the Council of the Institute for Fiscal Studies. He has written widely on economic and social policy. In 2011 he published a book, 'The Pinch: How the baby boomers took their children's future – and why they should give it back'.

Personal life
David is married to the artist Sarah Butterfield, with whom he has 2 children.

The Rt. Hon Dominic Grieve QC MP
Roles: Attorney General

Responsibilities
The Attorney General is chief legal adviser to the Crown and has a number of independent public interest functions, as well as overseeing the Law Officers' departments. These are:

- the Crown Prosecution Service
- the Serious Fraud Office

Her Majesty's Crown Prosecution Service Inspectorate
Other responsibilities include:

- acting as principal legal adviser on questions of EU and international law, human rights and devolution issues

- referring unduly lenient sentences to the Court of Appeal
- bringing proceedings for contempt of court
- intervening in certain proceedings to protect charities
- dealing with questions of law arising on government Bills
- legal aspects of all major international and domestic litigation involving the government

The Attorney General also holds the separate office of Advocate General for Northern Ireland. The Advocate General for Scotland has specific responsibility for Scottish law matters.

Current role holder:
The Rt. Hon Dominic Grieve QC MP
Dominic Grieve was appointed Attorney General in May 2010. He is the Conservative MP for Beaconsfield.

Education
Dominic was educated at Westminster School and Magdalen College, Oxford, where he studied modern history.

Political career
Dominic held a number of positions in the shadow cabinet including Shadow Attorney General and Shadow Secretary of State for Justice.

Career outside politics
He was called to the bar in 1980 and practised as a barrister before entering Parliament.

Personal life
Dominic is married with 2 children.

How government is run

Departments and their agencies are responsible for putting government policy into practice.

Government departments
Some departments, like the Ministry of Defence, cover the whole UK. Others don't – the Department for Work and Pensions doesn't cover Northern Ireland. This is because some aspects of government are devolved to Scotland, Wales and Northern Ireland.
Non-ministerial departments are headed by senior civil servants and not ministers. They usually have a regulatory or inspection function like the Charity Commission.

Executive agencies
These are part of government departments and usually provide government services rather than decide policy - which is done by the department that oversees the agency.
An example is the Driver and Vehicle Licensing Agency (overseen by the Department for Transport).

Other public bodies
These have varying degrees of independence but are directly accountable to ministers. There are 4 types of non-departmental public bodies (NDPBs).
Executive NDPBs do work for the government in specific areas - for example, the Environment Agency.
Advisory NDPBs provide independent, expert advice to ministers - for example, the Committee on Standards in Public Life.
Tribunal NDPBs are part of the justice system and have jurisdiction over a specific area of law - for example, the Competition Appeal Tribunal.
Independent monitoring boards are responsible for the running of prisons and treatment of prisoners - for example, Her Majesty's Inspectorate of Prisons.

24 ministerial departments
20 Non-ministerial department
334 Agencies & other public bodies

24 Ministerial departments:

Attorney General's Office
Works with 4 agencies and public bodies

Cabinet Office
Works with 20 agencies and public bodies

Department for Business, Innovation & Skills
Works with 47 agencies and public bodies

Department for Communities and Local Government
Works with 12 agencies and public bodies view all

Department for Culture, Media & Sport
Works with 44 agencies and public bodies view all

Department for Education
Works with 9 agencies and public bodies view all

Department for Environment, Food & Rural Affairs
Works with 39 agencies and public bodies view all

Department for International Development
Works with 2 agencies and public bodies view all

Department for Transport
Works with 24 agencies and public bodies view all

Department for Work & Pensions
Works with 13 agencies and public bodies view all

Department of Energy & Climate Change
Works with 8 agencies and public bodies view all

Department of Health
Works with 24 agencies and public bodies view all

Foreign & Commonwealth Office
Works with 12 agencies and public bodies view all

HM Treasury
Works with 8 agencies and public bodies view all

Home Office
Works with 27 agencies and public bodies view all

Ministry of Defence
Works with 28 agencies and public bodies view all

Ministry of Justice
Works with 38 agencies and public bodies view all

Northern Ireland Office
Works with 3 agencies and public bodies view all

Office of the Advocate General for Scotland

Office of the Leader of the House of Commons

Office of the Leader of the House of Lords

Scotland Office
Works with 1 public body view all

UK Export Finance
Works with 1 public body view all

Wales Office
Works with 1 public body

The Attorney General's Office

What we do

The Attorney General's Office (AGO) provides legal advice and support to the Attorney General and the Solicitor General (the Law Officers) who give legal advice to government. The AGO helps the Law Officers perform other duties in the public interest, such as looking at sentences, which may be too low.

Responsibilities

The Attorney General's Office (AGO) is a ministerial department, which supports the Attorney General and the Solicitor General (the Law Officers). The Law Officers are government ministers whom:

- provide legal advice to government
- superintend, or oversee, the main independent prosecuting departments - the Crown Prosecution Service and the Serious Fraud Office
- superintend, or oversee, Her Majesty's CPS Inspectorate, which inspects how cases are prosecuted
- superintend, or oversee, the Treasury Solicitor's Department, which provides legal services to government
- answer questions about their work in Parliament
- perform other functions in the public interest, such as looking at sentences which may be too low - these duties are independent of government

Neither we nor the Law Officers can provide legal advice to members of the public or business.

Consider unduly lenient (low) sentences

If a sentence given in a Crown Court appears to be very low, or unduly lenient, anyone can ask the Attorney General to examine the sentence, within 28 days of sentencing.

The Attorney or Solicitor General may then ask the Court of Appeal to look at the sentence. The Court may decide to keep the sentence the same, increase it, or issue guidance for future cases.

How to complain about a low Crown Court sentence

Complain about a low Crown Court sentence

You can ask for someone's Crown Court sentence to be reviewed if you think it's too low.
The Attorney General can review very low sentences given by the Crown Court in England and Wales if he's asked to.

Only certain types of case can be reviewed, including:

- murder
- rape
- robbery
- child sex crimes and child cruelty
- some serious fraud
- some serious drug crimes
- crimes committed because of the victim's race or religion

Anyone can ask for a sentence to be reviewed - they don't have to be involved in the case.

Only 1 person needs to ask for a sentence to be reviewed.

How to complain

Contact the Attorney General's Office as soon as possible after the sentence is passed. The time limit for making a complaint is 28 days after sentencing.

Provide as much information as you can about the case, e.g. the:

- name of the person who got the sentence
- date the sentence was given
- court where the case was held
- crime committed

Attorney General's Office

www.attorneygeneral.gov.uk
correspondence@attorneygeneral.gsi.gov.uk

Telephone: 020 7271 2492
Monday to Friday, 9am to 5pm
The Attorney General has 28 days to review a sentence and make a decision. Once the case has been reviewed, it may be sent to the Court of Appeal.

The Court of Appeal

The Court of Appeal may decide that the sentence:

- should stay the same
- is unreasonably low (called 'unduly lenient') and may increase it
- refuse to hear the case

Even if a case is passed on to the Court of Appeal it may not change the sentence.

Examine cases of contempt of court

Contempt of court is where inappropriate reporting risks making a trial unfair or where someone does not respect a court or disrupts its work by words or actions.

The Attorney General can take legal action in the public interest if certain types of contempt of court have been committed.

Types of contempt of court dealt with by the Attorney General's Office

The Attorney General and Solicitor General (the Law Officers) can be asked to look at some types of contempt of court.

Introduction

Contempt of court is where someone does not respect a court or disrupts its work by words or actions.

The Attorney General can take legal action in the public interest if contempt of court has been committed.

The main types of contempt are publication contempt, juror contempt and contempt in civil cases.

Publication contempt

Sometimes material is published which risks damaging a trial. This could be in a newspaper, television, and radio or on the Internet.

The material could have broken the laws concerning contempt of court if it could affect the way a jury thinks about a case, or prejudice it so much that a trial cannot take place or has to be stopped.

The material could be in contempt of court and the Law Officers can prosecute whoever published the material.

Juror contempt

A juror may commit contempt if he or she disobeys an order of the Judge or tells someone who is not on the jury details of the jury's thoughts and decisions on the case that they are considering.

Sometimes a judge will deal with contempt by a juror straight away - for example, a juror who disrupts the trial or is not on time. When a more detailed investigation is needed, a judge will often ask the Attorney General for advice.

Contempt in civil cases

In a civil case where the punishment is financial, somebody connected to the case can be in contempt by making a false written statement. The Attorney's role is limited to deciding if there has been a contempt of court.

Deal with vexatious litigants

People who keep bringing unnecessary court cases can be classed as vexatious litigants. The Attorney General can apply to the High Court to designate someone as a vexatious litigant by getting a court order to prevent them from issuing proceedings without agreement from the court.

Inquests

An inquest is a limited, fact-finding inquiry into an unexpected death. It is intended to establish who has died, and how, when and where the death occurred.

If somebody connected to the dead person thinks the inquest did not come to the correct conclusion, for example if new evidence emerges, they can ask the Attorney to consider asking the High Court to look at the evidence again. He will do this if he thinks a new inquest is necessary. He cannot order a new inquest himself.

The Attorney does this as part of his public interest role, independently of government and strictly on the basis of the evidence.

Charity law

The Attorney can help the courts when considering cases involving charities. He can also ask the Charity Tribunal to clarify any matter of charity law.

Consents to prosecute

A few serious offences need the consent of the Attorney General before somebody can be charged. Prosecutors must first decide whether there is enough evidence for a charge.

The Attorney General is not involved in the vast majority of individual cases in England and Wales.

Legal guidance on consents to prosecute

Consent of the Attorney General to prosecute: how to apply

Guidance created in 2012, for those who wish to begin a private prosecution for offences where the Attorney General's consent is required. Only applies to England, Northern Ireland and Wales

Introduction

Some offences cannot be prosecuted without the agreement of the Attorney General. These are called 'Attorney General consent cases' and consent can be given by either the Attorney General or the Solicitor General (known as the Law Officers).

The timing of when consent is required varies depending on the charge, but as a matter of good practice, Attorney General's consent should be obtained at the earliest reasonable opportunity. You should always check the time by which consent needs to be in place.

The Crown Prosecution Service has more detailed guidance on consent to prosecute.

Public prosecuting authorities should refer to their own internal guidance on seeking Attorney General's consent. In the guidance given here, 'prosecutor' means the person or organisation seeking the consent of the Attorney General to prosecute.

Consent is needed for the prosecution of an attempt or conspiracy to commit an offence which itself requires consent. Consent is also needed for offences of aiding, abetting, counselling or procuring a substantive offence, which requires consent.

A conspiracy in England and Wales may involve the doing of an act by one or more of the parties, or the happening of an event, in a place outside England and Wales which constitutes an offence in that other place. In these circumstances, the consent of the Attorney General is required to prosecute the conspiracy in England and Wales.

A list of offences which require Attorney General's consent can be found on the Crown Prosecution Service web site under 'Legal resources'.

However, you should always ensure that you satisfy yourself, by referring to current legislation or up-to-date practitioner textbooks, which offences require consent.

The prosecutor's role in applying for Attorney General's consent
The prosecutor is to:

- review the case and recommend suitable charges
- highlight public interest factors which may affect the decision to prosecute
- supply documents in accordance with the procedure set out below

How to apply for Law Officers' consent

The following is a checklist of material that should be provided (where relevant) to the Attorney General's Office. Original documents should not be sent to the Attorney General's Office.

- the draft charges or indictment

- a typed submission from the prosecutor, which must: contain an explanation of each charge in relation to each person it is proposed to prosecute, and the evidence that the prosecutor says makes it more likely than not that a magistrates' court or jury will convict that person of the charge

- list all the public interest factors which tend in favour of a prosecution and those which tend against - a list of some of the public interest factors which might be relevant can be found in the Code for Crown Prosecutors although there may be others than the ones on that list

- contain a summary of the facts

- identify all the issues in the case

- cross-refer to statements, exhibits and other documents supplied - the relevant page numbers must be referred to in brackets - markings must be then made in the margins on the cross-referenced page, highlighting the exact passage referred to highlight any issues as to timing

- bring to the Attorney's attention any other issues or sensitivities surrounding the matter

- describe how the prosecution intends to put the case at court

- copies of key documents, including statements, documents and exhibits which show the evidence against the person it is proposed to prosecute

- the details of the prosecutor making the application

It is particularly important that the name and address of the person it is proposed to prosecute is stated accurately.

Applications for consent should be sent to:

Deputy Director, Criminal Law
Attorney General's Office
20 Victoria Street
London
SW1H 0NF

Where possible, documents should be submitted by email to the Attorney General's Office.

If items are submitted by post only, if possible, an email should be sent to the Attorney General's Office confirming that they have been sent.

A lawyer at the Attorney General's Office will then review the papers before placing them before the Attorney General or Solicitor General. If there are any items missing from the papers, or more information is needed before the papers are looked at by a Law Officer, these will be requested.

Timing of application for Law Officers' consent

It is essential that the Law Officers are allowed sufficient time to consider the case. The length of time required will depend on the nature and complexity of the case and the quality of the application. A minimum of 2 weeks will normally be required in a straightforward case.

Appointing specialist lawyers to act for the Government

The Law Officers approve the appointment of highly qualified lawyers – counsel – who carry out government work and belong to groups, called panels, according to the type of work they do. This is done with the assistance of the Treasury Solicitor's Department.

Further information on the panels

How to nominate a lawyer to join the panels

Who we work with

The departments superintended by the Law Officers are the:

- Crown Prosecution Service (CPS)
- Serious Fraud Office (SFO)
- Treasury Solicitor's Department (TSol)
- Her Majesty's Crown Prosecution Service Inspectorate (HMCPSI)
- Government Legal Service (GLS)

Protocol between the Attorney General and prosecuting departments

Published in 2009, this protocol sets out how the Attorney General and the directors of the prosecuting departments, (which are the Crown Prosecution Service (CPS), and the Serious Fraud Office (SFO) work with each other. It covers:

- general responsibilities
- strategy
- planning and performance
- responsibility for prosecution decisions
- development of policy
- dealing with the media
- dealing with complaints

We also work with the Ministry of Justice and the Home Office to develop criminal justice policy and promote efficiency and effectiveness.

Cabinet Office

We support the Prime Minister and Deputy Prime Minister, and ensure the effective running of government. We are also the corporate headquarters for government, in partnership with HM Treasury, and we take the lead in certain critical policy areas.

CO is a ministerial department, supported by 20 agencies and public bodies:

- Prime Minister's Office, 10 Downing Street
- Deputy Prime Minister's Office

Ministerial department:

Office of the Leader of the House of Commons
Office of the Leader of the House of Lords

Executive agency:

Government Procurement Service

Executive non-departmental public body:

Civil Service Commission
Big Lottery Fund

Advisory non-departmental public body:

The Committee on Standards in Public Life
Advisory Committee on Business Appointments
Boundary Commission for England
House of Lords Appointments Commission
Security Vetting Appeals Panel
Review Body on Senior Salaries
Boundary Commission for Wales
Social Mobility and Child Poverty Commission

Other:

Privy Council Office
Commissioner for Public Appointments
The McKay Commission
The Parliamentary and Health Service Ombudsman
Government Estates Management

What we do

We support the Prime Minister and Deputy Prime Minister, and ensure the effective running of government. We are also the corporate headquarters for government, in partnership with HM Treasury, and we take the lead in certain critical policy areas.

Responsibilities

We have responsibility for:

- supporting collective government, helping to ensure the effective development, co-ordination and implementation of policy

- supporting the National Security Council and the Joint Intelligence Organisation, co-ordinating the government's response to crises and managing the UK's cyber security

- promoting efficiency and reform across government through innovation, better procurement and project management, and by transforming the delivery of services

- promoting the release of government data, and making the way government works more transparent

- creating an exceptional Civil Service, improving its capability and effectiveness

- promoting social action and National Citizen Service, and growing the social investment market

- political and constitutional reform

Priorities

In 2012 and 2013, our priorities are:

- to establish and implement the coalition government's overall strategy and policy priorities

- to reform the UK's constitutional and political system - implementing the coalition's commitments on lobbying, the Royal Succession laws, party funding and other areas

- to improve the integrity and efficiency of the electoral system, including managing the move to individual electoral registration in 2015

- to maintain a robust, decentralised UK, including co-ordinating

- to achieve greater efficiency savings across government

- to promote open data and transparency both nationally and internationally, through the UK's chairmanship of the Open Government Partnership

- to launch the Centre for Social Action, which will promote volunteering opportunities through its campaigns, and to increase the scale of National Citizen Service to provide more places for young people

- to contribute to UK growth and agree our strategy for continued contribution in future years

- to implement the Civil Service Reform Plan and publish a one year on report

Who we are

We employ around 2,050 staff. There are also around 380 people working for the Government Procurement Service, an executive agency.

Our main offices are in London, but we have staff based around the country. We are supported by a number of advisory non-departmental bodies.

Priorities

Our main priorities are to:

- deliver the government's legislative programme
- respond to the Joint Committee on Parliamentary Privilege

Who we are

Our team is based in the Palace of Westminster and 1 Horse Guards Road, London.

Although resourced by Cabinet Office, the Leader and the Deputy Leader of the Commons are not Cabinet Office ministers. Together with the Leader of the House of Lords, the Chief Whips and their respective deputies in both houses, our ministers and offices are otherwise known as the Parliamentary Business Managers.

The Leader is an ex-officio member of the House of Commons Commission and the Speaker's Committee on IPSA, and as Lord Privy Seal acts as the Chair of the Board of Trustees for the Chevening Estate.

Office of the Leader of the House of Lords

What we do

We provide support to the Leader of the House of Lords. The Leader of the House is appointed by the Prime Minister, is a member of the Cabinet and is responsible for the conduct of government business in the Lords. The Leader advises the House on procedure and order, and he and his office are available to assist and advise all members of the House.
Responsibilities

We support the Leader in his parliamentary and ministerial duties, which include:

- leading the government benches in the House of Lords

- delivery of the government's business in the Lords (jointly responsible with the Lords Chief Whip)

- repeating in the Lords statements made by the Prime Minister in the Commons

- giving guidance to the House on matters of procedure and order

- taking part in formal ceremonies in the House, like the State Opening of Parliament Chair, Board of Trustees for Chequers and Dorneywood

- as Chancellor of the Duchy of Lancaster, responsible to the Sovereign for the administration of the Duchy (a collection of land, property and assets held in trust for the Sovereign as private income)

We also provide private office support to the Rt. Hon Lord McNally in his capacity as Deputy Leader.

Who we are

We are a small team based in the Palace of Westminster and 1 Horse Guards Road, London.

Together with the Leader of the House of Commons, the Chief Whips and their respective deputies in both houses, our ministers and offices are otherwise known as the Parliamentary Business Managers.

Government Procurement Service

The Government Procurement Service (GPS) saves money for the public sector by improving supplier management, and is responsible for agreeing centralised contracts for government departments.
GPS is an executive agency of the Cabinet Office
http://gps.cabinetoffice.gov.uk/

Civil Service Commission

The Civil Service Commission regulates recruitment to the Civil Service, ensuring appointments are fair. It also hears complaints under the Civil Service Code. CSC is an executive non-departmental public body of the Cabinet Office
http://civilservicecommission.independent.gov.uk/

Big Lottery Fund

Every year the Big Lottery Fund (BIG) gives out millions of pounds from the UK's National Lottery to good causes, with money going to community groups and health, education and environment projects.
BIG is an executive non-departmental public body of the Cabinet Office
http://www.biglotteryfund.org.uk

The Committee on Standards in Public Life

The Committee on Standards in Public Life (CSPL) advises government on ethical standards across the whole of public life in the UK. It monitors and reports on issues relating to the standards of conduct of all public office holders. CSPL is an advisory non-departmental public body of the Cabinet Office
http://www.public-standards.gov.uk/

Advisory Committee on Business Appointments

The Advisory Committee on Business Appointments (ACOBA) considers applications under the business appointment rules about new jobs for former ministers, senior civil servants and other Crown servants. ACOBA is an advisory non-departmental public body of the Cabinet Office
http://acoba.independent.gov.uk

Boundary Commission for England

The Boundary Commission for England (BCE) is required by the Parliamentary Constituencies Act 1986 to review the parliamentary constituencies in England every 5 years. BCE is an advisory non-departmental public body of the Cabinet Office
http://consultation.boundarycommissionforengland.independent.gov.uk/

House of Lords Appointments Commission

The House of Lords Appointments Commission (HOLAC) recommends individuals for appointment as non-party-political life peers and vets nominations for life peers to ensure the highest standards of propriety. HOLAC is an advisory non-departmental public body of the Cabinet Office
http://lordsappointments.independent.gov.uk/

Security Vetting Appeals Panel

The Security Vetting Appeals Panel is an independent avenue of appeal for Civil Service staff and contractors whose security clearance has been refused or withdrawn. SVAP is an advisory non-departmental public body of the Cabinet Office
http://webarchive.nationalarchives.gov.uk/+/www.direct.gov.uk/en/Dl1/Directories/DG_065029

Review Body on Senior Salaries

The Review Body on Senior Salaries (SSRB) provides independent advice to the Prime Minister, the Lord Chancellor and the Secretary of State for Defence on the pay of senior civil servants, the judiciary, senior officers of the armed forces and others. It also advises the Prime Minister on the pay and pensions of MPs and their allowances, on peers' allowances, and on the pay, pensions and allowances of ministers and others in England. SSRB is an advisory non-departmental public body of the Cabinet Office
http://www.ome.uk.com/Senior_Salaries_Review_Body.aspx

Boundary Commission for Wales

The Boundary Commission for Wales (BCW) carries out boundary reviews of parliamentary constituencies in Wales, and submits its recommendations to the government. BCW is an advisory non-departmental public body of the Wales Office and the Cabinet Office
http://bcomm-wales.gov.uk/

Social Mobility and Child Poverty Commission

What we do

The Social Mobility and Child Poverty (SMCP) Commission monitors the progress of government and others in improving social mobility and reducing child poverty in the United Kingdom.

Responsibilities

We are responsible for:

- publishing an annual report setting out our views on progress made in improving social mobility and reducing child poverty in the UK, including against the targets in the Child Poverty Act 2010, and describing the measures taken by the Scottish and Welsh governments

- providing published advice to ministers (at their request) on how to measure socio-economic disadvantage, social mobility and child poverty

- acting as an advocate for social mobility beyond government by challenging employers, the professions and universities amongst others to play their part in improving life chances

Priorities

In 2013, our main priorities will be:

- holding the government and others to account through providing an authoritative 'state of the nation' analysis of social mobility and child poverty in our first annual report

- creating a business manifesto for social mobility and using it to encourage firms to put and keep the issue on the agenda, as well as working closely with specific professions and the university sector to drive change

- Influencing policy via credible and independent advice. We have responded to the government consultation on better measures of child poverty and are currently developing advice to ministers on the 3 or 4 most impactful steps the government could reasonably take to improve social mobility

Who we are

The Social Mobility and Child Poverty Commission is chaired by the Rt. Hon Alan Milburn and deputy chaired by Baroness Gillian Shephard.

It includes 7 other members drawn from across business, academia and the voluntary sector. It is supported by a small secretariat based in London.

Privy Council Office

The Privy Council is how interdepartmental agreement is reached on items of government business which, for historical or other reasons, fall to ministers as privy counsellors rather than as departmental ministers. The Privy Council Office (PCO) provides secretariat services for the Council, including the arrangements leading to the making of all Royal Proclamations and Orders in Council. PCO works with the Cabinet Office
http://privycouncil.independent.gov.uk/

Commissioner for Public Appointments

The Commissioner for Public Appointments regulates the processes by which ministers make appointments to the boards of national and regional public bodies. The commissioner aims to ensure that such appointments are made on merit after a fair, open and transparent process. Commissioner for Public Appointments works with the Cabinet Office
http://publicappointmentscommissioner.independent.gov.uk/

McKay Commission

The McKay Commission (TMC) was set up to consider how the House of Commons might deal with legislation which affects only part of the UK, following the devolution of certain legislative powers to Scotland, Northern Ireland and Wales. TMC works with the Cabinet Office
http://tmc.independent.gov.uk/

The Parliamentary and Health Service Ombudsman
The Parliamentary and Health Service Ombudsman investigates complaints that individuals have been treated unfairly or have received poor service from government departments, other public organisations and the NHS in England. The Ombudsman works with the Cabinet Office
http://www.ombudsman.org.uk/

Government Estates Management

What we do

We are responsible for providing solutions to specialist estates management issues across government. Responsibilities

We work to develop a government estate that is:

- safe - health and safety is a critical issue for government workers and the public

- secure - whether it is a facility or an area of land, government property needs to be protected from intrusion, damage and unauthorised use

- economical - limited resources mean that public sector bodies need to make tough decisions about priorities

- efficient - to maximise value for money, it's essential for public bodies to increase the efficiency of their estate services and investments

- sustainable - the government has set high standards for the public sector to reduce its impact on the environment and ensure a sustainable future

Priorities

GEM's advisory team provides a range of services to clients. We are committed to:

- promoting best practices in estates management

- delivering value-added services to our client

- providing consultancy advice on issues involving the government estate

- managing public expectations in relation to estates management

Department for Business Innovation & Skills

What we do

The Department for Business, Innovation & Skills (BIS) is the department for economic growth. The department invests in skills and education to promote trade, boost innovation and help people to start and grow a business. BIS also protects consumers and reduces the impact of regulation.

Responsibilities

We are responsible for:

- working with further and higher education providers to give students the skills they need to compete in a global employment market

- supporting innovation and developing the UK's science and research industry, which is important to help economic growth

- making sure consumer law is fair for both consumers and businesses, and that consumers know their rights and are able to use them effectively

- supporting British businesses to increase productivity and compete anywhere in the world

- better regulation - by cutting the amount of regulation and making it easy to understand we can help businesses cut time, save money and be more efficient

Priorities

Our priorities for 2012 to 2013 include:

- supplying £100 million to universities for long-term research projects

- introducing a new loans system for further education students

- creating a single Manufacturing Advisory Service (MAS) in England to replace the 8 previous regional services

- making the UK one of the fastest and easiest countries in the world to set up a new business

- extending the right to request flexible working and develop a new system of shared parental leave

- ending the culture of 'tick-box' regulation, and instead target inspections on high-risk organisations through co-regulation and improving professional standards

- giving the public and businesses the opportunity to challenge the worst regulations

For all of our priorities, have a look at our business plan for 2012 to 2015.

Who we are

We have around 2,500 staff working for BIS plus around 500 people working for UK Trade & Investment in the UK.

Our partner organisations include 9 executive agencies employing around 14,500 staff.

We have BIS offices in London, Sheffield, Billingham, Cardiff, Darlington, Glasgow, Manchester, Nottingham, Runcorn and Watford.

BIS is supported by 49 agencies and public bodies. Read more about them:

Non-ministerial department
Office of Fair Trading
UK Trade & Investment
Competition and Markets Authority

Executive agency
Companies House
UK Space Agency
The Insolvency Service
National Measurement Office
Skills Funding Agency
Intellectual Property Office
Met Office
HM Land Registry
Ordnance Survey

Executive non-departmental public body
Higher Education Funding Council for England
Acas
Arts and Humanities Research Council
British Hallmarking Council
Construction Industry Training Board
Economic and Social Research Council
Engineering and Physical Sciences Research Council
Engineering Construction Industry Training Board
Medical Research Council
Natural Environment Research Council
Office for Fair Access
Science and Technology Facilities Council
Student Loans Company
Technology Strategy Board
UK Atomic Energy Authority
UK Commission for Employment and Skills
Capital for Enterprise Ltd
Biotechnology & Biological Sciences Research Council
Competition Service
Competition Commission

Consumer Focus

Tribunal non-departmental public body
Competition Appeal Tribunal
Central Arbitration Committee
Copyright Tribunal
Insolvency Practitioners' Tribunal

Other
Certification Office
Office of Manpower Economics
UK Green Investment Bank
Groceries Code Adjudicator

Office of Fair Trading

The Office of Fair-Trading (OFT) promotes and protects consumer interests throughout the UK, while ensuring that businesses are fair and competitive. Its mission is to make markets work well for consumers.
OFT is a non-ministerial department of the Department for Business, Innovation & Skills
http://www.oft.gov.uk

UK Trade & Investment

UK Trade & Investment (UKTI) works with UK-based businesses to ensure their success in international markets and encourage the best overseas companies to look to the UK as their global partner of choice.
UKTI is a non-ministerial department of the Department for Business, Innovation & Skills and the Foreign & Commonwealth Office
http://www.ukti.gov.uk/

Competition and Markets Authority

The Competition and Markets Authority (CMA) will work independently of government to promote competition for the benefit of consumers. It will aim to deliver a faster, more responsive competition regime focused on what matters to people and businesses. The CMA will function fully from 1 April 2014 and start sharing its development and plans from 1 October 2013.
CMA is a non-ministerial department of the Department for Business, Innovation & Skills

Companies House

Companies House incorporates and dissolves limited companies, registers the information companies are legally required to supply, and makes that information available to the public.
CH is an executive agency of the Department for Business, Innovation & Skills
http://www.companieshouse.gov.uk/

UK Space Agency

The UK Space Agency is at the heart of UK efforts to explore and benefit from space. It funds the National Space Technology Programme and works with educational and community organisations.
UKSA is an executive agency of the Department for Business, Innovation & Skills
http://www.bis.gov.uk/ukspaceagency

The Insolvency Service

The Insolvency Service (INSS) regulates the insolvency profession. It pays statutory redundancy to employees of insolvent companies, conducts investigations in the public interest and provides practical information on insolvency procedures in England and Wales.
INSS is an executive agency of the Department for Business, Innovation & Skills
http://www.bis.gov.uk/insolvency

National Measurement Office

The National Measurement Office (NMO) ensures fair and accurate measurements are available and used for transactions regulated by law. One of its main activities is preparing legislation under the Weights and Measures Act 1985 and European Communities Act 1972.
NMO is an executive agency of the Department for Business, Innovation & Skills
http://www.bis.gov.uk/nmo

Skills Funding Agency

The Skills Funding Agency (SFA) funds and promotes adult further education and skills training in England (excluding higher education).
SFA is an executive agency of the Department for Business, Innovation & Skills
http://skillsfundingagency.bis.gov.uk/

Intellectual Property Office

The Intellectual Property Office (IPO) is responsible for intellectual property rights in the UK, including patents, designs, trademarks and copyright. It can help you get the right type of protection for your creation or invention.
IPO is an executive agency of the Department for Business, Innovation & Skills
http://www.ipo.gov.uk

Met Office

The Met Office is the UK's national weather service. It provides weather and climate-related services to the Armed Forces, government departments, the public, civil aviation, shipping, industry, agriculture and commerce. Met Office is an executive agency of the Department for Business, Innovation & Skills
http://www.metoffice.gov.uk/

HM Land Registry

The Land Registry (HMLR) registers the ownership of land and property in England and Wales. It keeps and maintains the Land Register, where more than 23 million titles – the evidence of ownership – are documented. HMLR is an executive agency of the Department for Business, Innovation & Skills
http://www.landregistry.gov.uk/

Ordnance Survey

Ordnance Survey is Great Britain's national mapping agency. It carries out the official surveying of GB, providing the most accurate and up-to-date geographic data, relied on by government, business and individuals. Ordnance Survey is an executive agency of the Department for Business, Innovation & Skills
OS is an executive agency of the Department for Business, Innovation & Skills
http://www.ordnancesurvey.co.uk/

Higher Education Funding Council for England

The Higher Education Funding Council for England (HEFCE) distributes public money for teaching and research to universities and colleges. It promotes high quality education and research, within a financially healthy sector. HEFCE is an executive non-departmental public body of the Department for Business, Innovation & Skills
http://www.hefce.ac.uk/

Advisory, Conciliation and Arbitration Service
Acas stands for the Advisory, Conciliation and Arbitration Service. The service aims to improve organisations and working life through better employment relations, working with employers and employees to solve problems and improve performance.
Acas is an executive non-departmental public body of the Department for Business, Innovation & Skills
http://www.acas.org.uk/

Arts and Humanities Research Council

The Arts and Humanities Research Council (AHRC) is a national funding agency supporting arts and humanities research and study in the UK. Each year it makes about 700 research awards, 2,000 postgraduate scholarships, and many knowledge transfers awards.
AHRC is an executive non-departmental public body of the Department for Business, Innovation & Skills
http://www.ahrc.ac.uk/

British Hallmarking Council

We supervise the Hallmarking activities of the 4 Assay Offices and ensure there is adequate provision of Hallmarking within the UK.
BHC is an executive non-departmental public body of the Department for Business, Innovation & Skills
http://www.bis.gov.uk/britishhallmarkingcouncil

Construction Industry Training Board

The Construction Industry Training Board (CITB) is the Sector Skills Council and Industry Training Board for the construction industry. It works with construction companies to improve skills, increase competitive edge and respond to the many challenges employers' face.
CITB is an executive non-departmental public body of the Department for Business, Innovation & Skills
http://www.citb.co.uk

Economic and Social Research Council

The Economic and Social Research Council (ESRC) is the UK's largest organisation funding research on economic and social issues, supporting independent, high quality research which influences business, the public sector and the charity and voluntary sector. It currently supports over 4,000 researchers and postgraduate students.
ESRC is an executive non-departmental public body of the Department for Business, Innovation & Skills
http://www.esrc.ac.uk/

Engineering and Physical Sciences Research Council

The Engineering and Physical Sciences Research Council (EPSRC) is the main UK government agency for funding research and training in engineering and the physical sciences, investing more than £850 million a year in a broad range of subjects – from mathematics to materials science, and from information technology to structural engineering.
EPSRC is an executive non-departmental public body of the Department for Business, Innovation & Skills
http://www.epsrc.ac.uk/

Engineering Construction Industry Training Board

The Engineering Construction Industry Training Board (ECITB) ensures there are enough trained people to meet industry needs. It gives professional advice and offers skills development and qualifications to help individuals in the sector succeed in their chosen careers.
ECITB is an executive non-departmental public body of the Department for Business, Innovation & Skills
http://www.ecitb.org.uk/

Medical Research Council

The Medical Research Council (MRC) is a national funding agency dedicated to improving human health by supporting research across the entire spectrum of medical sciences, in universities and hospitals, in MRC units, centres and institutes in the UK, and in MRC units in Africa.
MRC is an executive non-departmental public body of the Department for Business, Innovation & Skills
http://www.mrc.ac.uk/

Natural Environment Research Council
The Natural Environment Research Council (NERC) is the UK's main agency for funding and managing research, training and knowledge exchange in atmospheric, Earth, biological, terrestrial and aquatic sciences.
NERC is an executive non-departmental public body of the Department for Business, Innovation & Skills
http://www.nerc.ac.uk/

Office for Fair Access

The Office for Fair Access (OFFA) safeguards and promotes fair access to higher education by approving and monitoring access agreements. All English universities and colleges that want to charge higher fees must have an access agreement with us.
OFFA is an executive non-departmental public body of the Department for Business, Innovation & Skills
http://www.offa.org.uk/

Science and Technology Facilities Council

The Science and Technology Facilities Council (STFC) co-ordinates research on some of the most significant challenges facing society, such as future energy needs, monitoring and understanding climate change, and global security. It offers grants and support in particle physics, astronomy and nuclear physics.
STFC is an executive non-departmental public body of the Department for Business, Innovation & Skills
http://www.stfc.ac.uk/

Student Loans Company

The Student Loans Company (SLC) is a non-profit making government-owned organisation that administers loans and grants to students in universities and colleges in the UK.
SLC is an executive non-departmental public body of the Department for Business, Innovation & Skills
http://www.slc.co.uk/

Technology Strategy Board

The Technology Strategy Board (TSB) stimulates technology-enabled innovation in the areas that should boost UK growth and productivity. It advises government on how to accelerate the exploitation of new technologies.
TSB is an executive non-departmental public body of the Department for Business, Innovation & Skills
http://www.innovateuk.org/

UK Atomic Energy Authority

The UK Atomic Energy Authority carries out fusion research in the UK on behalf of the government and manages the JET fusion project on behalf of the EU at the Culham Centre for Fusion Energy (CCFE).
UKAEA is an executive non-departmental public body of the Department for Business, Innovation & Skills
http://www.uk-atomic-energy.org.uk/

UK Commission for Employment and Skills

The UK Commission for Employment and Skills (UKCES) is a social partnership of commissioners that include CEOs and representatives from trade unions and the voluntary sector. The commission helps to raise skill levels to create more and better jobs and stimulate economic growth.
UKCES is an executive non-departmental public body of the Department for Business, Innovation & Skills
http://www.ukces.org.uk/

Capital for Enterprise Ltd

Capital for Enterprise (CfEL) is a fund management company for venture capital and debt guarantee schemes. It acts on behalf of the public and private sectors, bringing together expertise in SME finance markets (debt, equity and hybrids) with an understanding of public policy objectives.
CfEL is an executive non-departmental public body of the Department for Business, Innovation & Skills
http://www.capitalforenterprise.gov.uk/

Biotechnology & Biological Sciences Research Council
The Biotechnology and Biological Sciences Research Council (BBSRC) is a national funding agency investing in bioscience research and training in the UK. The Council aims to further scientific knowledge, promote economic growth and improve the quality of life in the UK and beyond.
BBSRC is an executive non-departmental public body of the Department for Business, Innovation & Skills
http://www.bbsrc.ac.uk/

The Competition Service

(CS) hears appeals on rulings by the Office of Fair Trading and the regulators of the telecommunications, electricity, gas, water, railways and air traffic services, under the Competition Act 1998 and other legislation. It also reviews decisions made by the Secretary of State, the OFT and the Competition Commission in respect of merger and market references. The government proposes to close, merge or reforms this body as part of the Public Bodies Reform Programme.
CS is an executive non-departmental public body of the Department for Business, Innovation & Skills
http://www.catribunal.org.uk/244/Competition-Service.html Competition Service

Competition Commission

The Competition Commission (CC) ensures healthy competition between companies in the UK for the ultimate benefit of consumers and the economy. It conducts in-depth investigations into mergers and markets, and also has certain functions with regard to the major regulated industries.
CC is an executive non-departmental public body of the Department for Business, Innovation & Skills
http://www.competition-commission.org.uk/

Consumer Focus
Consumer Focus is the statutory consumer champion for England, Wales, Scotland and (for postal consumers) Northern Ireland. It investigates complaints that are of wider consumer interest and can make the provider's response public.
Consumer Focus is an executive non-departmental public body of the Department for Business, Innovation & Skills
http://www.consumerfocus.org.uk

Council for Science and Technology
The Council for Science and Technology (CST) advises the government on developing science, engineering, technology and mathematics (STEM) in the UK, improving STEM education and making more effective use of research and scientific advice.
CST is an advisory non-departmental public body of the Department for Business, Innovation & Skills
http://www.bis.gov.uk/cst

Low Pay Commission

The Low Pay Commission (LPC) advises government about the National Minimum Wage and makes rate recommendations, taking into account the impact on the economy. The commission has a long-term research programme including fact-finding visits to all parts of the country.
LPC is an advisory non-departmental public body of the Department for Business, Innovation & Skills
http://www.lowpay.gov.uk/

Industrial Development Advisory Board

What we do

The Industrial Development Advisory Board (IDAB) advises ministers on applications from companies proposing to start capital investment projects in the Assisted Areas in England and who have applied for regional selective assistance under the Grant for Business Investment scheme or the Regional Growth Fund.

The Industrial Development Advisory Board (IDAB) advises Ministers on applications from companies who are proposing to undertake capital investment projects in the Assisted Areas in England and have applied for regional selective assistance under the Grant for Business Investment (GBI) scheme or the Regional Growth Fund.

We are a statutory body that provides robust, independent, business advice to Ministers on large business investment decisions. The main focus of our work is large applications for investment support in England's Assisted Areas, though we also look at a range of other projects where Ministers want a commercial view. We also look at relevant schemes of support in their development phase.

The Board has a long and distinguished history of service to successive Governments. It first met in 1972. We see the key objective of our role as ensuring that taxpayers' support is given only to projects that truly merit it and that it represents best value for money.

Board members are chosen to provide a range of expertise from industry, banking and the wider community. All are experts in their field. Members are unpaid and give significant amounts of their time on a voluntary basis.

Land Registration Rule Committee

The Land Registration Rule Committee (LRRC) advises and assists in the making of Land Registration Rules and Land Registration Fee Orders and draft amendments for the Lord Chancellor and the Secretary of State under the Land Registration Act 2002.
LRRC is an advisory non-departmental public body of the Department for Business, Innovation & Skills
http://www.landregistry.gov.uk/professional/law-and-practice/act-and-rules/land-registration-rule-committee

Regulatory Policy Committee

The Regulatory Policy Committee (RPC) helps government by reviewing evidence and analysis supporting new regulatory proposals before final ministerial decisions.
RPC is an advisory non-departmental public body of the Department for Business, Innovation & Skills
http://regulatorypolicycommittee.independent.gov.uk/

Export Guarantees Advisory Council

What we do

We advise the Secretary of State for Business, Innovation and Skills (BIS) on UK Export Finance's operations.

What we do
We advise ministers on the operations of UK Export Finance.

Responsibilities

The Export Guarantees Advisory Council (EGAC) is a statutory body that provides advice to UK Export Finance and its ministers on the policies UK Export Finance applies when doing business including:

- environmental impacts and human rights
- anti-bribery and corruption
- sustainable lending
- disclosure (freedom of information)

Ministers have a statutory duty to consult EGAC on matters related to the provision of reinsurance by UK Export Finance to the private credit insurance market.

The council doesn't provide advice on decisions UK Export Finance makes to support individual export transactions and projects, although it does carry out reviews to understand how UK Export Finance's principles and policies are applied in practice. As appropriate, it also gives advice on how these might be further developed.

Priorities

Our main function is to provide advice on UK Export Finance's work, so our priorities reflect the work UK Export Finance has set out for 2013 to 2014.

Who we are

The council has 8 members, each representing a separate area of expertise. The members come from industry, government and academia, and are appointed by UK Export Finance's ministers.

Competition Appeal Tribunal

The UK Competition Appeal Tribunal (CAT) is a specialist judicial body with a cross-disciplinary expertise in law, economics, business and accountancy, whose function is to hear and decide cases involving competition or economic regulatory issues.
CAT is a tribunal non-departmental public body of the Department for Business, Innovation & Skills
http://www.catribunal.org.uk/

Central Arbitration Committee

The Central Arbitration Committee (CAC) judges applications relating to recognition of trade unions. Its role is to promote fair and efficient arrangements in the workplace, by resolving collective disputes (in England, Scotland and Wales) either by voluntary agreement or, if necessary, through adjudication.
CAC is a tribunal non-departmental public body of the Department for Business, Innovation & Skills
http://www.cac.gov.uk/

Copyright Tribunal

The Copyright Tribunal makes rulings in unresolved cases on the terms and conditions of licences offered to applicants by collective licensing bodies in the copyright and related rights area. It can also settle disputes over royalties' payable, for example by publishers of TV programme listings to broadcasting organisations.
Copyright Tribunal is a tribunal non-departmental public body of the Department for Business, Innovation & Skills
http://www.ipo.gov.uk/ctribunal.htm

Insolvency Practitioners' Tribunal

The Insolvency Practitioners' Tribunal (IPT) is a specialist body, which hears appeals from people who have had their accreditation as an insolvency practitioner removed.
IPT is a tribunal non-departmental public body of the Department for Business, Innovation & Skills

Certification Office

The Certification Office (CERTOFF) maintains a list of trade unions and employers' associations.
CERTOFF works with the Department for Business, Innovation & Skills
http://www.certoffice.org/

Office of Manpower Economics

The Office of Manpower Economics (OME) offers independent advice on public sector pay and conditions to the 6 Pay Review Bodies and the Police Negotiating and Police Advisory (England & Wales) Boards. Together these make recommendations affecting some 2.5 million public sector workers with an aggregate pay bill of around £95 billion.
OME works with the Department for Business, Innovation & Skills
http://www.ome.uk.com/

UK Green Investment Bank

The UK Green Investment Bank (GIB) is the world's first investment bank dedicated to greening the economy. With government funding of £3 billion, the GIB invests in innovative, environmentally friendly areas for which there is a lack of support from private markets. This includes offshore wind power generation, waste-handling plants, energy efficiency measures, biofuels, biomass, carbon capture and storage, marine energy and renewable heat generation.
GIB works with the Department for Business, Innovation & Skills
http://www.greeninvestmentbank.com/

Groceries Code Adjudicator

What we do

The Groceries Code Adjudicator is the UK's first independent adjudicator to oversee the relationship between supermarkets and their suppliers. It ensures that large supermarkets treat their direct suppliers lawfully and fairly, investigates complaints and arbitrates in disputes.

The Groceries Code Adjudicator is the new independent adjudicator that oversees the relationship between supermarkets and their suppliers. It ensures that large supermarkets treat their direct suppliers lawfully and fairly by upholding and enforcing the [Groceries Supply Code of Practice].

Responsibilities

We have powers to enforce the Groceries Supply Code of Practice, in particular we:

- investigate confidential complaints from any source about how supermarkets treat their suppliers
- make recommendations to retailers if a complaint is upheld
- require retailers to publish details of a breach of the code
- in the most serious cases, impose a fine on the retailer
- arbitrate disputes between retailers and suppliers

Who we are

The Groceries Code Adjudicator Act, which created the GCA, came into force on June 25 2013.

If a supplier is concerned that there has been a breach of the code, they can complain to the GCA. We can also receive information about potential breaches from the code from anyone, and any complaints we receive will be kept strictly confidential.

We will only be able to launch investigations after we have completed our consultation and finalised our guidance. We anticipate this will be by the end of the year.

If you are considering sending us a complaint or information about a potential breach of the code, please use our checklist to ensure the item is under the remit of the adjudicator and that the retailer is one of those that has to abide by the code.

You can also view a PowerPoint presentation that explains the powers, remit and functions of the Groceries Code Adjudicator, including what types of complaint are covered by the GCA.

We work on these topics

Food and farming
Britain needs to ensure a sustainable supply of food for the UK market and export. Supporting and developing British farming and encouraging sustainable food production (including fisheries) will ensure a secure, environmentally sustainable and healthy supply of food with improved standards of animal welfare.

Department for Communities and Local Government

What we do

We work to move decision-making power from central government to local councils. This helps put communities in charge of planning, increases accountability and helps citizens to see how their money is being spent.

Responsibilities

We are responsible for:

- supporting local government by giving them the power to act for their community - without interference from central government
- helping communities and neighbourhoods to solve their own problems so neighbourhoods are strong, attractive and thriving
- working with local enterprise partnerships and enterprise zones to help the private sector grow
- making the planning system work more efficiently and effectively
- supporting local fire and rescue authorities so that they're able to respond to emergencies and reduce the number and impact of fires

Priorities

In 2012 to 2013, our priorities will be:

- putting local councils and businesses in charge of economic growth and bringing new business and jobs to their areas
- getting the housing market moving again so there are more homes to buy and to rent at prices people can afford
- ensuring Council Tax payers get value for money and making their local council accountable to them
- turning round the lives of troubled families, giving them the chance of a better life and reducing the cost to the taxpayer
- bringing people together in strong united, communities

DCLG is a ministerial department, supported by 12 agencies and public bodies.

Department for Communities and Local Government

Executive agency

Planning Inspectorate
Queen Elizabeth II Conference Centre

Executive non-departmental public body

Homes and Communities Agency
Housing Ombudsman
Leasehold Advisory Service
London Thames Gateway Development Corporation
West Northamptonshire Development Corporation

Advisory non-departmental public body

Building Regulations
Advisory Committee

Tribunal non-departmental public body

Valuation Tribunal

Public corporation
Architects Registration Board
Audit Commission

Other
Local Government
Ombudsman

Planning Inspectorate

What we do

The Planning Inspectorate deals with planning appeals, national infrastructure planning applications, examinations of local plans and other planning-related and specialist casework in England and Wales.
This site contains corporate information only. If you are looking for guidance on appeals or any other type of casework we deal with, or wish to use our online appeals service, please go to the Planning Portal.

For information on national infrastructure projects please go to the National Infrastructure Planning site.

Responsibilities

We are responsible for:

- national infrastructure planning, which includes large-scale projects such as harbours, power generating stations (including wind farms) and electricity transmission lines
- planning and enforcement appeals

- examining local plans
- listed building consent appeals
- advertisement appeals
- reporting on planning applications that are called in for DCLG's Secretary of State to decide
- rights of way orders

Priorities

In 2012 to 2013, our main priorities will be to:

- improve the experiences of our customers by improving our systems, business processes and productivity
- use modern technology and 'digital by default' services to replace our casework management system
- share our IT with other areas of government
- explore different ways of delivering existing and new services and opportunities for generating income
- develop our workforce through improved performance management and a new plan for learning and development

Who we are

We have around 730 staff and 100 contractors, who work from home or from our offices in Bristol or Cardiff.

Department for Culture Media & Sport

What we do

The Department for Culture, Media & Sport (DCMS) is here to help make Britain the world's most creative and exciting place to live, visit and do business. We protect and promote our cultural and artistic heritage and help businesses and communities to grow by investing in innovation and highlighting Britain as a fantastic place to visit. Alongside this, we protect our deeply held beliefs in freedom and equality. We help to give the UK a unique advantage in the global race for economic success.

Responsibilities

We are responsible for:

- making it easier for everyone to enjoy our national culture, play sport and have access to world-leading mobile and online communications
- making it easier for the media, creative, tourism and telecoms industries to grow by reducing restrictions, providing advice and supporting innovation, while protecting the interests of citizens
- protecting free access to cultural institutions, art and broadcasting that challenges and provokes, and funding our future elite athletes
- the Government Art Collection, which places art in British government buildings and official residences around the world, to promote British art and history while contributing to cultural diplomacy
- We also lead on issues relating to women, sexual orientation and transgender equality matters through the Government Equalities Office (GEO), which is part of DCMS.

Priorities

In 2013, our priorities include:

- creating a fairer and more equal society, including opening up marriage to same-sex couples
- helping to provide a lasting legacy for the 2012 London Olympic and Paralympic Games (working with the Cabinet Office and colleagues across government)
- supporting vibrant and sustainable arts and culture nationally by continuing to fund arm's length bodies like the Arts Council, giving incentives to the creative industries and by sponsoring the UK city of culture programme (Derry - Londonderry in 2013)
- helping roll out the next generation of mobile communications (4G) and working to transform the UK's broadband network by 2015
- sponsoring ongoing national and international campaigns promoting UK tourism

Who we are

Our headquarters are in London.

We have around 380 staff working for DCMS, but most of the work that people know us for is carried out by the 47 public bodies that support us.

Executive agency
Royal Parks

Executive non-departmental public body

Arts Council England
British Library
British Museum
English Heritage
Gambling Commission
Geffrye Museum
Horniman Museum
Imperial War Museum
National Gallery
National Heritage Memorial Fund
National Lottery Commission
Science Museum Group
National Museums Liverpool
National Portrait Gallery
Natural History Museum
Olympic Delivery Authority
Royal Armouries Museum
Sir John Soane's Museum
Sports Grounds Safety Authority
UK Sport
Visit Britain
Wallace Collection
British Film Institute
Sport England
UK Anti-Doping
Equality and Human Rights Commission
Victoria and Albert Museum
Public Lending Right
Olympic Lottery Distributor
Heritage Lottery Fund
Royal Museums Greenwich

Advisory non-departmental public body

Visit England
The Theatres Trust
The Reviewing Committee on the Export of Works of Art and Objects of Cultural Interest
Treasure Valuation Committee
Advisory Council on Libraries

Tribunal non-departmental public body

Horserace Betting Levy Board

Public corporation

Channel 4
S4C
BBC
Historic Royal Palaces

Other
Ofcom
Government Equalities Office

Royal Parks

The Royal Parks manages the 5,000 acres of London parkland that make up the 8 Royal Parks: Bushy Park (with the Longford River), The Green Park, Greenwich Park, Hyde Park, Kensington Gardens, The Regent's Park (and Primrose Hill), Richmond Park and St James's Park. It also tends to a number of other spaces in London, including Victoria Tower Gardens, Brompton Cemetery, the gardens of 10, 11 and 12 Downing Street, and Grosvenor Square Gardens.
Royal Parks is an executive agency of the Department for Culture, Media & Sport
http://www.royalparks.gov.uk/

Arts Council England
Arts Council England champions, develops and invests in artistic and cultural experiences to enrich people's lives. It supports a range of activities across the arts, museums and libraries - from theatre to digital art - reading to dance music to literature, and crafts to collections.
Arts Council England is an executive non-departmental public body of the Department for Culture, Media & Sport
http://www.artscouncil.org.uk/

The British Library

The British Library (BL) is the national library of the United Kingdom and one of the world's largest libraries. Its collections include more than 150 million items, in over 400 languages including books, magazines, manuscripts, maps, music scores, newspapers, patents, databases, philatelic items, prints and drawings and sound recordings.
BL is an executive non-departmental public body of the Department for Culture, Media & Sport
http://www.bl.uk/

British Museum

The British Museum (BM) was the first national public museum in the world. Its permanent collection, over 8 million works, is amongst the largest and most comprehensive in existence and originates from every continent, illustrating and documenting the story of human culture from its beginnings to the present.
BM is an executive non-departmental public body of the Department for Culture, Media & Sport
http://www.britishmuseum.org

English Heritage

English Heritage (EH) preserves aspects of the built environment, complementing the work of Natural England, which protects the natural environment. It also advises the government on policy and in cases such as registering listed buildings and scheduled ancient monuments.
EH is an executive non-departmental public body of the Department for Culture, Media & Sport
http://www.english-heritage.org.uk/

Gambling Commission

The Gambling Commission (GC) regulates arcades, betting, bingo, casinos, gaming machine providers, gambling software providers, lottery operators and external lottery managers and remote gambling (online and by phone) that uses British-based equipment.
GC is an executive non-departmental public body of the Department for Culture, Media & Sport
http://www.gamblingcommission.gov.uk/

Geffrye Museum

Located in London's East End, the Geffrye Museum (GMus) depicts the quintessential style of English middle-class living rooms. Its collections of furniture, textiles, paintings and decorative arts are displayed in a series of period rooms from 1600 to the present day.
GMus is an executive non-departmental public body of the Department for Culture, Media & Sport
http://www.geffrye-museum.org.uk/

Horniman Museum

Opened in 1901, the Horniman was designed in the Arts and Crafts style. It was founded by Frederick Horniman, who had inherited his father's tea business, which by 1891 had become the world's biggest tea trading company. It specialises in anthropology, natural history and musical instruments and has a collection of 350,000 objects.
Horniman is an executive non-departmental public body of the Department for Culture, Media & Sport
http://www.horniman.ac.uk/

Imperial War Museum

The Imperial War Museum (IWM) is unique in its coverage of conflicts, especially those involving Britain and the Commonwealth, from World War 1 to the present day. It provides for, and encourages, the study and understanding of the history of modern war and 'wartime experience'.
IWM is an executive non-departmental public body of the Department for Culture, Media & Sport
http://www.iwm.org.uk/

National Gallery

The National Gallery houses the national collection of Western European painting from the 13th to 19th centuries. It cares for the collection, enhancing it for future generations, primarily by acquisition, and also studies it whilst encouraging access to the pictures for the education and enjoyment of the widest possible public.
National Gallery is an executive non-departmental public body of the Department for Culture, Media & Sport
http://www.nationalgallery.org.uk/

National Heritage Memorial Fund

The National Heritage Memorial Fund (NHMF) saves the most outstanding parts of our heritage at risk of loss to the nation, as a memorial to those who have given their lives for the UK.
NHMF is an executive non-departmental public body of the Department for Culture, Media & Sport
http://www.nhmf.org.uk/

National Lottery Commission

The National Lottery Commission (NLC) is responsible for licensing and regulating the National Lottery. They protect the integrity of the Lottery; protect players; maximise funds to good causes, and also run the competition process to select the operator of the Lottery.
NLC is an executive non-departmental public body of the Department for Culture, Media & Sport
http://www.natlotcomm.gov.uk/

Science Museum Group

The Science Museum Group is devoted to the history and contemporary practice of science, medicine, technology, industry and media. With 5 million visitors each year and an unrivalled collection, it consists of: Science Museum, Museum of Science and Industry, National Railway Museum (York), National Media Museum and National Railway Museum (Shildon) - the most significant group of museums of science and innovation worldwide.
Science Museum Group is an executive non-departmental public body of the Department for Culture, Media & Sport
http://www.sciencemuseum.org.uk/about_us/smg.aspx

National Museums Liverpool

National Museums Liverpool (NML) is a diverse group of museums and galleries. Its collections are among the most important and varied in Europe, and contain everything from Impressionist paintings and rare beetles to a lifejacket from the Titanic and artefacts from ancient Egypt.
NML is an executive non-departmental public body of the Department for Culture, Media & Sport
http://www.liverpoolmuseums.org.uk/

National Portrait Gallery

The National Portrait Gallery (NPG) aims 'to promote through the medium of portraits the appreciation and understanding of the men and women who have made and are making British history and culture, and to promote the appreciation and understanding of portraiture in all media'. It holds the most extensive collection of portraits in the world.
NPG is an executive non-departmental public body of the Department for Culture, Media & Sport
http://www.npg.org.uk/

Natural History Museum

The Natural History Museum (NHM) is home to life and earth science specimens comprising some 70 million items within 5 main collections: Botany, Entomology, Mineralogy, Palaeontology and Zoology. The museum is a world-renowned centre of research, specialising in taxonomy, identification and conservation. Given the age of the institution, many of the collections have great historical as well as scientific value, such as specimens collected by Darwin. The Natural History Museum Library contains extensive books, journals, manuscripts, and artwork collections linked to the work and research of the scientific departments.
NHM is an executive non-departmental public body of the Department for Culture, Media & Sport
http://www.nhm.ac.uk/

Olympic Delivery Authority

What we do
We are working to transform the Olympic and Paralympic Village into more than 2,800 new homes, close out £6 billion of contracts, and dismantle temporary venues. We were responsible for the construction of venues and infrastructure for London 2012, including the Olympic Park, planning and funding transport for the Games, and regulating advertising and trading.

Responsibilities

We are:

- building new permanent venues for the Games and beyond: the Olympic Stadium, Aquatics Centre, International Broadcast Centre/Main Press Centre, Velodrome, Copper Box, and BMX Track - all in the Olympic Park; and the Lee Valley White Water Centre in Hertfordshire
- building temporary arenas/facilities that are being dismantled and/or relocated after the Games: the Water Polo Arena; Basketball Arena; facilities at Eton Manor; and the shooting venue at The Royal Artillery Barracks
- improvement works to existing sports venues at Eton Dorney and Weymouth and Portland
- planning, funding and building transport infrastructure and operations to support the Games
- planning and enforcing the regulation of advertising and trading in and around London 2012 venues during the Games
- Priorities
- In 2013 and 2014, our priority is to complete the transformation of the Olympic Village into East Village, installing new kitchens and removing temporary floors and partitions – the heart of a new community in our capital city, with a school and health facilities alongside world-class sports facilities.

Who we are

The Olympic Delivery Authority (ODA) was established by the London Olympic Games and Paralympic Games Act, which received Royal Assent in March 2006.

The Act was passed to ensure the necessary planning and preparation for the Games could take place. As a public body, the ODA is accountable to government, the Greater London Authority (GLA) and other stakeholders for its work.

The ODA now employs around 80 staff, based at Canary Wharf in London.

Royal Armouries

As the National Museum of Arms and Armour, Royal Armouries is Britain's oldest public museum and traces its roots to the Tower of London. Royal Armouries is home to the national collections of arms and armour, including artillery, and to the National Firearms Centre. The collection is split across three UK sites – Royal

Armouries Museum in Leeds; it's ancestral home at the Tower of London; and Fort Nelson near Portsmouth. It is the only UK museum to have a permanent presence in the US at the Frazier History Museum in Louisville, Kentucky. It is the only UK museum to have a permanent presence in the US at the Frazier History Museum in Louisville, Kentucky.
RA is an executive non-departmental public body of the Department for Culture, Media & Sport
http://www.royalarmouries.org/

Sir John Soane's Museum

Soane's is the idiosyncratic house-museum of the great neo-classical architect Sir John Soane (1753 – 1837). The house still displays his collection of antiquities, furniture, models and paintings in the same state in which they were left at the time of his death as well as preserving over 30,000 architectural drawings and a fine library.
Soane's is an executive non-departmental public body of the Department for Culture, Media & Sport
http://www.soane.org/

Sports Grounds Safety Authority

The Sports Grounds Safety Authority (SGSA) helps to secure the conditions for safe and enjoyable experiences for spectators at all sports grounds in England and Wales, and campaigns for safe sports grounds around the world.
SGSA is an executive non-departmental public body of the Department for Culture, Media & Sport
http://www.safetyatsportsgrounds.org.uk/

UK Sport

UK Sport (UKSP) supports Britain's best Olympic and Paralympic sports and athletes, co-ordinating the bids for and staging of major international sporting events in the UK. It invests around £100 million each year in high performance sport.
UKSP is an executive non-departmental public body of the Department for Culture, Media & Sport
http://www.uksport.gov.uk/

Visit Britain

Visit Britain (VB) is the national tourism agency, responsible for marketing Britain worldwide and developing Britain's visitor economy. It works with UK Trade & Investment as well as airline travels operators, global brands and the official tourism bodies for London, England, Scotland and Wales.
VB is an executive non-departmental public body of the Department for Culture, Media & Sport
http://www.visitbritain.org/

Wallace Collection

The Wallace Collection is a national museum in an historic London town house. In 25 galleries, unsurpassed French 18th-century painting (including Old Masters), furniture, porcelain and a world class armoury are on display.
Wallace Collection is an executive non-departmental public body of the Department for Culture, Media & Sport
http://www.wallacecollection.org/

British Film Institute

The British Film Institute (BFI) is the lead organisation for film in the UK and use Lottery funds to support film production, distribution, education and audience development. Since 1933 they've cared for the BFI National Archive, and celebrated the best of British and international filmmaking through festivals, film restoration, DVD releases and cinema programming.
BFI is an executive non-departmental public body of the Department for Culture, Media & Sport
http://www.bfi.org.uk

Sport England

Sport England (SE) helps people and communities across the country get a sporting habit for life. It also protects existing sports provision and must be consulted on any planning applications that affect playing fields in England.

SE is an executive non-departmental public body of the Department for Culture, Media & Sport
http://www.sportengland.org

UK Anti-Doping

UK Anti-Doping (UKAD) implements and manages anti-doping policy in the UK. It works with athletes and national sports bodies to ensure compliance with the World Anti-Doping (WADA) Code.
UKAD is an executive non-departmental public body of the Department for Culture, Media & Sport
http://www.ukad.org.uk

Equality and Human Rights Commission

The Equality and Human Rights Commission (EHRC) monitors human rights, protecting equality across 9 grounds - age, disability, gender, race, religion and belief, pregnancy and maternity, marriage and civil partnership, sexual orientation and gender reassignment.
EHRC is an executive non-departmental public body of the Department for Culture, Media & Sport
http://www.equalityhumanrights.com/

Victoria and Albert Museum

The Victoria and Albert Museum (V&A / VAM) is the world's largest museum of decorative arts and design, housing a permanent collection of over 4.5 million objects. Named after Queen Victoria and Prince Albert, it was founded in 1852, and has since grown to cover 12.5 acres and 145 galleries. Its collection spans 5,000 years of art, from ancient times to the present day, in virtually every medium, from the cultures of Europe, North America, Asia and North Africa.
VAM is an executive non-departmental public body of the Department for Culture, Media & Sport
http://www.vam.ac.uk

Public Lending Right

The Public Lending Right (PLR) is the right for authors to receive payment under PLR legislation for the loans of their books by public libraries.
PLR is an executive non-departmental public body of the Department for Culture, Media & Sport
http://www.plr.uk.com/

Olympic Lottery Distributor

The Olympic Lottery Distributor (OLD) used money raised by the National Lottery to deliver the infrastructure for the London 2012 Olympic and Paralympic Games and their legacy.
OLD is an executive non-departmental public body of the Department for Culture, Media & Sport
http://www.olympiclotterydistributor.org.uk/

Heritage Lottery Fund

Using money raised through the National Lottery, the Heritage Lottery Fund (HLF) gives grants to sustain and transform the UK's heritage. Museums, parks, historic places, archaeology, natural environment and cultural traditions all receive investment.
HLF is an executive non-departmental public body of the Department for Culture, Media & Sport
http://www.hlf.org.uk

Royal Museums Greenwich

Royal Museums Greenwich (RMG) comprises the National Maritime Museum, the Royal Observatory, and the Queen's House. Together they work to illustrate the importance of the sea, ships, time and the stars, and their relationship with people.
RMG is an executive non-departmental public body of the Department for Culture, Media & Sport
http://www.rmg.co.uk

Advisory non-departmental public body

VisitEngland

VisitEngland (VE) is the national tourist board for England, responsible for marketing England to domestic and established overseas markets and for improving England's tourism product.
VE is an advisory non-departmental public body of the Department for Culture, Media & Sport
http://www.visitengland.com

The Theatres Trust

The Theatres Trust (TTT) is the national advisory body for theatres, promoting the value of theatre buildings and championing their future. It provides a range of specialist advisory services to help theatres and are a statutory consultee on planning applications.
TTT is an advisory non-departmental public body of the Department for Culture, Media & Sport
http://www.theatrestrust.org.uk/

The Reviewing Committee on the Export of Works of Art and Objects of Cultural Interest

The Reviewing Committee on the Export of Works of Art and Objects of Cultural Interest (RCEWA) advises the government on the export of cultural property. If an artwork is sold to a foreign buyer, it also advises on whether to delay the granting of an export licence in order to allow time for a British buyer to raise funds to buy the work instead and keep it in the UK.
RCEWA is an advisory non-departmental public body of the Department for Culture, Media & Sport
http://www.artscouncil.org.uk/what-we-do/supporting-museums/cultural-property/export-controls/reviewing-committee/

Treasure Valuation Committee

The Treasure Valuation Committee (TVC), comprising of independent antiques or coin experts and a leading metal detectorist, establishes the likely market value of each treasure find. A reward of this value can then be made to the finders of treasure and to the owners of find sites unless there are grounds for no reward or a reduced award to be made.
TVC is an advisory non-departmental public body of the Department for Culture, Media & Sport
http://finds.org.uk/

Advisory Council on Libraries

The Advisory Council on Libraries (ACL) gave advice to the government on issues connected to library facilities. The government proposes to close, merge or reforms this body as part of the Public Bodies Reform Programme.
ACL is an advisory non-departmental public body of the Department for Culture, Media & Sport
http://www.culture.gov.uk/what_we_do/libraries/3408.aspx

Tribunal non-departmental public body

Horserace Betting Levy Board

The Horserace Betting Levy Board (HBLB) is required to collect a statutory levy, known as the Horserace Betting Levy, from horseracing bookmakers and the Tote successor company which it then distributes for the improvement of horseracing and breeds of horses and for the advancement of veterinary science and education.
HBLB is a tribunal non-departmental public body of the Department for Culture, Media & Sport
http://www.hblb.org.uk/

Public corporation

Channel 4

Channel 4 (C4) is public service broadcaster and works across television, film and digital media. In addition to the main Channel 4 service, its portfolio includes E4, More4, Film4 and 4Music, as well as online activities that includes channel4.com, Channel 4's bespoke video-on-demand service 4oD and standalone digital projects.
C4 is a public corporation of the Department for Culture, Media & Sport
http://www.channel4.com

S4C

S4C is the only Welsh language public service broadcaster. It commissions independent producers from across Wales to make the majority of its programmes. S4C broadcasts sport, drama, music, factual, entertainment and events programmes, across a range of platforms, including online.
S4C is a public corporation of the Department for Culture, Media & Sport
http://www.s4c.co.uk

BBC

The BBC (British Broadcasting Corporation) is a British public service broadcaster. Its main responsibility is to provide impartial public service broadcasting in the UK, Channel Islands and Isle of Man.
BBC is a public corporation of the Department for Culture, Media & Sport
http://www.bbc.co.uk

Historic Royal Palaces

Historic Royal Palaces (HRP) manages Britain's unoccupied royal palaces: the Tower of London, Hampton Court Palace, the Banqueting House, Kensington Palace and Kew Palace.
HRP is a public corporation of the Department for Culture, Media & Sport
http://www.hrp.org.uk

Other

Ofcom

Ofcom is the regulator and competition authority for the UK communications industries. It regulates the TV and radio sectors, fixed line telecoms, mobiles, postal services, plus the airwaves over which wireless devices operate.
Ofcom works with the Department for Culture, Media & Sport
http://www.ofcom.org.uk

Government Equalities Office

What we do

The Government Equalities Office (GEO) is responsible for equality strategy and legislation across government. We work to take action on the government's commitment to remove barriers to equality and help to build a fairer society, leading on issues relating to women, sexual orientation and transgender equality.

Responsibilities

We are responsible for:

- improving equality and reducing discrimination and disadvantage for all in the UK, at work, in public and political life, and in people's life chances - we co-ordinate the Inter-Ministerial Group on Equalities, which works to implement the Equality Strategy
- taking the lead on the Equality Act 2010 and being the lead department on gender and LGBT issues in government
- supporting and implementing international equality measures in the UK, including our international commitments to the UN Convention on the Elimination of All Forms of Discrimination against Women (CEDAW), the Beijing Declaration and Platform for Action, and the European Union Roadmap for Equality between Women and Men

Priorities

Our priorities for 2013 include:

- opening up marriage for same-sex couples
- helping women to fulfil their potential in the workplace and helping businesses get the full economic benefit of women's skills
- addressing the discrimination and inequalities that LGBT people face

- making it easier for disabled people to stand for election
- promoting the rights of British citizens abroad and using our influence to promote international equality
- For all of our priorities, have a look at the government equality strategy.

Who we work with

The Government Equalities Office is part of the Department for Culture, Media and Sport. Our lead minister, Maria Miller, is also Secretary of State for Culture, Media and Sport. We are based in London and have around 100 staff.

We work across government, but in particular we work closely with:

- the Department for Communities and Local Government (DCLG), which leads on integration, race and faith policy and community issues
- the Department for Work and Pensions (DWP), which leads on disability discrimination policy and legislation and general age policy outside the workplace
- the Department for Business, Innovation & Skills (BIS), which provides the broad policy for further and higher education and has responsibility for the Equality Act's provisions relating to age exceptions to the Act's working provisions
- the Department for Education, which is responsible for the Equality Act's provisions relating to schools and children
- the Department for Transport, which is responsible for the Equality Act's provisions on disability and transport

We also work closely with:

- the Ministry of Justice (MOJ), which leads on human rights policy
- the devolved administrations in Wales, Scotland and Northern Ireland

Department for Education

What we do
We are responsible for education and children's services in England. We work to achieve a highly educated society in which opportunity is equal for children and young people, no matter what their background or family circumstances.

Responsibilities
We are responsible for:

- teaching and learning for children in the early years and in primary schools
- teaching and learning for young people under the age of 19 years in secondary schools and in further education
- supporting professionals who work with children and young people
- helping disadvantaged children and young people to achieve more
- making sure that local services protect and support children

Our priorities
In 2013, our priorities are to:

- increase the number of high quality schools
- introduce fair funding
- reform the school curriculum and qualifications
- reduce bureaucracy and improve accountability
- train and develop the professionals who work with children
- improve services for children in the early years
- improve support for children, young people and families, focusing on the most disadvantaged

Who we are
We are a ministerial department with 3 executive agencies:

Education Funding Agency (EFA)

Standards and Testing Agency (STA)
National College for Teaching and Leadership (NCTL)
Our staff are based at our ministerial offices in London and in a number of other locations around England. We work closely with national and local agencies who look after children, with local authorities, and with the professionals who work in schools, children's services and health services.

DfE is a ministerial department, supported by 9 agencies and public bodies.

Non-ministerial department

Ofqual

The Office of Qualifications and Examinations Regulation (Ofqual) maintains standards in educational qualifications, including GCSEs and A levels in England and a wide range of vocational qualifications in England and Northern Ireland. It also regulates the National Curriculum assessments in England.
Ofqual is a non-ministerial department of the Department for Education
http://www.ofqual.gov.uk/

Ofsted

The Office for Standards in Education, Children's Services and Skills (Ofsted) regulates and inspects childcare and children's social care. It also inspects schools, colleges, initial teacher education, work-based learning and skills training, adult and community learning, education and training in prisons and other secure establishments, and the Children and Family Court Advisory Support Service (Cafcass). Additionally, Ofsted assesses children's services in local areas, and inspects services for looked-after children, safeguarding and child protection.
Ofsted is a non-ministerial department of the Department for Education
http://www.ofsted.gov.uk/

Executive agency

Education Funding Agency

The Education Funding Agency (EFA) administers education revenue and capital funding for learners between the ages of 3 and 19, or up to 25 for those with special educational needs and disabilities. It also supports building and maintenance programmes for schools, academies, free schools and sixth-form colleges.
EFA is an executive agency of the Department for Education
http://www.education.gov.uk/aboutdfe/executiveagencies/efa

Standards & Testing Agency

The Standards and Testing Agency (STA) is responsible for the development and delivery of all statutory assessment tests from early years to the end of key stage 3.
STA is an executive agency of the Department for Education
http://www.education.gov.uk/aboutdfe/executiveagencies/b00198511/sta

National College for Teaching and Leadership

NCTL is an executive agency of the Department for Education
http://www.education.gov.uk/nationalcollege

Executive non-departmental public body

Cafcass

The Children and Family Court Advisory and Support Service (Cafcass) looks after the interests of children involved in family proceedings. It is independent of the courts and social services, but works under the rules of the Family Court and legislation to work with children and their families, and then advise the courts on what is considered to be in the best interests of individual children.
Cafcass is an executive non-departmental public body of the Department for Education
http://www.cafcass.gov.uk/

The Office of the Children's Commissioner

The Office of the Children's Commissioner promotes the rights, views and interests of children in policies or decisions affecting their lives. They particularly represent children who are vulnerable or who find it hard to make their views known.
The Office of the Children's Commissioner is an executive non-departmental public body of the Department for Education
http://www.childrenscommissioner.gov.uk/

Advisory non-departmental public body

School Teachers' Review Body

The School Teachers' Review Body (STRB) looks into pay, professional duties and working time of school teachers in England and Wales and reports to the Secretary of State.
STRB is an advisory non-departmental public body of the Department for Education
http://www.education.gov.uk/schools/careers/payandpensions/a0013922/the-role-of-the-school-teachers-review-body-strb

Social Mobility and Child Poverty Commission

What we do

The Social Mobility and Child Poverty (SMCP) Commission monitors the progress of government and others in improving social mobility and reducing child poverty in the United Kingdom.

Responsibilities

We are responsible for:

- publishing an annual report setting out our views on progress made in improving social mobility and reducing child poverty in the UK, including against the targets in the Child Poverty Act 2010, and describing the measures taken by the Scottish and Welsh governments
- providing published advice to ministers (at their request) on how to measure socio-economic disadvantage, social mobility and child poverty
- acting as an advocate for social mobility beyond government by challenging employers, the professions and universities amongst others to play their part in improving life chances

Priorities

In 2013, our main priorities will be:

- holding the government and others to account through providing an authoritative 'state of the nation' analysis of social mobility and child poverty in our first annual report
- creating a business manifesto for social mobility and using it to encourage firms to put and keep the issue on the agenda, as well as working closely with specific professions and the university sector to drive change
- influencing policy via credible and independent advice. We have responded to the government consultation on better measures of child poverty and are currently developing advice to ministers on the 3 or 4 most impactful steps the government could reasonably take to improve social mobility

Who we are

The Social Mobility and Child Poverty Commission is chaired by the Rt. Hon Alan Milburn and deputy chaired by Baroness Gillian Shephard.

It includes 7 other members drawn from across business, academia and the voluntary sector. It is supported by a small secretariat based in London.

Department for Environment Food & Rural Affairs

What we do

We are the UK government department responsible for policy and regulations on environmental, food and rural issues. Our priorities are to grow the rural economy, improve the environment and safeguard animal and plant health.

Defra is a ministerial department, supported by 39 agencies and public bodies.

Responsibilities

We are responsible for policy and regulations on:

- the natural environment, biodiversity, plants and animals
- sustainable development and the green economy
- food, farming and fisheries
- animal health and welfare
- environmental protection and pollution control
- rural communities and issues

Although Defra only works directly in England, it works closely with the devolved administrations in Wales, Scotland and Northern Ireland, and generally leads on negotiations in the EU and internationally.

Priorities

Our priorities are to:

- grow the rural economy
- improve the environment
- safeguard plant health
- safeguard animal health

Who we are

We have around 10,000 staff, including those at our executive agencies. Our staff are mainly based in London, York, Bristol and Alnwick, but we have many other offices throughout England.

Our headquarters building is Nobel House, in Smith Square, London SW1.

Expenditure data

Defra publishes a range of corporate information on data.gov including information on staffing and salaries.

Non-ministerial department

Office for Water Services

The Water Services Regulation Authority (Ofwat) is a non-ministerial government department. We are the economic regulators for the water and sewerage sectors in England and Wales. We are responsible for making sure that the companies we regulate provide consumers with a good quality and efficient service at a fair price.
Ofwat is a non-ministerial department of the Department for Environment, Food & Rural Affairs
http://www.ofwat.gov.uk/

Forestry Commission

The Forestry Commission is responsible for protecting and expanding Britain's woods and forests and for managing nearly 1 million hectares of public forest.
Forestry is a non-ministerial department of the Department for Environment, Food & Rural Affairs
http://www.forestry.gov.uk/

Executive agency

Animal Health and Veterinary Laboratories Agency

AHVLA works to prevent and control farm animal disease in England, Scotland and Wales protect the health and welfare of farmed animals and safeguard public health from food-borne disease. Its range of activities includes scientific research, welfare inspections, and the registration and licensing of imports of endangered wildlife. The agency also provides an emergency response to outbreaks of notifiable animal diseases.
AHVLA is an executive agency of the Department for Environment, Food & Rural Affairs
http://www.defra.gov.uk/ahvla/

Centre for Environment Fisheries and Aquaculture Science

The Centre for Environment Fisheries and Aquaculture Science (CEFAS) provides scientific and technical support, consultancy and advice to Defra and other customers, in the fields of fisheries' science and management, environmental assessment, aquaculture and fish health.
Cefas is an executive agency of the Department for Environment, Food & Rural Affairs
http://www.cefas.defra.gov.uk/

The Food and Environment Research Agency

The Food and Environment Research Agency (Fera) supports and develops a sustainable food chain and a healthy natural environment and protects the global community from biological and chemical risks. It provides evidence, analysis and professional advice to the government, international organisations and the private sector.
Fera is an executive agency of the Department for Environment, Food & Rural Affairs
http://www.fera.defra.gov.uk/

Rural Payments Agency

The Rural Payments Agency (RPA) funds the Common Agricultural Policy (CAP) schemes run by all the UK paying agencies. It is responsible for dealing with monies from the Guarantee Section of the European Agriculture Guidance and Guarantee Fund (EAGGF), providing operational advice in support of policy formation.
RPA is an executive agency of the Department for Environment, Food & Rural Affairs
http://rpa.defra.gov.uk/

Rural Payments Agency

The Rural Payments Agency (RPA) funds the Common Agricultural Policy (CAP) schemes run by all the UK paying agencies. It is responsible for dealing with monies from the Guarantee Section of the European Agriculture Guidance and Guarantee Fund (EAGGF), providing operational advice in support of policy formation.
RPA is an executive agency of the Department for Environment, Food & Rural Affairs
http://rpa.defra.gov.uk/

Veterinary Medicines Directorate

The Veterinary Medicines Directorate (VMD) protects public health, animal health and the environment. It promotes animal welfare by assuring the safety, quality and efficacy of veterinary medicines in the United Kingdom. Certain enforcement and food safety matters are devolved to Scotland, Wales and Northern Ireland.
VMD is an executive agency of the Department for Environment, Food & Rural Affairs
http://www.vmd.defra.gov.uk/

Executive non-departmental public body

Marine Management Organisation

The Marine Management Organisation (MMO) promotes the government's vision for clean, safe, productive and biologically diverse oceans and seas and has sole or shared responsibility that include: marine planning, marine licensing and fisheries quotas.

MMO is an executive non-departmental public body of the Department for Environment, Food & Rural Affairs
http://www.marinemanagement.org.uk/

Consumer Council for Water

Consumer Council for Water (CCWater) represents water and sewerage consumers in England and Wales and takes up unresolved complaints.
CCWater is an executive non-departmental public body of the Department for Environment, Food & Rural Affairs
http://www.ccwater.org.uk/

Environment Agency

The Environment Agency (EA) protects and improves the environment and promotes sustainable development. It plays a central role in implementing the government's environmental strategy in England. The Environment Agency plays a lead role in managing flood risk and works to minimise the impact of flooding.
EA is an executive non-departmental public body of the Department for Environment, Food & Rural Affairs
http://www.environment-agency.gov.uk/

Gangmasters Licensing Authority

The Gangmasters Licensing Authority (GLA) protects workers from exploitation: its licensing scheme regulates businesses who provide workers to agriculture, horticulture, forestry, shellfish gathering and food and drink processing and packaging.
GLA is an executive non-departmental public body of the Department for Environment, Food & Rural Affairs
http://gla.defra.gov.uk/

Joint Nature Conservation Committee
The Joint Nature Conservation Committee (JNCC) is the statutory adviser to the government and devolved administrations on UK and international nature conservation. Its work contributes to maintaining and enriching biological diversity, conserving geological features and sustaining natural systems.
JNCC is an executive non-departmental public body of the Department for Environment, Food & Rural Affairs
http://jncc.defra.gov.uk/

Natural England

Natural England works with farmers, planners, researchers and scientists and the public to create a better natural environment for people and wildlife across all of England's urban, country and coastal landscapes.
NE is an executive non-departmental public body of the Department for Environment, Food & Rural Affairs
http://www.naturalengland.org.uk/

Agriculture and Horticulture Development Board

The Agriculture and Horticulture Development Board (AHDB) helps to make Great Britain's livestock, dairy and agriculture sectors more successful, providing market information to improve supply chain transparency and stimulating demand in the UK and export markets.
AHDB is an executive non-departmental public body of the Department for Environment, Food & Rural Affairs
http://www.ahdb.org.uk/

Sea Fish Industry Authority

The Sea Fish Industry Authority (Seafish) supports the seafood industry to work for a sustainable, profitable future. It offers regulatory guidance and services to all parts of the seafood industry, including catching and aquaculture, processors, importers, exporters and distributors of seafood, as well as restaurants and retailers. It is sponsored by the Scottish government, Welsh Assembly and the Northern Ireland Department of Agriculture and Rural Development, as well as Defra.
Seafish is an executive non-departmental public body of the Department for Environment, Food & Rural Affairs
http://www.seafish.org/

Agricultural Wages Committee (x15)

There are 15 Agricultural Wage Committees (AWCs) across England. Their members are local agricultural workers nominated by their union Unite and agricultural employers nominated by the National Farmers' Union. The committees can grant permits to trainee or disabled workers, exempting an employer from paying them the full statutory minimum wage, and can make other exemptions. Following completion of the Enterprise and Regulatory Reform Act, AWCs in England are due to be abolished. However, they remain in place for a transitional period. Applications to AWCs for revaluation's of benefits in kind attributable to a house can continue to be made until 1 October 2013. After that date, no further applications will be allowed and once any pending applications have been dealt with, an Order will be made to bring into force the provisions in the Enterprise and Regulatory Reform Act which will abolish AWCs in England.
AWC is an executive non-departmental public body of the Department for Environment, Food & Rural Affairs

National Forest Company

The National Forest Company (NFC) leads the creation of The National Forest, a new, wooded landscape across 200 square miles of central England. The area has been transformed through the planting of millions of trees (8 million by October 2012) and the creation of many other valuable habitats.
NFC is an executive non-departmental public body of the Department for Environment, Food & Rural Affairs
http://www.nationalforest.org

Board of Trustees of the Royal Botanic Gardens Kew

The Board of Trustees of the Royal Botanic Gardens Kew is responsible for ensuring that Kew Gardens operates within the guidelines set out by government, and secures maximum value for money.
Board of Trustees of the Royal Botanic Gardens Kew is an executive non-departmental public body of the Department for Environment, Food & Rural Affairs
http://www.kew.org/about-kew/who-we-are/board-of-trustees/index.htm

Tribunal non-departmental public body

*Agricultural
Land Tribunal*
The Agricultural Land Tribunal (ALT) deals with applications from close relatives of a deceased or retiring tenant to succeed to an agricultural tenancy, applications from landlords for consent to a notice to quit or a certificate of bad husbandry, and applications from tenants for approval to carry out long-term improvements. The government proposes to reform this body as part of the Public Bodies Reform Programme.
ALT is a tribunal non-departmental public body of the Department for Environment, Food & Rural Affairs
http://archive.defra.gov.uk/foodfarm/farmmanage/alt/

Plant Varieties and Seeds Tribunal

The Plant Varieties and Seeds Tribunal (PVST) considers decisions made by the government about seed certifications or by the Controller of Plant Breeders' Rights. The government proposes to close, merge or reforms this body as part of the Public Bodies Reform Programme.
PVST is a tribunal non-departmental public body of the Department for Environment, Food & Rural Affairs
http://webarchive.nationalarchives.gov.uk/+/www.direct.gov.uk/en/Dl1/Directories/DG_10012171

Other

Covent Garden Market Authority

CGMA works with the Department for Environment, Food & Rural Affairs
http://www.newcoventgardenmarket.com/

Broads Authority

The Broads Authority conserves and enhances the natural beauty, wildlife and cultural heritage of the Broads and promotes opportunities for the understanding and enjoyment of the Broads by the public. It also protects the interests of navigation.
Broads Authority works with the Department for Environment, Food & Rural Affairs
http://www.broads-authority.gov.uk/

Dartmoor National Park Authority

The Dartmoor National Park Authority (DNPA) conserves and enhances the natural beauty, wildlife and cultural heritage of Dartmoor and promotes opportunities for the understanding and enjoyment of the area by the public. It also protects the interests of navigation.
DNPA works with the Department for Environment, Food & Rural Affairs
http://www.dartmoor-npa.gov.uk/

Exmoor National Park Authority

The Exmoor National Park Authority conserves and enhances the natural beauty, wildlife and cultural heritage of Exmoor and promotes opportunities for the understanding and enjoyment of the area by the public.
Exmoor works with the Department for Environment, Food & Rural Affairs
http://www.exmoor-nationalpark.gov.uk/

Lake District National Park Authority

The Lake District National Park Authority (LDNP) conserves and enhances the natural beauty, wildlife and cultural heritage of the Lake District and promotes opportunities for the understanding and enjoyment of the area by the public.
LDNP works with the Department for Environment, Food & Rural Affairs
http://www.lakedistrict.gov.uk/

New Forest National Park Authority

The New Forest National Park Authority (NFNPA) conserves and enhances the natural beauty, wildlife and cultural heritage of the New Forest and promotes opportunities for the understanding and enjoyment of the area by the public.
NFNPA works with the Department for Environment, Food & Rural Affairs
http://www.newforestnpa.gov.uk/

North York Moors National Park Authority

The North York Moors National Park (NYMNP) authority conserves and enhances the natural beauty, wildlife and cultural heritage of the North York Moors and promotes opportunities for the understanding and enjoyment of the area by the public.
NYMNP works with the Department for Environment, Food & Rural Affairs
http://www.northyorkmoors.org.uk/

Drinking Water Inspectorate

The Drinking Water Inspectorate (DWI) is the independent regulator of drinking water in England and Wales, ensuring that water companies supply safe drinking water that is acceptable to consumers and meets the standards set down in law.
DWI works with the Department for Environment, Food & Rural Affairs
http://www.dwi.gov.uk

Forest Research

Forest Research provides research services relevant to UK and international forestry interests, informing and supporting forestry's contribution to government policies. It provides the evidence base for UK forestry practices and supports innovation.
Forest Research works with the Forestry Commission and the Department for Environment, Food & Rural Affairs
http://www.forestry.gov.uk/forestresearch

Northumberland National Park Authority

Northumberland National Park Authority conserves and enhances the natural beauty, wildlife and cultural heritage of the Northumberland uplands – 405 square miles of hills and valleys stretching from Hadrian's Wall northwards to the Cheviot Hills on the border with Scotland. It also promotes opportunities for the understanding and enjoyment of the area by the public.

Northumberland National Park Authority works with the Department for Environment, Food & Rural Affairs
http://www.northumberlandnationalpark.org.uk

Peak District National Park Authority

The Peak District National Park (PDNP) authority conserves and enhances the natural beauty, wildlife and cultural heritage of the Peak District and promotes opportunities for the understanding and enjoyment of the area by the public.
PDNP works with the Department for Environment, Food & Rural Affairs
http://www.peakdistrict.gov.uk/

South Downs National Park Authority

The South Downs National Park (SDNP) authority conserves and enhances the natural beauty, wildlife and cultural heritage of the South Downs and promotes opportunities for the understanding and enjoyment of the area by the public.
SDNP works with the Department for Environment, Food & Rural Affairs
http://www.southdowns.gov.uk

Yorkshire Dales National Park Authority
The Yorkshire Dales National Park (YDNP) authority conserves and enhances the natural beauty, wildlife and cultural heritage of the Yorkshire Dales and promotes opportunities for the understanding and enjoyment of the area by the public.
YDNP works with the Department for Environment, Food & Rural Affairs
http://www.yorkshiredales.org.uk/

Department for International Development

What we do

The Department for International Development (DFID) leads the UK's work to end extreme poverty. We're ending the need for aid by creating jobs, unlocking the potential of girls and women and helping to save lives when humanitarian emergencies hit.

Responsibilities

We are responsible for:

- honouring the UK's international commitments and taking action to achieve the Millennium Development Goals
- making British aid more effective by improving transparency, openness and value for money
- targeting British international development policy on economic growth and wealth creation
- improving the coherence and performance of British international development policy in fragile and conflict-affected countries
- improving the lives of girls and women through better education and a greater choice on family planning
- preventing violence against girls and women in the developing world
- helping to prevent climate change and encouraging adaptation and low-carbon growth in developing countries

Priorities

Education
By 2015 we will:

- help 9 million children in primary school, at least half of which will be girls
- help 2 million children in lower secondary school
- train more than 190,000 teachers and improve the quality of education and children's learning

Health
By 2015 we will:

- help immunise more than 55 million children against preventable diseases

- save the lives of at least 50,000 women in pregnancy and childbirth and 250,000 new-born babies
- help at least 10 million more women to use modern methods of family planning by 2015
- help halve malaria deaths in 10 of the worst affected countries

Economic growth and the private sector
By 2015 we will:

- provide more than 50 million people with the means to help work their way out of poverty
- help up to half of the countries in Africa benefit from freer trade
- secure the right to land and property for more than 6 million people

Governance and conflict
To make countries safer and fairer we will:

- devote 30% of our aid to war-torn and unstable countries by 2014
- support freer and fairer elections in 13 countries
- help 10 million women to access justice through the courts, police and legal assistance
- help 40 million people to hold authorities to account

Climate and environment
Our 4 main areas of focus are:

- helping the poorest people adapt to the effects of climate change on their lives and livelihoods
- helping poor countries develop in ways that avoid or reduce harmful greenhouse gas emissions and enabling millions of people to benefit from clean energy
- protecting the world's forests and the livelihoods of the 1.2 billion people who depend on them
- encouraging global action on climate change

Water and sanitation
By 2015 we will:

- give 15 million people access to clean drinking water
- improve access to sanitation for 25 million people
- improve hygiene for 15 million to help stop people getting sick

Who we are
The Department for International Development (DFID) was set up in 1997. We employ around 2,700 staff who work in our offices in London, East Kilbride and globally.

Where we work

We work directly in 29 countries across Africa, Asia and the Middle East:

Afghanistan
We work in Afghanistan to protect our national security by helping the Afghans take control of theirs. We also work closely with the international community and other partners to support the development of Afghan security, governance, infrastructure, economy and the provision of essential services.

Bangladesh
We work with Bangladesh as forces for good in the world and for our mutual prosperity and security, and to make Britain the partner of choice for Bangladesh.

Burma
We aim to work with Government, political parties, and wider civil society to support a peaceful transition to a democratic, accountable government and a functioning market economy, enabling significant improvements in respect for human rights and fundamental freedoms, and in the economic and social prospects of ordinary people.

Democratic Republic of Congo
As permanent member of the UN Security Council, member of the EU and a major donor, the UK supports a stable DRC at peace with its neighbours, with legitimate and effective state institutions that serve its citizens

and which sees sustainable economic growth leading to improved health, education and living conditions for all Congolese citizens.

Ethiopia
We work to develop and maintain longstanding relations between the United Kingdom and Ethiopia, Djibouti and Somaliland. We deal with a wide range of political, commercial, security and economic questions of interest to the UK and Ethiopia, Djibouti and Somaliland.

Ghana
We represent the British government in relation with the Ghanaian government and support the range of British interests in Ghana. We develop and maintain the important and longstanding relationship between the UK and Ghana. We deal with a wide range of political, commercial, security and economic questions of interest to the UK and Ghana.

India
We enhance the India-UK relationship - that is stronger, wider, and deeper - generating more jobs, more growth and more security for our two nations. The UK-India relationship is founded on a broad range of mutual interests. We work closely together on issues as diverse as education and research, energy security and climate change, security and defence, international relations.

Kenya
We represent the British government in its relations with the Kenyan government and support British interests in Kenya. This stems from our shared history, enduring friendship and vital political, economic, commercial & cultural interests.

Kyrgyzstan
We develop and sustain the important bilateral relationship between the UK and the Kyrgyz Republic, supporting security, democratisation and prosperity. Our work includes efforts to deepen democracy and embed an international rules-based system in Kyrgyz legislation; supporting defence and security co-operation, working to reduce conflict, encouraging sustainable economic growth, and providing modern and efficient services to British nationals.

Liberia
We work closely with the Liberian Government and international partners to further the country's recent progress with security and prosperity. On security we are supporting the training of the Liberian security forces as the UN operation (UNMIL) draws down. On prosperity the UK supports UK companies investing in and trading with Liberia.

Malawi
We work to make a positive difference in Malawi in pursuit of the UK's global objectives, with mutual benefit to the prosperity of Malawi and the UK.

To do this we work in partnership with the government and people of Malawi, together with our international partners, to reduce poverty, encourage growth, and support good governance and respect for human rights, while improving local and international security and stability.

We aim to provide a professional service that wins respect from those we engage with and work for.

Mozambique
We support Mozambique's stability, prosperity, democratic development and poverty reduction. We encourage bilateral trade and investment, and improved political, economic and cultural ties. We project a modern and positive image of the UK; and provide friendly and efficient services to our partners and customers.

Nepal
We represent the UK and support British interests in Nepal.

Nigeria
We improve the bilateral strategic partnership, with a view to seizing common opportunities and addressing mutual threats. We support shared goals on prosperity, security, migration, development and co-operation in the international field and support the interests of British nationals working and living in Nigeria.

Occupied Palestinian Territories
We work to improve the United Kingdom's security and prosperity through a just peace between a stable, democratic Palestinian State and Israel, based on 1967 borders, ending the Occupation by agreement. Our aim is to improve the ties of friendship between the Palestinian and British peoples.

Pakistan
Our mission is to secure constructive Pakistani engagement with the international and regional security agendas, to support sustainable development, democracy and human rights in Pakistan, to improve UK economic interests and to provide high-quality public services.

We do this by ensuring close co-operation between all elements of the UK team, working in a secure, happy, cost-effective and best-practice environment.

Rwanda
We aim to help Rwanda's development into a democratic, prosperous country, with good governance and respect for human rights, playing a responsible role in the region's politics including in support of peacekeeping. In so doing, we seek to improve possibilities for UK trade and investment, supporting Rwanda's own goal of becoming a middle income country.

Sierra Leone
We work with the government of Sierra Leone to create prosperity that helps to prevent national and regional conflict, and is regarded as a regional model for effective democracy.

Somalia
We oversee the work and implementation of the UK-Somalia strategy.

South Africa
The UK agencies in South Africa work together to implement the UK-South Africa Strategy agreed by the British and South African Foreign Ministers in 2011 for a five year period. This work is in-line with the British government's wider foreign policy Priorities.

We work together with South Africa internationally, regionally and nationally on three strands of partnership: sustainable development, security, and governance and society.

Sudan
We help develop a Sudan at peace with itself and neighbours, meeting the needs and aspirations of its people.

South Sudan
We work closely with the Republic of South Sudan government on a wide range of issues which support international peace and stability efforts in South Sudan. This covers the political, security, economic, humanitarian and human rights challenges in South Sudan as well as negotiations between Sudan and South Sudan.

Tajikistan
We develop the UK's bilateral political and economic relationship with Tajikistan. We deal with a wide range of political, consular, commercial, security, defence and economic issues, which are of interest to the United Kingdom and Tajikistan. The Department for International Development (DFID) manages the UK's aid programme to Tajikistan and Kyrgyzstan.

Tanzania
We develop and maintain relations between the United Kingdom and Tanzania. We deal with a wide range of political, commercial, security and economic questions of interest to the UK and Tanzania.

We support British nationals in Tanzania, both in the mainland and Zanzibar.

Uganda
We maintain and develop close and co-operative relations between the UK and Uganda, in accordance with British government policies.

Vietnam
Progress the UK-Vietnam Strategic Partnership to support international peace and security and achieve our prosperity goals. Provide a modern and efficient consular service for British nationals in Vietnam.

Yemen
This Embassy works to promote British interests and support British nationals in Yemen. It works to support Yemen's political transition and its fight against terrorism and provides assistance to reduce Yemen's humanitarian and economic crises.

The FCO, DfID and MOD teams work in the areas of conflict prevention, reform of the military and security sectors, capacity building and empowerment of disadvantaged and marginalised sectors of society. They do this through participating directly in working groups, bilateral programmes, and contributing to and supporting international agencies.

Zambia
We work closely with the government and people of Zambia for our mutual benefit, representing the UK and supporting UK interests in Zambia, including commercial interests.

We deal with a wide range of political, social, economic, investment, trade and security questions of interest to the UK and Zambia, working with the UK's Department for International Development and the British Council. We provide consular assistance to British nationals and take in visa applications from foreign nationals wishing to visit the UK.

Zimbabwe
Our goal in Zimbabwe is to encourage a peaceful, democratic society where the rule of law and human rights are adhered to, laying the foundations for long term sustainable development.

Case studies
Our case studies explore the impact of DFID's work and provide real-life examples of our policies in practice.

Funding
We fund many organisations that are working to end poverty.

Reporting fraud
Our Counter Fraud and Whistle blowing Unit (CFWU) is the central point for raising concerns, suspicions and/or allegations of fraud or corrupt practices. This includes both internal and external cases where DFID funds, assets or interests (including DFID's reputation) are involved, as well as any breach of the Civil Service Code.

All suspicions of fraud or corruption must be reported.

The CFWU has a dedicated secure email address for raising all concerns and suspicions of fraud: fraud@dfid.gov.uk

Alternatively, any concerns can be reported by:

- calling the confidential hotline on +44 (0)1355 843747
- writing to the Head of Internal Audit, Abercrombie House, Eaglesham Road, East Kilbride, G75 8EA United Kingdom

Your information will be treated in confidence and you do not have to provide your name, however the provision of such information will assist us in taking forward your concerns.

Our guide to rules and tools (Blue Book)
The guide to rules and tools (known as the Blue Book) sets out core information about how to do things in DFID.

Corporate communications
The UK aid logo is designed to help publicly acknowledge that the development programmes we and our partners deliver are funded by UK taxpayers.

Staff in DFID and our partner governments and organisations can download the artwork for the UK aid logo and instructions on how and when to use it.

All organisations delivering DFID-funded programmes must use the UK aid logo in accordance with our standards for use.

No other organisation is permitted to use the logo without our permission

Executive non-departmental public body

Commonwealth Scholarship Commission in the UK

The Commonwealth Scholarship Commission in the UK manages Britain's contribution to the Commonwealth Scholarship and Fellowship Plan, established in 1959, and supports around 700 awards annually.
CSCUK is an executive non-departmental public body of the Department for International Development
http://cscuk.dfid.gov.uk/

Advisory non-departmental public body

Independent Commission for Aid Impact

The Independent Commission for Aid Impact (ICAI) is the independent body responsible for scrutiny of UK aid. ICAI focuses on maximising the impact of the UK aid budget for intended beneficiaries and getting the best value for money for the UK taxpayer.
ICAI is an advisory non-departmental public body of the Department for International Development
http://icai.independent.gov.uk/

Department for Transport London offices

What we do

We work with our agencies and partners to support the transport network that helps the UK's businesses and gets people and goods travelling around the country. We plan and invest in transport infrastructure to keep the UK on the move.

DFT is a ministerial department, supported by 24 agencies and public bodies.

Responsibilities

We are responsible for:

- providing policy, guidance, and funding to English local authorities to help them run and maintain their road networks, improve passenger and freight travel, and develop new major transport schemes
- investing in, maintaining and operating around 4,300 miles of the motorway and trunk road network in England through the Highways Agency
- setting the strategic direction for the rail industry in England and Wales – funding investment in infrastructure through Network Rail, awarding and managing rail franchises, and regulating rail fares
- improving English bus services through funding and regulation
- working to make our roads less congested and polluted by promoting lower carbon transport, including cycling and walking
- encouraging the use of new technology such as smart ticketing and low carbon vehicles
- maintaining high standards of safety and security in transport
- supporting the maritime sector by producing the overall strategy and planning policy for ports in England and Wales
- setting national aviation policy, working with airlines, airports, the Civil Aviation Authority and NATS (the

UK's air traffic service)

Priorities

Our priorities are:

- continuing to develop and lead the preparations for a high speed rail network
- improving the existing rail network and creating new capacity to improve services for passengers
- tackling congestion on our roads
- continuing to improve road safety
- encouraging sustainable local travel

- promoting lower carbon transport, such as walking and cycling as well as introducing more environmentally-friendly buses and trains
- supporting the development of the market for electric and other ultra-low emission vehicles
- supporting the development of aviation, improving passenger experience at airports
- maintaining high standards of safety and security for passengers and freight

Who we are

The Department for Transport and our agencies employ around 18,245 staff and 354 non-payroll staff, who work in locations across the country.

What we do

We work with our agencies and partners to support the transport network that helps the UK's businesses and gets people and goods travelling around the country. We plan and invest in transport infrastructure to keep the UK on the move.

Responsibilities

We are responsible for:

- providing policy, guidance, and funding to English local authorities to help them run and maintain their road networks, improve passenger and freight travel, and develop new major transport schemes
- investing in, maintaining and operating around 4,300 miles of the motorway and trunk road network in England through the Highways Agency
- setting the strategic direction for the rail industry in England and Wales – funding investment in infrastructure through Network Rail, awarding and managing rail franchises, and regulating rail fares
- improving English bus services through funding and regulation
- working to make our roads less congested and polluted by promoting lower carbon transport, including cycling and walking
- encouraging the use of new technology such as smart ticketing and low carbon vehicles
- maintaining high standards of safety and security in transport
- supporting the maritime sector by producing the overall strategy and planning policy for ports in England and Wales
- setting national aviation policy, working with airlines, airports, the Civil Aviation Authority and NATS (the UK's air traffic service)

Priorities

Our priorities are:

- continuing to develop and lead the preparations for a high speed rail network
- improving the existing rail network and creating new capacity to improve services for passengers
- tackling congestion on our roads
- continuing to improve road safety
- encouraging sustainable local travel
- promoting lower carbon transport, such as walking and cycling as well as introducing more environmentally-friendly buses and trains
- supporting the development of the market for electric and other ultra-low emission vehicles
- supporting the development of aviation, improving passenger experience at airports
- maintaining high standards of safety and security for passengers and freight

Driver & Vehicle Licensing Agency

Who we are

The Department for Transport and our agencies employ around 18,245 staff and 354 non-payroll staff, who work in locations across the country.

Department for Transport London offices

Non-ministerial department

Office of Rail Regulation

The Office of Rail Regulation (ORR) is the independent safety and economic regulator for Britain's railways. It is responsible for ensuring that railway operators comply with health and safety law. It regulates Network Rail's activities and funding requirements, regulates access to the railway network and licenses the operators of railway assets. ORR is also the competition authority for the railways and enforces consumer protection law in relation to the railway.
ORR is a non-ministerial department of the Department for Transport
http://www.rail-reg.gov.uk/

Executive agency

What we do
We maintain registers of drivers and vehicles in Great Britain. This information helps us improve road safety, reduce vehicle-related crime, support environmental initiatives and limit vehicle tax evasion.

Responsibilities

We are responsible for:

- maintaining records of licensed drivers and registered vehicles
- issuing licences to drivers and the maintenance of the vehicle driving entitlements
- maintaining records of driver endorsements, disqualification's and medical conditions
- issuing registration certificates to vehicle keepers
- collecting and enforcing vehicle excise duty (also known as road tax and the road fund licence)
- helping the police and intelligence authorities deal with vehicle related crime
- registering and issuing tachograph cards
- issuing vehicle registration marks
- selling attractive vehicle registration marks (also known as personalised registrations)
- selling anonymised data
- limiting vehicle tax evasion to no more than 1%

Priorities

From 2012 to 2013, our priorities will be:

- to reduce personal and economic loss from road accidents through improved road safety
- to reduce vehicle related crime
- to reduce harm to the environment caused by vehicles

Who we are
We are an executive agency of the Department for Transport (DfT). Our main headquarters is located in Swansea, with a network of 39 local offices across the country. At the end of March 2013, we employed around 5,612 staff.

Highways Agency

The Highways Agency (HA) operates, maintains and improves 7000km of strategic road network, which comprises the majority of England's motorways and major 'A' roads.
HA is an executive agency of the Department for Transport
http://www.highways.gov.uk/

Maritime and Coastguard Agency

The Maritime and Coastguard Agency (MCA) works to prevent the loss of life on the coasts and at sea, and implements the government's maritime safety policy in the UK. The Coastguard provides a 24 hour maritime search and rescue service around the UK coast. MCA inspects ships to ensure they meet safety rules, certifies seafarers, registers vessels and is responsible for co-ordinating responses to pollution from shipping and offshore installations.
MCA is an executive agency of the Department for Transport
http://www.dft.gov.uk/mca/

Vehicle & Operator Services Agency

We improve road safety by ensuring drivers, vehicle operators and MOT garages understand and comply with roadworthiness standards. We also provide a range of vehicle licensing, testing and enforcement services. We are merging with the Driving Standards Agency to become a single agency in 2014.
VOSA is an executive agency of the Department for Transport
http://www.dft.gov.uk/vosa/

Vehicle Certification Agency

The Vehicle Certification Agency (VCA) is the designated UK national authority for approving new road vehicles, agricultural tractors, off-road vehicles and components as well as a leading certification body offering management systems certification to ISO 9001, ISO/TS 16949, ISO 14001, Acorn, EMAS, ISO 50001 and OHSAS 18001.
VCA is an executive agency of the Department for Transport
http://www.dft.gov.uk/vca/

Driving Standards Agency

What we do

We improve road safety in Great Britain by setting standards for driving and motorcycling, and for the education and training of drivers and riders. We also carry out theory and practical driving and riding tests. We will merge with the Vehicle and Operator Services Agency into a single agency in 2014.

Responsibilities
We are responsible for:

- setting the standard for safe and responsible driving and riding
- carrying out theory and practical driving tests for all types of motor vehicles
- maintaining the register of approved driving instructors
- approving training bodies and instructors to provide compulsory basic training and direct access scheme courses for motorcyclists
- running the tests that allow people to join and stay on the voluntary register of large goods vehicle instructors
- running the tests that allow people to join and stay on the voluntary register of driver trainers who train drivers of car and van fleets
- setting the standards for the drink-drive rehabilitation scheme, running the scheme and approving the courses that offenders can take

Priorities

In 2013 to 2015, our main priorities will be to:

- take forward the Department for Transport's motoring services strategy
- offer candidates a theory test appointment within 2 weeks of their preferred date, and keep 99.5% of those appointments
- offer candidates a car driving test appointment within 9 weeks of their preferred date, and keep 99% of those appointments
- increase the take-up of digital services to 90%
- carry out 95% of planned Driver Certificate of Professional Competence training centre audits and 90% of planned course audits
- maintain customer satisfaction
- cut our carbon emissions by at least 20% compared with 2009-10

Who we are

We employ around 2,300 staff around Great Britain and run tests from around 400 practical driving test centres. Theory tests are carried out at around 150 theory test centres.

Executive non-departmental public body

Directly Operated Railways Limited

Directly Operated Railways Limited (DOR) oversees the management and development of the East Coast rail franchise until it is re-let to a new private operator.
DOR is an executive non-departmental public body of the Department for Transport
http://www.directlyoperatedrailways.co.uk

High Speed Two Limited

High Speed Two Limited (HS2 Ltd) is responsible for developing proposals for a new national high speed rail network. It is a company limited by guarantee and wholly funded by grant-in-aid from the government.
HS2 is an executive non-departmental public body of the Department for Transport
http://www.hs2.org.uk/

British Transport Police Authority

The British Transport Police Authority (BTPA) is the independent body responsible for ensuring an efficient and effective British Transport Police force. The BTPA oversees the police force, sets its targets and allocates funding for its budget. It also deals with complaints, recruitment, independent custody visiting and Freedom of Information requests.
BTPA is an executive non-departmental public body of the Department for Transport
http://btpa.police.uk/

Trinity House

Trinity House is the General Lighthouse Authority for England, Wales, the Channel Islands and Gibraltar. It provides marine navigation aids to assist the safe passage of mariners through waters in these areas. It is also responsible for marking and dispersing wrecks, which are a danger to navigation.
TLS is an executive non-departmental public body of the Department for Transport
http://www.trinityhouse.co.uk/th/about/index.html

Northern Lighthouse Board

The Northern Lighthouse Board is the General Lighthouse Authority for Scotland and the Isle of Man. It provides marine navigation aids to assist the safe passage of mariners through waters in these areas. It is also responsible for marking and dispersing wrecks, which are a danger to navigation.
NLB is an executive non-departmental public body of the Department for Transport
http://www.nlb.org.uk/

Passenger Focus

Passenger Focus is the independent passenger watchdog, set up by the government to protect the interests of Britain's rail, bus and tram passengers. It offers information and advice to passengers and will pursue complaints on behalf of passengers that train companies have failed to resolve.
PF is an executive non-departmental public body of the Department for Transport
http://www.passengerfocus.org.uk

Railway Heritage Committee

The Railway Heritage Committee (RHC) identifies and designates railway records and artefacts, which are historically significant and should be permanently preserved and finds them a suitable home. The Committee is due to be abolished in 2013 with its designation powers being transferred to the Board of Trustees of the Science Museum.
RHC is an executive non-departmental public body of the Department for Transport
http://www.dft.gov.uk/rhc/

Tribunal non-departmental public body

Traffic Commissioners

What we do

Traffic Commissioners are responsible for the licensing and regulation of those who operate heavy goods vehicles, buses and coaches, and the registration of local bus services. They are assisted in this work by deputy Traffic Commissioners, who preside over a number of public inquiries.

Responsibilities

Traffic Commissioners have responsibility in their region or country for:

- the licensing of the operators of heavy goods vehicles (HGVs) and of buses and coaches (public service vehicles or PSVs)
- the registration of local bus services
- granting vocational licences and taking action against drivers of HGVs and PSVs
- the environmental suitability of centres designated as parking locations for HGVs

Priorities
Traffic Commissioners' shared priorities are:

- to ensure that people operating HGVs and PSVs are reputable, competent, and adequately funded
- to encourage all operators to adopt robust systems, so that there is fair competition and that the operation of goods and public service vehicles is safe
- to consider on behalf of the Secretary of State for Transport the fitness of drivers or those applying for passenger carrying vehicle or large goods vehicle driving licences based on their conduct
- to consider, and where appropriate impose, traffic regulation conditions to prevent danger to road users and/or reduce traffic congestion and/or pollution
- to ensure public inquiry proceedings are fair and free from any unjustified interference or bias
- to engage with stakeholders - listening to industry, meeting with local authorities, trade organisations, passenger groups and operators and presenting seminars

Public corporation

BRB (Residuary) Ltd

BRB (Residuary) Ltd dealt with obligations in respect of liabilities acquired by British Rail and was responsible for management and disposal of railway land and buildings, which were surplus to the needs of the operational railway. It is under review as a result of the Cabinet Office public bodies reform plans.
BRBR is a public corporation of the Department for Transport
http://www.brbr.co.uk/

Civil Aviation Authority

The Civil Aviation Authority (CAA) is responsible for the regulation of aviation safety in the UK, determining policy for the use of airspace, the economic regulation of Heathrow, Gatwick and Stansted airports, the licensing and financial fitness of airlines and the management of the ATOL financial protection scheme for holidaymakers.
CAA is a public corporation of the Department for Transport
http://www.caa.co.uk/

London and Continental Railways Ltd
The London and Continental Railways Ltd (LCR) is a government-owned construction company that was responsible for the Channel Tunnel and the HS1 rail network, and now manages regeneration projects at King's Cross Central.
LCR is a public corporation of the Department for Transport
http://www.lcrhq.co.uk/

Other

Air Accidents Investigation Branch

The Air Accidents Investigation Branch (AAIB) investigates civil aircraft accidents and serious incidents in the UK and overseas with a view to the preservation of life and the avoidance of accidents in the future. It does not apportion blame or liability.
AAIB works with the Department for Transport
http://www.aaib.gov.uk

Rail Accident Investigation Branch

The Rail Accident Investigation Branch (RAIB) is the independent railway accident investigation organisation for the UK. It investigates railway accidents and incidents on the UK's railways to improve safety, not to establish blame. RAIB's purpose for investigating an accident or incident is to improve the safety of the railways, and to prevent further accidents from occurring.
RAIB works with the Department for Transport
http://www.raib.gov.uk

Trust ports

Trust ports (TP) are independent statutory bodies, each governed by their own, unique, statutes and controlled by a local independent board. There are no shareholders or owners and any surplus is ploughed back into each port for the benefit of its stakeholders. There are over 100 trust ports in the UK. The Secretary of State for Transport retains responsibility for appointing chairs and non-executive members to the boards of the small number of ports considered to be nationally significant.
TP works with the Department for Transport

Marine Accident Investigation Branch

The Marine Accident Investigation Branch (MAIB) determines the causes of marine accidents with a view to improving safety. Reports of its investigations, which do not apportion blame or liability, are published online together with accident statistics and other information about its work.
MAIB works with the Department for Transport
http://www.maib.gov.uk

Airports Commission

What we do

The Airports Commission examines the need for additional UK airport capacity and recommends to government how this can be met in the short, medium and long term.

Responsibilities

We are responsible for:

- submitting a report to the government by the end of 2013, identifying and recommending options for maintaining the UK's status as an international hub for aviation and immediate actions to improve the use of existing runway capacity in the next 5 years
- submitting a final report to the government by summer 2015 assessing the environmental, economic and social costs and benefits of various solutions to increase airport capacity - considering operational, commercial and technical viability

Priorities

Our main priorities are to:

- take a UK-wide perspective considering the national, regional and local implications of any proposals
- provide interested parties and members of the public with opportunities to submit evidence and proposals and to set out views relevant to our work
- build a consensus in support of our approach and recommendations

Who we are

The Airports Commission is an independent commission chaired by Sir Howard Davies and includes 5 other members.

Department for Work & Pensions

What we do

The Department for Work and Pensions (DWP) is responsible for welfare and pension policy and is a key player in tackling child poverty. It is the biggest public service delivery department in the UK and serves over 20 million customers.

Responsibilities

We are responsible for:

- understanding and tackling the root causes of poverty rather than its symptoms
- encouraging people to work and making work pay
- encouraging disabled people and those with ill health to work and be independent
- providing a decent income for people of pension age and promoting saving for retirement
- providing value for money and reducing levels of fraud and error
- reducing work-related death and serious injury in workplaces through the Health and Safety Executive

Priorities

Our priorities are:

- welfare reform – simplifying the welfare system and ensuring work pays
- getting Britain working
- helping to reduce poverty and improve social justice
- reforming pensions
- enabling disabled people to fulfil their potential
- improving our service to the public

Who we are

We provide our services in a number of ways, for example through Jobcentre Plus, The Pension Service, the Child Maintenance Service and partner organisations.

Jobcentre Plus

Jobcentre Plus helps people move from benefits into work and helps employers fill vacancies. It also deals with benefits for people who are unemployed or unable to work because of a health condition or disability.

The Pension Service

The Pension Service provides pensions, benefits and retirement information for current and future pensioners in the UK and abroad. This includes:

- State Pension
- Pension Credit
- Winter Fuel Payment
- Cold Weather Payment
- Contact the Pension Service

Child Support Agency and Child Maintenance Service

Child maintenance is financial support that helps towards a child's everyday living costs when the parents have separated. For people who can't make their own, family-based arrangements, the Child Support Agency and Child Maintenance Service:

- calculate how much maintenance the paying parent should pay to the receiving parent
- collect the maintenance payments, if necessary

www.gov.uk/child-maintenance

Child Maintenance Options

Our Child Maintenance Options service provides impartial information and support to help both parents make informed choices about child maintenance. It can also help them to set up their own, family-based arrangements.
www.cmoptions.org

DWP is a ministerial department, supported by 13 agencies and public bodies.

Executive non-departmental public body

Health and Safety Executive

The Health and Safety Executive (HSE) is the national independent watchdog for work-related health, safety and illness. It acts in the public interest to reduce work-related death and serious injury across Great Britain's workplaces.
HSE is an executive non-departmental public body of the Department for Work & Pensions
http://www.hse.gov.uk/

The Pensions Advisory Service

The Pensions Advisory Service (TPAS) gives information and guidance to members of the public on state, company and personal pensions. It helps any member of the public who has a problem with their occupational or private pension arrangement.
TPAS is an executive non-departmental public body of the Department for Work & Pensions
http://www.pensionsadvisoryservice.org.uk/

The Pensions Regulator

The Pensions Regulator (TPR) is the UK regulator of work-based pension schemes. It works with trustees, employers, pension specialists and business advisers, giving guidance on what is expected of them.
TPR is an executive non-departmental public body of the Department for Work & Pensions
http://www.thepensionsregulator.gov.uk/

National Employment Savings Trust (NEST) Corporation

The National Employment Savings Trust (NEST) Corporation is the trustee of the NEST occupational pension scheme. The scheme, which is run on a not-for-profit basis, ensures that all employers have access to suitable, low-charge pension provision to meet their new duty to enrol all eligible workers into a workplace pension automatically.
NEST Corporation is an executive non-departmental public body of the Department for Work & Pensions
http://www.nestpensions.org.uk/

Remploy Ltd

Remploy is one of the UK's leading providers of employment and employment services for disabled people and those with barriers to work.
Remploy is an executive non-departmental public body of the Department for Work & Pensions
http://www.remploy.co.uk

Independent Living Fund

The Independent Living Fund (ILF) delivers financial support to disabled people so they can choose to live in their communities rather than in residential care.
ILF is an executive non-departmental public body of the Department for Work & Pensions
http://www.dwp.gov.uk/ilf

Advisory non-departmental public body

Equality 2025

Equality 2025 (E2025), a body of publicly appointed disabled people, offers strategic, confidential advice to government on issues that affect disabled people.
E2025 is an advisory non-departmental public body of the Department for Work & Pensions
http://odi.dwp.gov.uk/equality-2025/index.php

Industrial Injuries Advisory Council

The Industrial Injuries Advisory Council (IIAC) is a scientific advisory body that gives independent advice to DWP and the Department for Social Development in Northern Ireland on matters relating to Industrial Injuries benefit and its administration.
IIAC is an advisory non-departmental public body of the Department for Work & Pensions
http://iiac.independent.gov.uk/

Social Security Advisory Committee

The Social Security Advisory Committee (SSAC) gives impartial advice to the government on proposals for social security regulations. SSAC is independent of the government, the DWP and sectional interests.
SSAC is an advisory non-departmental public body of the Department for Work & Pensions
http://ssac.independent.gov.uk/

Social Mobility and Child Poverty Commission

What we do

The Social Mobility and Child Poverty (SMCP) Commission monitors the progress of government and others in improving social mobility and reducing child poverty in the United Kingdom.

Responsibilities

We are responsible for:

- publishing an annual report setting out our views on progress made in improving social mobility and reducing child poverty in the UK, including against the targets in the Child Poverty Act 2010, and describing the measures taken by the Scottish and Welsh governments
- providing published advice to ministers (at their request) on how to measure socio-economic disadvantage, social mobility and child poverty
- acting as an advocate for social mobility beyond government by challenging employers, the professions and universities amongst others to play their part in improving life chances

Priorities

In 2013, our main priorities will be:

- holding the government and others to account through providing an authoritative 'state of the nation' analysis of social mobility and child poverty in our first annual report
- creating a business manifesto for social mobility and using it to encourage firms to put and keep the issue on the agenda, as well as working closely with specific professions and the university sector to drive change
- influencing policy via credible and independent advice. We have responded to the government consultation on better measures of child poverty and are currently developing advice to ministers on the 3 or 4 most impactful steps the government could reasonably take to improve social mobility

Who we are

The Social Mobility and Child Poverty Commission is chaired by the Rt. Hon Alan Milburn and deputy chaired by Baroness Gillian Shephard.

It includes 7 other members drawn from across business, academia and the voluntary sector. It is supported by a small secretariat based in London.

Tribunal non-departmental public body

Pension Protection Fund Ombudsman

PPFO is a tribunal non-departmental public body of the Department for Work & Pensions
http://www.ppfo.org.uk/

Pensions Ombudsman

The Pensions Ombudsman (PO) impartially investigates complaints from members of pension schemes (including personal pensions) or their beneficiaries, employers or trustees. As the Pension Protection Fund Ombudsman, the same person investigates complaints about the way people and their cases have been handled by the Pension Protection Fund and conducts appeals against decisions issued by the Financial Assistance Scheme.
PO is a tribunal non-departmental public body of the Department for Work & Pensions
http://www.pensions-ombudsman.org.uk/

Public corporation

Pension Protection Fund

The Pension Protection Fund (PPF) pays compensation to members of eligible defined benefit pension schemes, when there is a qualifying insolvency event in relation to the employer and where there are insufficient assets in the pension scheme to cover Pension Protection Fund levels of compensation.
PPF is a public corporation of the Department for Work & Pensions
http://www.pensionprotectionfund.org.uk

Department of Energy & Climate Change

What we do

The Department of Energy & Climate Change (DECC) works to make sure the UK has secure, clean, affordable energy supplies and promote international action to mitigate climate change.

Responsibilities
We are responsible for:

- energy security – making sure UK businesses and households have secure supplies of energy for light and power, heat and transport
- action on climate change – leading government efforts to mitigate climate change, both through international action and cutting UK greenhouse gas emissions by at least 80% by 2050 (including by sourcing at least 15% of our energy from renewable sources by 2020)
- renewable energy – sourcing at least 15% of our energy from renewable sources by 2020
- affordability – delivering secure, low-carbon energy at the least cost to consumers, taxpayers and the economy
- fairness – making sure the costs and benefits of our policies are distributed fairly so that we protect the most vulnerable and fuel poor households and address competitiveness problems faced by energy intensive industries
- supporting growth – delivering our policies in a way that maximises the benefits to the economy in terms of jobs, growth and investment, including by making the most of our existing oil and gas reserves and seizing the opportunities presented by the rise of the global green economy
- managing the UK's energy legacy safely, securely and cost effectively

Priorities

From 2012 to 2013 our priorities will be:

- supporting investment in the UK's energy infrastructure – including through the Energy Bill, which will set in place the framework to bring forward the £110 billion needed in our electricity infrastructure over the next decade
- supporting consumers and keeping energy bills down, including through implementation of the Green Deal

- promoting action in the EU and internationally to maintain energy security and mitigate dangerous climate change as we chart the way towards a global deal on climate change in 2015

Who we are

The Department of Energy & Climate Change employs around 1600 staff based in London and Aberdeen.

DECC is a ministerial department, supported by 8 agencies and public bodies.

Non-ministerial department

Ofgem

The Office of Gas and Electricity Markets (Ofgem) regulates the monopoly companies which run the gas and electricity networks. It takes decisions on price controls and enforcement, acting in the interests of consumers and helping the industries to achieve environmental improvements.
Ofgem is a non-ministerial department of the Department of Energy & Climate Change
http://www.ofgem.gov.uk/

Executive non-departmental public body

Civil Nuclear Police Authority

The Civil Nuclear Police Authority (CNPA) employs and manages police officers and constables in the Civil Nuclear Constabulary and must ensure that their policing meets the need of the nuclear operating companies. This could involve denying unauthorised access to nuclear material or recovering control of nuclear material which may have been lost to unauthorised persons.
CNPA is an executive non-departmental public body of the Department of Energy & Climate Change
http://www.cnpa.police.uk/

The Coal Authority

The Coal Authority owns, on behalf of the country, the vast majority of the coal in Great Britain and licenses coal mining. It also manages the effects of past coal mining, including subsidence damage claims which are not the responsibility of licensed coal mine operators; deals with mine water pollution and other coal legacy issues and provides access to the mining information it holds. Its powers were extended in 2011 to enable it to deal with non-coal mine water pollution and subsidence when the necessary funding is made available.
The Coal Authority is an executive non-departmental public body of the Department of Energy & Climate Change
http://coal.decc.gov.uk/

Committee on Climate Change

The Committee on Climate Change (CCC) advises the government on emissions targets and reports to Parliament on progress made in reducing greenhouse gas emissions.
CCC is an executive non-departmental public body of the Department of Energy & Climate Change
http://www.theccc.org.uk/

Nuclear Decommissioning Authority

The Nuclear Decommissioning Authority (NDA) is responsible for the decommissioning and clean-up of civil nuclear facilities, ensuring that treatment and disposal follow government policy on the long-term management of nuclear waste.
NDA is an executive non-departmental public body of the Department of Energy & Climate Change
http://www.nda.gov.uk/

Advisory non-departmental public body

Committee on Radioactive Waste Management

The Committee on Radioactive Waste Management (CoRWM) provides independent scrutiny and advice to the government on the long-term management of higher activity radioactive wastes.
CoRWM is an advisory non-departmental public body of the Department of Energy & Climate Change

http://corwm.decc.gov.uk/

Fuel Poverty Advisory Group

What we do
We advise on the effectiveness of policies aimed at reducing fuel poverty, and encourage greater co-ordination across the organisations working to reduce fuel poverty.

Responsibilities

Our role is to:

- consider and report on the effectiveness of current policies aimed at reducing fuel poverty
- consider and report on the case for greater co-ordination across organisations to help reduce fuel poverty
- identify barriers to reducing fuel poverty and to developing effective partnerships – and propose solutions
- consider and report on any additional policies needed to reduce fuel poverty
- encourage key organisations to help reduce fuel poverty
- consider and report on the results of work to monitor fuel poverty

Priorities

Our priorities are encouraging organisations to help reduce fuel poverty and identifying any barriers to them working together to do this.

Who we are

FPAG is made up of a wide range of member organisations, with a chairman and senior representatives from the energy industry, charities and consumer bodies. Each member represents his or her organisation, but is expected to take an impartial view.

FPAG is an advisory Non Departmental Public Body. Members are representative ex officio members, rather than individuals. The Chair and members of the Group are unpaid.

Derek Lickorish was re-appointed as Chair of FPAG on 10 July 2011 for a further three years. FPAG membership was renewed on the 1st April 2012, whereby member organisations were re-appointed for a further three years.

Member organisations of the Fuel Poverty Advisory Group:
Chair: Derek Lickorish MBE
Public Utilities Access Forum (PUAF)
National Grid
Scottish Power
Scottish and Southern Energy
British Gas
E.ON UK
National Energy Action
RWEnpower
Child Poverty Action Group
National Heart Forum
Association for the Conservation of Energy
Age UK
Consumerfocus
Local Government Association
Carillion Energy Services
Citizens Advice
EDF Energy
Energy Efficiency Partnership for Homes

Nuclear Liabilities Financing Assurance Board

What we do

We provide impartial scrutiny and advice on the suitability of the Funded Decommissioning Programme (FDP), submitted by operators of new nuclear power stations. The Board advises the Secretary of State on the financial arrangements that operators submit for approval, and on the regular review of funding.
Responsibilities
DECC created the independent Nuclear Liabilities Financing Assurance Board (NLFAB) to provide impartial scrutiny and advice on the suitability of the Funded Decommissioning Programmes (FDPs), submitted by operators of new nuclear power stations.

We advise the Secretary of State on:

* the financial arrangements that operators submit for approval
* the regular review and ongoing scrutiny of funding

Priorities

The NLFAB's priority is to ensure that operators of new nuclear power stations have secure financing arrangements in place to meet the full costs of decommissioning and their full share of waste management costs.

Any operator of a new nuclear power station must have a Funded Decommissioning Programme, approved by the Secretary of State, in place before construction of a new nuclear power station begins.

Department of Health

What we do

The Department of Health (DH) helps people to live better for longer. We lead, shape and fund health and care in England, making sure people have the support, care and treatment they need, with the compassion, respect and dignity they deserve.

Our responsibilities

* we lead across health and care by creating national policies and legislation, providing the long-term vision and ambition to meet current and future challenges, putting health and care at the heart of government and being a global leader in health and care policy
* we support the integrity of the system by providing funding, assuring the delivery and continuity of services and accounting to Parliament in a way that represents the best interests of the patient, public and taxpayer.
* we champion innovation and improvement by supporting research and technology, promoting honesty, openness and transparency, and instilling a culture that values compassion, dignity and the highest quality of care above everything
* above all, DH encourages staff in every health and care organisation, including our own, to understand and learn from people's experience of health and care and to apply this to everything we do

Our priorities
Our priorities for 2013 to 2014 are:

* preventing people from dying prematurely by improving mortality rates for the big killer diseases, to be amongst the best in Europe, through improving prevention, diagnosis and treatment
* improving the standard of care throughout the system so that quality of care is considered as important as quality of treatment, through greater accountability, better training, tougher inspections and more attention paid to what patients say
* improving treatment and care of people with dementia, to be among the best in Europe through early diagnosis, better research and better support
* bringing the technology revolution to the NHS to help people, especially those with long term conditions, manage their health and care

Who we are

DH is a ministerial department, supported by 24 agencies and public bodies. The department employs 2,160 staff who works in locations across the country.

DH is a ministerial department, supported by 24 agencies and public bodies.

Non-ministerial department

Food Standards Agency

The Food Standards Agency (FSA) is responsible for food safety and food hygiene across the UK. It works with local authorities to enforce food safety regulations and its staff work in UK meat plants to check the standards are being met. The FSA also has responsibility for labelling policy in Scotland, Wales and Northern Ireland, and for nutrition policy in Scotland and Northern Ireland. Responsibility for nutrition policy in Wales lies with the Welsh Government.
FSA is a non-ministerial department of the Department of Health
http://www.food.gov.uk/

Executive agency

Medicines and Healthcare Products Regulatory Agency

The Medicines and Healthcare Products Regulatory Agency (MHRA) protects and promotes public health and patient safety by ensuring that medicines, healthcare products and medical equipment meet appropriate standards of safety, quality, performance and effectiveness and are used safely. The MHRA was formed from a merger of the Medicines Control Agency and the Medical Devices Agency on 1 April 2003.
MHRA is an executive agency of the Department of Health
http://www.mhra.gov.uk

Public Health England

What we do

We work with national and local government, industry and the NHS to protect and improve the nation's health and support healthier choices. We are addressing inequalities by focusing on removing barriers to good health.

Responsibilities

We are responsible for:

- making the public healthier by encouraging discussions, advising government and supporting action by local government, the NHS and other people and organisations
- supporting the public so they can protect and improve their own health
- protecting the nation's health through the national health protection service, and preparing for public health emergencies
- sharing our information and expertise with local authorities, industry and the NHS, to help them make improvements in the public's health
- researching, collecting and analysing data to improve our understanding of health and come up with answers to public health problems
- reporting on improvements in the public's health so everyone can understand the challenge and the next steps
- helping local authorities and the NHS to develop the public health system and its specialist workforce

Priorities

In 2013 and 2014, our priorities will be:

- helping people to live longer and more healthy lives by reducing preventable deaths and the burden of ill health associated with smoking, high blood pressure, obesity, poor diet, poor mental health, insufficient exercise, and alcohol

- reducing the burden of disease and disability in life by focusing on preventing and recovering from the conditions with the greatest impact, including dementia, anxiety, depression and drug dependency
- protecting the country from infectious diseases and environmental hazards, including the growing problem of infections that resist treatment with antibiotics
- supporting families to give children and young people the best start in life, through working with health visiting and school nursing, family nurse partnerships and the Troubled Families programme
- improving health in the workplace by encouraging employers to support their staff, and those moving into and out of the workforce, to lead healthier lives
- promoting the development of place-based public health systems
- developing our own capacity and capability to provide professional, scientific and delivery expertise to our partners

Who we are

We employ 5,500 staff, mostly scientists, researchers and public health professionals. We have 15 local centres and 4 regions (north of England, south of England, Midlands and east of England and London). We work closely with public health professionals in Wales, Scotland and Northern Ireland, and internationally.

Public Health England was established on 1 April 2013 to bring together public health specialists from more than 70 organisations into a single public health service.

Executive non-departmental public body

Care Quality Commission

The Care Quality Commission (CQC) regulates all health and social care services in England. The commission ensures the quality and safety of care in hospitals, dentists, ambulances, and care homes, and the care given in people's own homes.
CQC is an executive non-departmental public body of the Department of Health
http://www.cqc.org.uk/

Human Fertilisation and Embryology Authority

The Human Fertilisation and Embryology Authority (HEFA) oversees the use of gametes and embryos in fertility treatment and research. It licenses fertility clinics and centres carrying out in vitro fertilisation (IVF), other assisted conception procedures and human embryo research.
HFEA is an executive non-departmental public body of the Department of Health
http://www.hfea.gov.uk/

Human Tissue Authority

The Human Tissue Authority (HTA) ensures that human tissue is used safely and ethically, and with proper consent. It regulates organisations that remove, store and use tissue for research, medical treatment, post-mortem examination, teaching and display in public. It approves organ and bone marrow donations from living people.
HTA is an executive non-departmental public body of the Department of Health
http://www.hta.gov.uk/

Monitor

Monitor is the sector regulator for healthcare. Its main duty is to protect and promote the interests of patients by making sure healthcare services are effective, efficient and economic. Its work includes licensing healthcare providers and ensuring they are well-led in terms of quality and finances; making sure essential healthcare services continue to be available even if a provider gets into financial difficulty; and safeguarding patient choice.
Monitor is an executive non-departmental public body of the Department of Health
http://www.monitor.gov.uk/

National Institute for Health and Care Excellence

The National Institute for Health and Care Excellence (NICE) provides national guidance and advice to improve health and social care.
NICE is an executive non-departmental public body of the Department of Health

http://www.nice.org.uk/

NHS England

NHS England authorises the new clinical commissioning groups, which are the drivers of the new, clinically led commissioning system introduced by the Health and Social Care Act. Prior to 1 April 2013, NHS England was known as the NHS Commissioning Board.
NHS England is an executive non-departmental public body of the Department of Health
http://www.england.nhs.uk/

Health and Social Care Information Centre

The Health and Social Care Information Centre (HSCIC) collects, analyses and publishes national data and statistical information for commissioners, analysts and clinicians. It also provides systems and infrastructure at a national level and sets standard for health and social care.
HSCIC is an executive non-departmental public body of the Department of Health
http://www.hscic.gov.uk/

Advisory non-departmental public body

Advisory Committee on Clinical Excellence Awards

What we do

The Advisory Committee on Clinical Excellence Awards (ACCEA) advises health ministers on the presentation of clinical excellence awards to consultants working in the NHS.
What we do
We advise ministers on the making of clinical excellence awards to consultants and academic GPs working in the NHS. The awards are given for quality, excellence, and exceptional personal contributions.

Responsibilities

We are responsible for:

- approving the criteria for assessing candidates
- overseeing the process for judging nominations
- considering all nominations for platinum (level 12) awards
- recommending consultants for national awards: bronze, silver, gold and platinum (levels 9 to 12)
- recommending consultants for renewal of awards, taking into account advice from chairs and vice chairs of the regional sub-committees
- supporting employer-based awards processes to ensure a fair, open and transparent scheme
- considering the development of the scheme

Priorities

From 2013 our priorities will be to:

- continue to deliver an effective clinical excellence awards scheme to an annual timetable
- maintain a viable clinical excellence awards scheme against a background of NHS financial pressure
- work with a wide range of stakeholders, both internal and external, to manage expectations and the sensitivities arising from review of clinical excellence awards
- support the development of a new awards scheme and ensure transitional arrangements are in place for the current scheme
- continue to improve the effectiveness of the ACCEA secretariat internal business and financial processes
- continue to provide high quality support to ministers and accountability to Parliament

Administration of Radioactive Substances Advisory Committee

The Administration of Radioactive Substances Advisory Committee (ARSAC) helps certifies doctors and dentists to administer radioactive medicinal products.
ARSAC is an advisory non-departmental public body of the Department of Health
http://www.arsac.org.uk/

British Pharmacopoeia

British Pharmacopoeia (BP) provides official standards for pharmaceutical substances and medicinal products.
British Pharmacopoeia is an advisory non-departmental public body of the Department of Health
http://pharmacopoeia.mhra.gov.uk

Commission on Human Medicines

The Commission on Human Medicines (CHM) advises ministers on the safety and quality of medicinal products.
CHM is an advisory non-departmental public body of the Department of Health
http://www.mhra.gov.uk/Committees/Medicinesadvisorybodies/CommissiononHumanMedicines/index.htm

Committee on Mutagenicity of Chemicals in Food, Consumer Products and the Environment

The Committee on Mutagenicity of Chemicals in Food, Consumer Products and the Environment (COM) advises government on the stability of chemicals used in pesticides, pharmaceuticals and other products.
COM is an advisory non-departmental public body of the Department of Health
http://www.iacom.org.uk/

Independent Reconfiguration Panel

The Independent Reconfiguration Panel (IRP) advises ministers on proposals for health service change in England.
IRP is an advisory non-departmental public body of the Department of Health
http://www.irpanel.org.uk/

Review Body on Doctors' and Dentists' Remuneration

The Review Body on Doctors' and Dentists' Remuneration (DDRB) advises government on rates of pay for doctors and dentists.
DDRB is an advisory non-departmental public body of the Department of Health
http://www.dh.gov.uk/health/2011/11/information-for-the-review-body-on-doctors-and-dentists-remuneration-ddrb-review-for-2012/

NHS Pay Review Body

The NHS Pay Review Body (NHSPRB) advises on the pay of NHS staff.
NHSPRB is an advisory non-departmental public body of the Department of Health
http://www.ome.uk.com/example/NHS_Pay_Review_Body.aspx

Other

The Health Research Authority

The Health Research Authority (HRA) protects and promotes the interests of patients and the public in health research.
HRA works with the Department of Health
http://www.hra.nhs.uk/

NHS Trust Development Authority

The NHS Trust Development Authority (NHS TDA) will be responsible for overseeing the performance management and governance of NHS Trusts, including clinical quality, and managing their progress towards foundation trust status.
NHS TDA works with the Department of Health
http://www.ntda.nhs.uk/

NHS Blood and Transplant

NHS Blood and Transplant (NHSBT) improves the supply of donated blood, organs and tissues, and raises the quality, effectiveness and efficiency of blood and transplant services.

NHSBT works with the Department of Health
http://www.nhsbt.nhs.uk/

NHS Litigation Authority

The NHSLA administers 5 schemes that help NHS bodies pool the costs of any loss, damage or injury arising out of the carrying out of their functions.
NHSLA works with the Department of Health
http://www.nhsla.com

NHS Business Services Authority

The NHS Business Services Authority (NHSBSA) provides central services to NHS bodies, patients and the public, such as managing the NHS pension scheme, issuing European Health Insurance Cards (EHIC), and administering payments to pharmacists and dentists.

NHSBSA works with the Department of Health
http://www.nhsbsa.nhs.uk/

Health Education England

Health Education England (HEE) is the new national leadership organisation for education, training and workforce development in the health sector.
HEE works with the Department of Health
http://hee.nhs.uk/

Foreign & Commonwealth Office

What we do

The FCO promotes British interests overseas, supporting our citizens and businesses around the globe.
Responsibilities

We are responsible for:

- safeguarding Britain's national security by countering terrorism and weapons proliferation, and working to reduce conflict
- building Britain's prosperity by increasing exports and investment, opening markets, ensuring access to resources, and promoting sustainable global growth
- supporting British nationals around the world through modern and efficient consular services

Priorities

In 2012 and 2013, our priorities are organised around increasing security and prosperity and developing our consular presence. Specific priorities include:

- reducing the risk to the UK and UK interests overseas from international terrorism
- contributing to the success of Britain's effort in Afghanistan
- helping to build a stable and increasingly prosperous Pakistan
- playing a central role in international efforts to prevent the proliferation of weapons of mass destruction in Iran and elsewhere
- co-ordinating a UK government contribution to conflict prevention and supporting conflict resolution in fragile states
- promoting the British economy and lobbying for British business overseas and inward investment into the UK
- improving the global economic environment and advancing UK interests through trade agreements, an effective G20 and international development
- delivering a smaller and better consular service by managing resources more effectively to meet our customers' needs

Who we are

The Foreign & Commonwealth Office (FCO) has a world-wide network of embassies and consulates, employing over 14,000 people in nearly 270 diplomatic offices. We work with international organisations to promote British interests and global security, including the EU, NATO, the United Nations, the UN Security Council and the Commonwealth.

Our funding programmes

Our Strategic Programme Fund promotes action on global issues in areas of strategic importance to the UK. Current areas of focus include the Arab Partnership, commercial diplomacy, counter proliferation, counter terrorism, human rights, prosperity, bilateral programmes and the Overseas Territories. The funding allocation for the financial year 2012-13 will total £143.8 million.

HMG Conflict Funding is managed jointly by FCO, the Department for International Development and the Ministry of Defence, and is worth £644 million for 2012 to 2013. It covers conflict prevention work and the UK's contribution to international peacekeeping missions. You can find out more about this fund and how it will be used and managed in the future from the Written ministerial statement on conflict resources, 2012-13 and 2013-14.

We also support:

- outstanding scholars with leadership potential to take postgraduate courses in the UK on Chevening scholarships
- young Americans of high ability to study in the UK on Marshall scholarships
- victims of forced marriage with the Domestic Programme Fund
- natural resource management in the Overseas Territories with the Overseas Territories Environment and Climate Fund

FCO is a ministerial department, supported by 12 agencies and public bodies.

Non-ministerial department

UK Trade & Investment

UK Trade & Investment (UKTI) works with UK-based businesses to ensure their success in international markets and encourage the best overseas companies to look to the UK as their global partner of choice.
UKTI is a non-ministerial department of the Department for Business, Innovation & Skills and the Foreign & Commonwealth Office
http://www.ukti.gov.uk/

Executive agency

FCO Services
FCO Services (FCOS) deliver secure ICT, logistics and other services to maintain a secure working environment. FCOS works for the FCO and other government departments, non-governmental bodies and foreign governments.
FCOS is an executive agency of the Foreign & Commonwealth Office
http://www.fcoservices.gov.uk/

Wilton Park
Wilton Park provides a global forum for strategic discussion. It organises over 50 events a year in the UK and overseas, bringing together leading representatives from the worlds of politics, business, academia, diplomacy, civil society and media. Events focus on issues of international security, prosperity and justice.
Wilton Park is an executive agency of the Foreign & Commonwealth Office
http://www.wiltonpark.org.uk

Executive non-departmental public body

British Council
The British Council is the UK's international organisation for cultural relations and educational opportunities, building lasting relationships between the UK and other countries. It is an essential part of our international effort to promote British values and interests.

British Council is an executive non-departmental public body of the Foreign & Commonwealth Office
http://www.britishcouncil.org

Marshall Aid Commemoration Commission
The Marshall Aid Commemoration Commission (MACC) administers the British Marshall Scholarships, which finance young Americans of high ability to study for a graduate degree in the UK.
MACC is an executive non-departmental public body of the Foreign & Commonwealth Office
http://www.marshallscholarship.org/

Westminster Foundation for Democracy
The Westminster Foundation for Democracy (WFD) supports democratic practices and institutions in developing democracies. Working with partner organisations, it strengthens the institutions of democracy, principally political parties, parliaments and institutions that make up civil society.
Westminster Foundation for Democracy is an executive non-departmental public body of the Foreign & Commonwealth Office
http://www.wfd.org/

Great Britain China Centre
The Great Britain China Centre (GBCC) promotes understanding between China and the UK, helping UK organisations to engage and compete with Chinese counterparts.
GBCC is an executive non-departmental public body of the Foreign & Commonwealth Office
http://www.gbcc.org.uk/

Tribunal non-departmental public body

Foreign Compensation Commission
The Foreign Compensation Commission works out the amount of compensation British claimants are entitled to under international and British law for losses suffered abroad. It also helps in the settlement negotiations of British property losses overseas at the hands of foreign governments.
FCC is a tribunal non-departmental public body of the Foreign & Commonwealth Office
https://www.gov.uk/government/publications/foreign-compensation-commission-fcc

Public corporation

BBC World Service
The BBC World Service (BBCWS) is the world's leading international radio broadcaster, providing impartial news reports and analysis in English and 27 other languages.
BBCWS is a public corporation of the Foreign & Commonwealth Office
http://www.bbc.co.uk/worldservice/

Other

Secret Intelligence Service
The Secret Intelligence Service, often known as MI6, collects Britain's foreign intelligence. It provides the government with a global covert capability to promote and defend the national security and economic well being of the country.
SIS works with the Foreign & Commonwealth Office
https://www.sis.gov.uk/

Government Communications Headquarters
The Government Communications Headquarters (GCHQ) provides intelligence, protects information and informs relevant UK policy to keep society safe and successful in the internet age.
GCHQ works with the Foreign & Commonwealth Office
http://www.gchq.gov.uk/

Chevening Foundation
Chevening Scholarships are the UK government's global scholarships programme. Established in 1983, these scholarships support study at UK universities - mostly one-year Masters' degrees - for students with demonstrable potential to become future leaders, decision-makers and opinion formers.
Chevening works with the Foreign & Commonwealth Office
http://www.chevening.org/

HM Treasury

What we do
HM Treasury is the government's economic and finance ministry, maintaining control over public spending, setting the direction of the UK's economic policy and working to achieve strong and sustainable economic growth.

Responsibilities
We are responsible for:

- public spending: including departmental spending, public sector pay and pension, annually managed expenditure (AME) and welfare policy, and capital investment
- financial services policy: including banking and financial services regulation, financial stability, and ensuring competitiveness in the City
- strategic oversight of the UK tax system: including direct, indirect, business, property, personal tax, and corporation tax
- the delivery of infrastructure projects across the public sector and facilitating private sector investment into UK infrastructure
- ensuring the economy is growing sustainably

Priorities
In 2013 our priorities are:

- achieving strong and sustainable growth
- reducing the deficit and rebalancing the economy
- spending taxpayers' money responsibly
- creating a simpler, fairer tax system
- creating stronger and safer banks
- making corporate taxes more competitive
- making it easier for people to access and use financial services
- improving regulation of the financial sector to protect customers and the economy

Who we are
Our main offices are based in London, but we also have offices in Norwich and Edinburgh. Read more about the history of the Treasury and 11 Downing Street.

HMT is a ministerial department, supported by 8 agencies and public bodies.

Non-ministerial department

Royal Mint
The Royal Mint (RM) is the world's leading export mint, making coins and medals for an average of 60 countries every year. However, its first responsibility is to make and distribute United Kingdom coins as well as to supply blanks and official medals.
RM is a non-ministerial department of HM Treasury
http://www.royalmint.com/

NS&I
NS&I (National Savings and Investments), a state-owned savings bank in the UK, offers Premium Bonds and a range of other savings and investments, including Direct Saver and Children's Bonds.
NS&I is a non-ministerial department of HM Treasury
http://www.nsandi.com/

The Crown Estate
The Crown Estate is a diverse portfolio of UK buildings, shoreline, seabed, forestry, and agriculture and common land that generates valuable revenue for the government every year.
The Crown Estate is a non-ministerial department of HM Treasury
http://www.thecrownestate.co.uk/

The Crown Estate
The Crown Estate is a diverse portfolio of UK buildings, shoreline, seabed, forestry, agriculture and common land that generates valuable revenue for the government every year.
The Crown Estate is a non-ministerial department of HM Treasury
http://www.thecrownestate.co.uk/

Executive agency

UK Debt Management Office
The UK Debt Management Office (DMO) manages debt and cash for the UK Government, lending to local authorities and managing certain public sector funds.
DMO is an executive agency of HM Treasury
http://www.dmo.gov.uk/

Advisory non-departmental public body

Office for Budget Responsibility
The Office for Budget Responsibility (OBR) gives independent and authoritative analysis of the UK's public finances.
OBR is an advisory non-departmental public body of HM Treasury
http://budgetresponsibility.independent.gov.uk/

Royal Mint Advisory Committee
The Royal Mint Advisory Committee (RMAC) reviews new designs of coins, medals, seals and decorations and then recommends preferred designs to the government.
RMAC is an advisory non-departmental public body of HM Treasury
http://www.royalmint.com/aboutus/advisory-committee

Other

UK Financial Investments Ltd
UK Financial Investments Limited (UKFI) was set up in response to the financial crisis. It is responsible for managing the government's investments in The Royal Bank of Scotland (RBS) and Lloyds Banking Group (Lloyds) plc.
UKFI works with HM Treasury
http://www.ukfi.co.uk/

Home Office

What we do
The Home Office leads on immigration and passports, drug policy, crime policy and counter-terrorism and works to ensure visible, responsive and accountable policing in the UK.
The Home Office is the lead government department for immigration and passports, drugs policy, crime, counter-terrorism and police.

Responsibilities
We are responsible for:

- working on the problems caused by illegal drug use
- shaping the alcohol strategy, policy and licensing conditions
- keeping the United Kingdom safe from the threat of terrorism
- reducing and preventing crime, and ensuring people feel safe in their homes and communities
- securing the UK border and controlling immigration
- considering applications to enter and stay in the UK
- issuing passports and visas
- supporting visible, responsible and accountable policing by empowering the public and freeing up the police to fight crime

Priorities
In 2012 and 2013, our priorities are to:

- empower the public to hold the police to account for their role in cutting crime
- free up the police to fight crime more effectively and efficiently

- create a more integrated criminal justice system
- secure our borders and reduce immigration
- protect people's freedoms and civil liberties
- protect our citizens from terrorism

Who we are
Our main offices are based in London, but we also have staff based around the country.

We are supported by a number of agencies and public bodies.

Home Office is a ministerial department, supported by 27 agencies and public bodies.

Executive agency

HM Passport Office

What we do
HM Passport Office is the sole issuer of UK passports and responsible for civil registration services through the General Register Office.
Established in 2006, HM Passport Office provides accurate and secure records of key events and trusted passport operations.

The Identity and Passport Service became HM Passport Office in May 2013. Our new name makes clear our role in issuing passports to citizens of the United Kingdom on behalf of the Crown and is more recognisable as the official government service to British citizens at home and abroad. HM Passport Office will retain the General Register Office brand to oversee civil registration in England and Wales.

Responsibilities
We are responsible for:

- providing passport services for British nationals residing in the UK and, in association with our partners at the Foreign & Commonwealth Office, to those residing overseas
- administering civil registration in England and Wales

Priorities
In 2012 and 2013 our priorities will be to:

- process 90% of certificates within target
- process 99.5% of straightforward passport applications within 10 working days
- where additional information is required from customers, process 93% of applications within 29 working days
- process 99.5% of premium and fast track applications within 4 hours or 7 days
- achieve a customer satisfaction rating of at least 90%
- achieve a minimum standard of 53% on the staff engagement index
- demonstrate year on year reductions in unit cost
- increase the amount of passport fraud detected

Who we are
Each year we issue over 5 million passports - exceeding our customer service performance targets. We provide a passport validation service (PVS) to support the business community and government departments in preventing fraud. We have 7 regional passport offices and over 50 passport interview offices across the United Kingdom.

The General Register Office (GRO) joined with HM Passport Office in 2008. GRO oversees the system of civil registration in England and Wales: it administers the marriage laws and secures the provision of an efficient and effective system for the registration of births, stillbirths, adoptions, civil partnerships, marriages and deaths.

Purpose and principles
Our purpose is to provide accurate and secure records of key events and trusted passport services. We will do this by embedding the following principles into everything that we do:

- trusted and secure - we will maintain our high standards of integrity and reliability across all our products, services and the data we hold
- customer service - we are proud of the service we provide to customers and will deliver a modern and affordable service that meets the needs of today's society
- operational focus - we will create a more efficient and connected organisation with operational excellence at its core
- people - we value the contribution of all our people, treat them with respect and will support them through change
- cost - we will provide value for fee-payers and reduce our burden on the taxpayer

National Fraud Authority

What we do
The National Fraud Authority (NFA) works with wider government, law enforcement, and industry and voluntary/charity sectors to co-ordinate the fight against fraud in the UK.
We work with a huge range of stakeholders from across the wider government, law enforcement, industry and voluntary/charity sectors to focus and co-ordinate the fight against fraud in the UK. Fraudsters attack all economic sectors and parts of our society. Our fight against them is much more effective when we work together.

Responsibilities
We are responsible for:

- the implementation of the 'Fighting Fraud Together' strategy plan to reduce fraud
- the Annual Fraud Indicator (AFI) - a compendium of fraud loss indicators which strives to provide a best estimate of the scale of the problem and raise awareness

Action Fraud - the UK's national fraud and Internet crime reporting centre

Priorities
Our priorities are to:

- improve information sharing between and within the public and private sectors, in order to prevent and detect more fraud
- increase and improve the reporting of fraud through the Action Fraud reporting centre, and to harness the information collected to achieve better prevention and enforcement of fraud
- improve the level of support and advice given to fraud victims
- improve public and business awareness of fraud and self-protection from it
- build and exploit improved information and knowledge, providing a centre of expertise to raise the priority of fraud, secure and target counter fraud resource appropriately and achieve better prevention and enforcement of fraud
- address the key fraud enablers and high threat areas by prioritising and driving forward specific multi-partner interventions to reduce them
- ensure there is an appropriate balance in the criminal justice system between fraud prevention and disruption and the use of criminal justice powers and that the criminal and civil enforcement measures used against fraudsters are as effective as possible
- champion and co-ordinate the counter-fraud community, helping it become more joined up, more efficient and effective - we will do this by building relationships, sharing good practice, dealing with the gaps and overlays and helping to streamline the counter-fraud community landscape

Who we work with
We work with organisations with an interest in reducing the fraud threat. This work crosses boundaries of commercial activity and breaks down barriers between the public and private sectors. Our strategic role means co-operation and co-ordination are at the heart of our work.

The NFA works with stakeholder groups to expand the reach of the government's counter-fraud strategy. The NFA facilitates and co-ordinates activities with a wide range of public and private sector stakeholders. The enthusiastic involvement and engagement of these bodies has enabled us to openly discuss sensitive topics, broker agreements, deal with conflicts of interest and overlapping areas of responsibility and ensure delivery.

Our stakeholder community includes banks, retailers, insurance companies, trade associations, government departments and the police, as well as professional and statutory bodies, all working to achieve the goal of a hostile environment for fraudulent activity. Our relationship with the stakeholder community requires information to be willingly and openly exchanged between all the partners in this national effort to confront and eliminate fraudulent activity.

We continue to work closely with:

City of London Police
COLP has developed a great deal of expertise in dealing with fraud and is the acknowledged lead force within the UK for economic crime investigation. It provides a central resource for counter-fraud policing activity, with an overall objective to provide consistency and co-ordination to fraud investigations.

National Fraud Intelligence Bureau (NFIB)
The NFIB is a central place for analysing and assessing fraud. The NFIB is overseen by the City of London Police as part of its role as a national lead on fraud. Although funded by the Home Office, the NFIB database is populated from a large number of organisations within the public and private sectors, representing industry, commerce and government. The NFIB employs analysts from both law enforcement and private sector backgrounds to sift through the raw intelligence, searching for distinct patterns of fraudulent activity and behaviour. Once a trend has been spotted, such as a identifying a persistent offender, an intelligence report will be dispatched to the relevant police forces to be used in their investigation. Individuals, police, businesses, and charities report fraud directly into the NFIB by using the national fraud-reporting centre - Action Fraud.

In addition to the NFA and COLP we also work closely with a range of organisations within the counter fraud community:

Department for Business, Innovation and Skills (BIS), which is committed to fostering competitive markets in the UK, EU and world-wide

Crown Prosecution Service (CPS), which is responsible for prosecuting criminal, cases investigated by the police, HMRC and SOCA in England and Wales.

Department for Work and Pensions (DWP) which is responsible for welfare and pension policy and is a key player in tackling child poverty.

Financial Services Authority (FSA) which is an independent body that regulates the financial services industry in the UK which comprises approximately 30,000 firms.

Home Office, which is the lead government department for immigration and passports, drugs policy, counter-terrorism and police. It has responsibility for police funding (including funding of the Lead Force for Fraud) - NFA is an executive agency of the Home Office

HM Revenue and Customs (HMRC) which is responsible for ensuring the correct tax is paid at the right time, whether this relates to payment of taxes received by the department or entitlement to benefits paid Metropolitan Police Service (MPS) whose main task is to protect London from, and reduce the harm caused by, serious crime and criminal networks

Office of Fair Trading (OFT) whose mission is to make markets work well for consumers - it achieves this by promoting and protecting consumer interests throughout the UK, while ensuring that businesses are fair and competitive

Serious Fraud Office (SFO) which protects society from serious economic crime - it does this by preventing or disrupting economic crime in real time, investigating, prosecuting, recovering assets, and other outcomes, using proactive techniques as appropriate, in order to gain satisfaction for victims

Serious Organised Crime Agency (SOCA) which is an Executive Non-Departmental Public Body, which is sponsored by, but operationally independent from the Home Office - SOCA is an intelligence led agency with law enforcement powers and harm reduction responsibilities.

Attorney General's Office (AGO)
The Attorney General is the Chief Legal Adviser to the Crown and is a Minister of the Crown with responsibility for superintending the prosecuting departments, namely the Crown Prosecution Service and the Serious Fraud Office. He has a number of independent public interest functions.

These bodies represent a community of stakeholders that are in close contact with the NFA, feeding intelligence and information into the centre of the government's counter-fraud strategy. Representative organisations from the counter-fraud community and different sectors, with the NFA, have formed a number of task forces, forums and working groups, each focused on tackling particular fraud priority areas.

Executive non-departmental public body

Office of the Immigration Services Commissioner
The Office of the Immigration Services Commissioner (OISC) is responsible for regulating immigration advisers by ensuring they are fit and competent and act in the best interest of their clients.
OISC is an executive non-departmental public body of the Home Office
http://oisc.homeoffice.gov.uk/

Security Industry Authority
The Security Industry Authority (SIA) regulates and licenses the private security industry in the UK.
SIA is an executive non-departmental public body of the Home Office
http://www.sia.homeoffice.gov.uk/Pages/home.aspx

Serious Organised Crime Agency
The Serious Organised Crime Agency (SOCA) tackles serious organised crime including Class A drugs, human trafficking, major gun crime, fraud, computer crime and money laundering.
SOCA is an executive non-departmental public body of the Home Office
http://www.soca.gov.uk/

Independent Police Complaint Commission
The Independent Police Complaint Commission (IPCC) exists to increase public confidence in the police complaints system in England and Wales. It also investigates serious complaints and allegations of misconduct against the police and handles appeals.
IPCC is an executive non-departmental public body of the Home Office
http://www.ipcc.gov.uk

Disclosure & Barring Service

What we do
The Disclosure and Barring Service (DBS) helps employers make safer recruitment decisions and prevent unsuitable people from working with vulnerable groups, including children. It replaces the Criminal Records Bureau (CRB) and Independent Safeguarding Authority (ISA).
We are responsible for:

- processing requests for criminal records checks
- deciding whether it is appropriate for a person to be placed on or removed from a barred list
- placing or removing people from the DBS children's barred list and adults' barred list for England, Wales and Northern Ireland

Criminal record checks
We search police records and, in relevant cases, barred list information and then issue a DBS certificate to the applicant and employer to help them make an informed recruitment decision.

We recognise that information released on DBS certificates can be extremely sensitive and personal. Therefore a code of practice for recipients of DBS certificates has been developed to ensure that any information they contain is handled fairly and used properly.

Referrals
Referrals are made to us when an employer or organisation, e.g. a regulatory body, has concerns that a person has caused harm, or poses a future risk of harm to vulnerable groups, including children.

In these circumstances the employer must make a referral to the DBS, though this is not obligatory for regulatory bodies.

Barring

We make fair, consistent and thorough barring decisions that are an appropriate response to the harm that has occurred, as well as the risk of harm posed.

We are keenly aware of the impact barring or not barring can have both to the person under consideration and also those with whom they have or could have come into contact. Often very difficult and finely balanced decisions have to be made.

There are 2 main ways cases come to us:

Autobars - there are 2 types of automatic barring cases where a person has been cautioned or convicted for a 'relevant offence':

- automatic barring without representations offences will result in the person being placed in a barred list(s) by the DBS irrespective of whether they work in regulated activity
- automatic barring with representations offences may, subject to the consideration of representations and whether the DBS believes that the person has worked in regulated activity, is working in regulated activity or may in future work in regulated activity, this may also result in the person being placed on a DBS barred list(s)
- referrals from an organisation that has a legal duty or power to make referrals to DBS: typically there is a duty, in certain circumstances, on employers to make a referral to the DBS when they have dismissed or removed an employee from working in regulated activity, following harm to a child or vulnerable adult or where there is a risk of harm

Test for regulated activity

A new test for regulated activity has been introduced which means the DBS can only bar a person from working within regulated activity with children or adults if we believe the person is or has been, or might in the future be, engaged in regulated activity.

The only exception to this is where a person is cautioned or convicted for a relevant (automatic barring) offence and is not eligible to submit representations against their inclusion in a barred list.

Additionally, where a person is cautioned or convicted of a relevant (automatic barring) offence with the right to make representations, the DBS will ask the person to submit their representations and consider them before making a final barring decision.

Who we work with

We work with the police, who provide information that is held locally or on the police national computer. When disclosing information held locally, the police follow the quality assurance framework developed by the Association of Chief Police Officers (ACPO) and the DBS.

We also work with:

Department for Education - owns the safeguarding policy for children
Department of Health - owns the safeguarding policy for vulnerable groups
Capita - private sector partner that operates an administration infrastructure and call centre for our disclosure service
Registered bodies - organisations that have registered with the DBS checking service, and are the primary point of contact for:

- checking disclosure applications and validating information provided by the applicant
- establishing the identity of the applicant
- submitting fully completed application forms
- countersigning application forms to confirm entitlement

Advisory non-departmental public body

Advisory Council on the Misuse of Drugs

What we do

The Advisory Council on the Misuse of Drugs makes recommendations to government on the control of dangerous or otherwise harmful drugs, including classification and scheduling under the Misuse of Drugs Act 1971 and its regulations.

We are an independent expert body that advises government on drug-related issues in the UK. *[ACMD]: Advisory Council on the Misuse Drugs was established under the Misuse of Drugs Act 1971.

We consider any substance, which is being or appears to be misused and which is having or appears to be capable of having harmful effects sufficient to cause a social problem.

We also carry out in-depth inquiries into aspects of drug use that are causing particular concern in the UK, with the aim of producing considered reports that will be helpful to policy makers and practitioners.

Responsibilities
We are responsible for:

- making recommendations to government on the control of dangerous or otherwise harmful drugs, including classification and scheduling under the Misuse of Drugs Act 1971 and its regulations
- considering any substances which are being or appears to be misused and of which is having or appears to be capable of having harmful effects sufficient to cause a social problem
- carrying out in-depth inquiries into aspects of drug use that are causing particular concern in the UK, with the aim of producing considered reports that will be helpful to policy makers and practitioners

We produce reports on the following:

- drug-specific reports
- inquiry reports
- correspondence
- consultation responses
- annual reports

Priorities
Recovery
The Recovery Committee is the newest standing committee of the ACMD, formed in 2011 to support the ACMD to advise the government on:

- how people can best be supported to recover from dependence on drugs and alcohol
- how best to prevent drug and alcohol misuse and the harms it causes

Novel Psychoactive Substances
The Novel Psychoactive Substances Committee was set up in response to the emergence of novel psychoactive substances (NPS) that have rapidly and significantly changed the drug scene. The committee aims to monitor the prevalence and harms of NPS and where appropriate provide advice on this to government.

Police Advisory Board for England and Wales
The Police Advisory Board for England and Wales (PABEW) considers draft regulations under the Police Act 1996 with respect to matters such as recruitment, diversity and collaboration between forces. It also works with police managers and staff to respond to more general questions from the Home Secretary about changes to and reform of the police.
PAB is an advisory non-departmental public body of the Home Office
http://www.ome.uk.com/Police_Advisory_Board_for_England__Wales.aspx

Technical Advisory Board

What we do
The Technical Advisory Board (TAB) advises the Home Secretary on whether the obligations imposed on communications service providers (CSPs) under the terms of Regulation of Investigatory Powers Act (RIPA) are reasonable.

Responsibilities
We advise on the obligations placed on CSPs, including:

- the obligation to maintain interception capability (stated in Section 12 of the RIPA)
- the obligations and exemptions listed on the RIPA (Maintenance of Interception Capability) Order 2002

Most companies will receive a notice listing their obligations under the law, and giving them a date by which those obligations must be carried out.

We manage appeals from CSPs on notices they consider unreasonable under section 12 of RIPA, and advise the Home Secretary on each case.

Migration Advisory Committee
The Migration Advisory Committee (MAC) researches and reports on migration issues for the government, most often in the context of labour shortages and the points system for selective economic immigration. MAC is an advisory non-departmental public body of the Home Office
http://www.bia.homeoffice.gov.uk/aboutus/workingwithus/indbodies/mac/

National DNA Database Ethics Group

What we do
The National DNA Database Ethics Group is an advisory non-departmental public body. National DNA Database Ethics Group is established to provide independent advice on ethical issues surrounding the operations of the National DNA Database to Home Office ministers and the National DNA Database Strategy Board.

The application of quality standards is important to national forensic science intelligence databases. Of particular importance is the NDNAD, which is administered by the National Policing Improvement Agency (NPIA) and governed by the NDNAD strategy board.

The National DNA Database Ethics Group is an advisory non-departmental public body, established to provide independent advice on ethical issues surrounding the operations of the National DNA Database to Home Office ministers and the National DNA Database Strategy Board.

Responsibilities
The NDNAD Ethics Group provides independent ethical advice on the operations of the National DNA Database.

Priorities
Our priorities are to:

- advise on the implementation of the Protection of Freedoms Act 2012
- monitor, advise, and review the implementation of the deletion of profiles from the NDNAD
- provide ethical advice on elimination databases
- ensure all police and supplier databases containing DNA information are subject to robust governance requirements.
- provide support and advice on ethical matters to the Biometrics Commissioner and others as required
- continue to monitor the various agreements, including the Prüm Treaty, for the international exchange of DNA data and the use of the NDNAD
- monitor developments on crime scene DNA testing and other new technology
- continue to monitor the treatment of children and young people in relation to DNA sampling and retention with a view to ensuring that they are safeguarded and that their distinct rights are recognised
- continue to monitor and assess potential disproportionate or discriminatory effects of the use and operation of the NDNAD may have on ethnic minority groups and vulnerable people
- support the NDNAD Strategy Board in developing more transparent, ethical and user friendly information about the forensic use of DNA and the database

Who we are
The National DNA Database Ethics Group comprises members from different disciplines and professions led by an independent chair.

Police Negotiating Board
The Police Negotiating Board (PNB) negotiates agreements between employers of police (local authorities) and police staff, which it recommends to the Home Secretary to become part of police regulations. Some of the issues negotiated are: hours of duty, leave, pay and allowances, and pensions.
PNB is an advisory non-departmental public body of the Home Office
http://www.lge.gov.uk/lge/core/page.do?pageId=119225

Animals in Science Committee

What we do

The Animals in Science Committee roles are

- to advise the Secretary of State on all matters concerning the use of animals in scientific procedures
- to advise animal welfare bodies on sharing best practice within the UK and
- by exchanging information within the European Union to co-ordinate best practice

Responsibilities
The Animals in Science Committee is responsible for providing impartial, balanced and objective advice to the Secretary of State, to animal welfare bodies and within the European Union on issues relating to the Animals (Scientific Procedures) Act 1986 as amended.

Who we are
The Animals in Science Committee is an advisory non-departmental public body of the Home Office. The Chair of the Animals in Science Committee is Dr John Landers. The members are to be appointed. The Animals in Science Committee was established by the Animals (Scientific Procedures) Act 1986 as amended to comply with Directive EU 2010/63/EU which came in to force on the 1st January 2013. Article 49 of this Directive requires each EU country to set up a National Committee for the Protection of Animals used for Scientific Purposes. In this country the committee is known as the Animals in Science Committee and has superseded the Animal Procedures Committee.

Tribunal non-departmental public body

Investigatory Powers Tribunal
The Investigatory Powers Tribunal (IPT) investigates complaints about the alleged conduct of public bodies in relation to members of the public under the Regulation of Investigatory Powers Act (RIPA, 2000). This includes complaints about the use of intrusive powers such as phone tapping by intelligence services, law enforcement agencies and public authorities.
IPT is a tribunal non-departmental public body of the Home Office
http://www.ipt-uk.com/

Police Arbitration Tribunal
The Police Arbitration Tribunal (PAT) acts under the arbitration service Acas as the final recourse for negotiations between employers of police and police staff on which no agreement can be reached about hours of duty, leave or pay and allowances. The Home Secretary is not bound by the recommendations of the PAT.
PAT is a tribunal non-departmental public body of the Home Office
http://www.homeoffice.gov.uk/agencies-public-bodies/public-bodies-list/

Police Discipline Appeals Tribunal
The Police (Discipline) Appeals Tribunal hears appeals against the findings of internal disciplinary proceedings brought against members of the police force.
Police Discipline is a tribunal non-departmental public body of the Home Office
http://www.homeoffice.gov.uk/agencies-public-bodies/public-bodies-list/

Office of Surveillance Commissioners
The Office of Surveillance Commissioners (OSC) oversees the conduct of covert surveillance and covert human intelligence sources by public authorities in accordance with the Police Act 1997 and the Regulation of Investigatory Powers Act 2000 (RIPA).
OSC is a tribunal non-departmental public body of the Home Office
http://surveillancecommissioners.independent.gov.uk/

Other

HM Inspectorate of Constabulary
HM Inspectorate of Constabulary (HMIC) independently assesses police forces and policing, asking the questions that citizens would ask and publishing information to allow the public to compare the performance of their force against others.
HMIC works with the Home Office
http://www.hmic.gov.uk/

Independent Chief Inspector of Borders and Immigration
The Independent Chief Inspector of Borders and Immigration provides independent scrutiny of the work of the UK Border Agency and the Border Force. The Inspector is completely independent of these organisations, and reports directly to the Home Secretary.
Independent Chief Inspector works with the Home Office
http://icinspector.independent.gov.uk/

The Security Service
The Security Service, MI5, is responsible for protecting the UK against threats to national security.
MI5 works with the Home Office
https://www.mi5.gov.uk/

Independent Reviewer of Terrorism Legislation
The Independent Reviewer of Terrorism Legislation reviews the operation of the UK's laws on terrorism, and writes up the findings and recommendations in regular reports. These reports are then laid before Parliament, to inform the public and political debate.
Independent Reviewer works with the Home Office
https://terrorismlegislationreviewer.independent.gov.uk

Intelligence Services Commissioner
The Intelligence Services Commissioner (ISC) provides independent judicial oversight of the conduct of the Secret Intelligence Service (MI6), Security Service (MI5), Government Communications Headquarters (GCHQ) and a number of other public authorities.
ISC works with the Home Office
http://www.intelligencecommissioners.com/

Interception of Communications Commissioner
The Interception of Communications Commissioner ensures that government agencies act in accordance with their legal responsibilities when intercepting communications. The Commissioner also reviews the role of the Home Office Secretary of State in issuing interception warrants.
Interception Commissioner works with the Home Office
http://www.iocco-uk.info/

Biometrics Commissioner
The Biometrics Commissioner is responsible for reviewing government decisions to retain biometrics materials - such as DNA and fingerprints - for national security purposes. The Biometrics Commissioner, Alastair R MacGregor QC, was appointed on 4 March 2013. His role is to provide independent oversight of the new regime established by the Protection of Freedoms Act to govern the retention and use of DNA and fingerprints. Once the Act is fully in force in October his role will also include determination of applications from the authorities to retain biometric material. The Biometrics Commissioner's postal address is: Office of the Biometrics Commissioner PO Box 72256 LONDON SW1P 9DU Email address: Alastair.MacGregor@homeoffice.gsi.gov.uk
Biometrics Commissioner works with the Home Office

Surveillance Camera Commissioner
The Surveillance Camera Commissioner was created within the Protection of Freedoms Act 2012 to meet the Coalition agreement to further regulate CCTV. The act commits the Secretary of State to produce a code of practice about surveillance camera systems which will set out new guidelines for CCTV and automatic number plate recognition. The role of the Commissioner is to encourage compliance with the code, review how the code is working and to provide advice to ministers on whether or not the code needs amending. Andrew Rennison is the first Surveillance Camera Commissioner and can be contacted at SCC@homeoffice.gsi.gov.uk.
SCC works with the Home Office

Forensic Science Regulator

What we do
The Forensic Science Regulator ensures that the provision of forensic science services across the criminal justice system is subject to an appropriate regime of scientific quality standards.
Responsibilities
Responsibilities involve:

• identifying the requirement for new or improved quality standards

- leading on the development of new standards
- where necessary, providing advice and guidance so that providers of forensic science services can demonstrate compliance with common standards

Priorities

The Regulator's priorities and aims are to see that:

- forensic science services are delivered to appropriate standards (usually an international standard) tailored to meet the needs of the criminal justice system and subject to independent and effective assessments of quality
- high quality advice and guidance is provided to forensic science providers, ministers and others on the forensic science requirements of the criminal justice system
- there are effective means to investigate quality failures and to address any issues
- there is effective collaboration with the authorities in Scotland and Northern Ireland to achieve UK-wide quality standards
- the UK is a strong voice at the table on projects to develop European or international standards for forensic science

Who we are

Although sponsored by the Home Office, the Regulator is an public appointee and operate independently of the Home Office, on behalf of the criminal justice system as a whole. This independence allows us to make unbiased recommendations and decisions.

We collaborate with the authorities in Scotland and Northern Ireland who have expressed their willingness to be partners in the setting of quality standards which will be adopted within their justice systems.

The regulator is supported by a team of 4 civil servants (which includes 3 scientists) with additional support provided by shared services from the Home Office and Home Office Science Secretariat.

Ministry of Defence

What we do

We protect the security, independence and interests of our country at home and abroad. We work with our allies and partners whenever possible. Our aim is to ensure that the armed forces have the training, equipment and support necessary for their work, and that we keep within budget.

Responsibilities

We have 7 military tasks:

- defending the UK and its overseas territories
- providing strategic intelligence
- providing nuclear deterrence
- supporting civil emergency organisations in times of crisis
- defending our interests by projecting power strategically and through expeditionary interventions
- providing a defence contribution to UK influence
- providing security for stabilisation

Priorities

In 2012 and 2013 our priorities are:

- to continue to bring stability to Afghanistan as part of the international task force and prepare for hand over to the Afghans in 2014
- to fulfil our ongoing defence commitments at home and across the world
- to be fully prepared to take on a wide range of other military operations, as they develop
- to continue the transformation of defence through the restructuring of the armed forces to create a simpler and more effective organisation at a lower cost to the taxpayer

Who we are

The Ministry of Defence has 68,010 permanent and casual civilian personnel, including Royal Fleet Auxiliaries, Trading Funds and locally engaged civilians .

The UK Regular Forces comprise 170,710 full time trained and untrained personnel:

Royal Navy 33,960
Army 99,730
Royal Air Force 37,030
UK Regular Forces figures do not include Gurkhas, full-time or mobilised reservists.

Figures are correct as at 1 April 2013 and have been rounded to the nearest 10; numbers ending in 5 have been rounded to the nearest multiple of 20 to prevent systematic bias.

Figures are provided quarterly and the next update containing 1 July statistics will be released on 15 August 2013.

Full information can be found in Quarterly civilian personnel report and UK armed forces: Quarterly personnel report

MOD is a ministerial department, supported by 28 agencies and public bodies.

Executive agency

Defence Science and Technology Laboratory
The Defence Science and Technology Laboratory (Dstl) maximises the impact of science and technology for the defence and security of the UK.
Dstl is an executive agency of the Ministry of Defence
https://www.dstl.gov.uk/

Defence Support Group
The Defence Support Group (DSG) gives the department secure access to assured onshore capacity and capability for the through-life maintenance, repair, overhaul, upgrade and procurement support services for defence equipment.
DSG is an executive agency of the Ministry of Defence
http://www.dsg.mod.uk/

Service Children's Education
Service Children's Education (SCE) provides schools and educational support for the children of HM Armed Forces, MOD personnel and sponsored organisations stationed overseas.
SCE is an executive agency of the Ministry of Defence
http://www.sceschools.com/

Service Personnel and Veterans Agency

What we do
We provide pay, pension and support services to military personnel and the veterans community, directly serving around 900,000 members of the armed forces community.
Responsibilities
We are responsible for:

- assessing
- awarding
- paying
- maintaining
- all pensions relating to service in the armed forces.

This includes:

- Armed Forces Pension Schemes
- Reserve Forces Pension Scheme and, for those disabled or bereaved through service
- War disablement pensions
- other payments to veterans

Priorities
Our priorities are:

- customer focus - anticipating, understanding and responding to their needs
- efficiency - cohesion, coherence and optimal use of technology

- business excellence - continually improving
- employer of choice - well trained, valued and fully engaged staff

Who we are
We have 4 main UK sites, from Glasgow to Gosport, and we a tri-service (army, navy and air force) organisation.

UK Hydrographic Office
The UK Hydrographic Office (UKHO) produces a global range of electronic and paper nautical charts, publications and services for the Royal Navy and international mariner. They are a government Trading Fund.
UKHO is an executive agency of the Ministry of Defence
http://www.ukho.gov.uk/

Executive non-departmental public body

Royal Naval Museum
The Royal Naval Museum, in Portsmouth's Historic Dockyard, is one of Britain's oldest maritime museums. The Museum's aim is to preserve and present the history of the 'Fleet' - the ships and the men and women who manned them.
RNM is an executive non-departmental public body of the Ministry of Defence
http://www.nmrn.org.uk

National Army Museum
The National Army Museum (NAM) is the leading authority on the history of the British Army. It gathers, maintains and makes known the story of the British Army and its role and impact in world history.
NAM is an executive non-departmental public body of the Ministry of Defence
http://www.nam.ac.uk/

Royal Air Force Museum
The Royal Air Force Museum (RAFM) tells the story of British aviation, from early bi-planes to the latest strike-jets. It is based on two sites - Colindale in North London, and Cosford in Shropshire, and is free to visit.
RAFM is an executive non-departmental public body of the Ministry of Defence
http://www.rafmuseum.org.uk

Advisory non-departmental public body

Advisory Committee on Conscientious Objectors

What we do
We advise the Secretary of State for Defence on all conscientious objection claims. These claims are made by those in the armed forces whose application for permission to retire, resign or be discharged have been refused by the service authorities.
Responsibilities
We are responsible for advising on claims to conscientious objection by those who have been refused permission to:

- retire
- resign their commissions
- be discharged

Priorities
The committee deals with cases of those who object to further service and have been turned down; not those who are objecting to conscription or call-up on mobilisation for war.

Many of the conscientious objections are made on religious grounds.

Who we are
There are 6 committee members. There is a chair and a deputy chair (who must be legally qualified) and 4 lay members. Each time the committee meets the chair, deputy chair and at least 2 lay members must be present.

Central Advisory Committee on Pensions and Compensation

What we do
The Central Advisory Committee on Pensions and Compensation (CAC Pensions and Compensation) gives advice on all service pension and compensation schemes and on policy issues related to them.
Responsibilities
The committee now provides advice on policy issues and consults on all service pension and compensation schemes.

Who we are
The CAC is chaired by the Minister for Defence Personnel Veterans and Welfare and has representatives from:

The Royal British Legion (RBL)
The Soldiers, Sailors, Airmen and Families Association (SSAFA)
The Confederation of British Service Organisations (COBSEO)
The British Limbless Ex-Service Men's Association (BLESMA)
The Forces Family Federation (FFF)
The Independent Medical Expert Group (IMEG)
The Veterans Advisory and Pensions Committee (VA&PC)
The War Widows' Association (WWA)
The Forces Pension Society (FPS)
The Service Personnel and Veterans Agency (SPVA)
Ministry of Defence (MOD)

Defence Nuclear Safety Committee
The Defence Nuclear Safety Committee (DNSC) advises the Secretary of State for Defence (and other ministers) on all public safety matters relating to the construction, operation and maintenance of nuclear powered warships and the design, manufacture, transport, storage, handling and operational training related to nuclear weapon systems.
DNSC is an advisory non-departmental public body of the Ministry of Defence

Defence Scientific Advisory Council

What we do
We provide an independent advice and analysis to the Secretary of State for Defence on science, engineering and technology matters.
Responsibilities
We are responsible for providing advice on:

- all aspects of the MOD research and development programme, including direction, content, exploitation, balance and changes, and value for money
- the use of science, engineering, technology and analysis (SETA) resources within MOD
- ways of achieving cross-cutting capabilities across all defence lines of development; operational issues
- ad-hoc issues, including broad strategic issues, priorities and policies that could impact the MOD
- emerging external developments, innovation, opportunities and threats to MOD, both national and international

The defence science and technology office provides permanent secretariat services to the Defence Scientific Advisory Council (DSAC) Council.

Priorities
Our priorities change with the demands of Ministry of Defence (MOD) and defence issues.

We aim to give the best available independent advice on how well projects are meeting military needs in:

- the direction, content and exploitation of research
- the best use of SETA resources within the MOD
- operational and strategic issues
- external developments, opportunities and threats

Who we are
We have a chairman, deputy chairman and a number of independent council members.

National Employer Advisory Board
We advise the Secretary of State for Defence on issues like employing reservists, and to manage the Supporting Britain's Reservists and Employers campaign.
NEAB is an advisory non-departmental public body of the Ministry of Defence
http://www.sabre.mod.uk/Employers/How-SaBRE-can-support-you.aspx#.UIa06WnLyjY

Nuclear Research Advisory Council
The Nuclear Research Advisory Council (NRAC) reviews the Atomic Weapons Establishment's nuclear warhead research and techniques and checks we have the facilities needed to develop and maintain a UK nuclear weapon capability.
NRAC is an advisory non-departmental public body of the Ministry of Defence

Science Advisory Committee on the Medical Implications of Less-Lethal Weapons
The Science Advisory Committee on the Medical Implications of Less-Lethal Weapons (SACMILL) advises the government on the biophysical, biomechanical, pathological and clinical aspects of generic classes of Less Lethal Weapons, including medical implications and potential injuries.
SACMILL is an advisory non-departmental public body of the Ministry of Defence

Veterans Advisory and Pensions Committees (x13)
The Veterans Advisory and Pensions Committees (VAPC), formerly known as War Pensions Committees, have existed since the 1920s, supporting war pensioners and war widows and widowers, hearing their complaints on war pension issues and making recommendations to the government and its agencies. There are 13 VAPCs.
VAPC is an advisory non-departmental public body of the Ministry of Defence
http://www.veterans-uk.info/new_vapc/index.htm

Review Board for Government Contracts

What we do
The Review Board for Government Contracts (RBGC) reviews and maintains the Government Profit Formula used by MOD when pricing single source work. It also reviews the price of individual contracts that are referred to it under contract conditions, by one or both parties to the contract.

Responsibilities
We review the profit formula used in pricing non-competitive government contracts. We normally carry out a review every 3 years.

We also look at complaints that are referred to us if the price of a contract is not believed to be fair and reasonable by either party involved. We can decide if the pricing of a contract should be adjusted and by how much.

Priorities
We now carry out intermediate reviews of the profit formula at the end of the first and second year of each 3-year period. These reviews are usually limited to looking at the target rate of return and associated assumptions.

Who we are
The review board is made up of a chairman, 2 government-nominated members and 2 CBI-nominated members.

Advisory Group on Military Medicine
The Advisory Group on Military Medicine (AGMM) provides specialist advice to the department, as required, on the medical aspects of defence against chemical, biological and radiological threats.
AGMM is an advisory non-departmental public body of the Ministry of Defence

Armed Forces Pay Review Body
The Armed Forces Pay Review Body (AFPRB) provides independent advice to the Prime Minister and the Secretary of State for Defence on the pay and charges for members of the Naval, Military and Air Forces of the Crown.
AFPRB is an advisory non-departmental public body of the Ministry of Defence
http://www.ome.uk.com/example/Armed_Forces_Pay_Review_Body.aspx

Public corporation

Pipelines Agency

What we do

The Oil and Pipelines Agency (OPA) is responsible for managing the Government Pipeline and Storage System. It oversees all aspects of the facilities' operation and maintenance, ensuring that UK military requirements for aviation fuel are met.

Other

Royal Marines Museum
The Royal Marines Museum (RMM) explores the history of the Royal Marines from their origins in 1664 as Sea Soldiers through to current day operations around the world. It tells stories of past and present marines with a vast collection of objects, paintings and archive documents, containing over 1 million photographs and documents, and 30,000 objects.
RMM works with the Ministry of Defence
http://www.royalmarinesmuseum.co.uk/

Fleet Air Arm Museum
The Fleet Air Arm Museum, the world's second largest naval aviation museum, has 4 exhibition halls, over 90 aircraft and over 2 million records and 30,000 artefacts.
Fleet Air Arm Museum works with the Ministry of Defence
http://www.fleetairarm.com/

Service Complaints Commissioner
The Service Complaints Commissioner (SCC) was created by the Armed Forces Act 2006, following the deaths of four soldiers at Princess Royal Barracks, Deepcut. It aims to ensure all service men and women and their families have confidence in the complaints system and are treated properly.
SCC works with the Ministry of Defence
http://armedforcescomplaints.independent.gov.uk

Defence Academy of the United Kingdom
The Defence Academy of the United Kingdom (DA) is responsible for postgraduate education and the majority of command, staff, leadership, defence management, acquisition and technology training for members of the UK Armed Forces and MOD civil servants. It is also the MOD's main link with UK universities and international military educational institutions.
DA works with the Ministry of Defence
http://www.da.mod.uk

Service Prosecuting Authority
The Service Prosecuting Authority (SPA) initiates and conducts prosecutions in criminal cases involving alleged offences contrary to military discipline. It works in the service courts of first instance and the service appellate courts.
SPA works with the Ministry of Defence
http://spa.independent.gov.uk

Defence, Press and Broadcasting Advisory Committee
The Defence, Press and Broadcasting Advisory Committee (DPBAC) oversees a voluntary code which operates between the government departments which have responsibility for national security and the media. It uses the Defence Advisory Notice system as its vehicle.
DPBAC works with the Ministry of Defence
http://www.dnotice.org.uk

Royal Navy Submarine Museum
The Royal Navy Submarine Museum (RNSM) at Gosport traces the international history of submarine development, from the age of Alexander the Great to the present day, in particular the history of the Submarine Service from the tiny Holland 1 to the nuclear powered Vanguard class vessel.
RNSM works with the Ministry of Defence
http://www.submarine-museum.co.uk/

Defence Sixth Form College
Welbeck Defence Sixth Form College (DSFC) offers a unique programme of personal, physical and intellectual development, which provides its students with an education, designed to meet the needs of today's modern technical Armed Forces.
DSFC works with the Ministry of Defence
http://www.dsfc.ac.uk

Ministry of Justice

What we do
We work to protect the public and reduce re-offending, and to provide a more effective, transparent and responsive criminal justice system for victims and the public.
Responsibilities
We are responsible for these parts of the justice system:

- courts
- prisons
- probation services
- attendance centres

We also work in partnership with the other government departments and agencies to reform the criminal justice system, to serve the public and support the victims of crime. We are also responsible for making new laws, strengthening democracy, and safeguarding human rights.

Priorities
In 2013 our priorities are to:

- reduce re-offending by using the skills of the public, private and voluntary sectors
- reduce youth crime by putting education at the centre of youth justice
- build a prison system that delivers maximum value for money
- reduce the cost of legal aid and ensure it helps those cases that genuinely need it
- improve the way our courts are run and put the needs of victims first

Who we are
We are one of the largest government departments, employing around 76,000 people (including those in the Probation Service), with a budget of approximately £9 billion. Each year, millions of people use our services across the UK - including at 500 courts and tribunals, and 133 prisons in England and Wales.

We work with many other government agencies, including:

HM Courts and Tribunals Service
HM Prison Service
Probation Service
National Offender Management Service (NOMS)
Legal Aid Agency
Youth Justice Board

MOJ is a ministerial department, supported by 38 agencies and public bodies.

Executive agency

The National Archives
The National Archives (TNA) is the official archive and publisher for the UK government and for England and Wales. We are the guardians of some of our most iconic national documents, dating back over 1,000 years.
TNA is an executive agency of the Ministry of Justice
http://www.nationalarchives.gov.uk/

National Offender Management Service
The National Offender Management Service (NOMS) is responsible for adult offender management services for England and Wales within the framework set by the government. The agency manages HM Prison Service and the probation services and oversees privately run prisons.
NOMS is an executive agency of the Ministry of Justice

http://www.justice.gov.uk/about/noms/

Office of the Public Guardian
The Office of the Public Guardian (OPG) implements the Mental Capacity Act 2005 by administering powers of attorney, supervising deputies who manage the affairs of others and investigating and acting on allegations of abuse by attorneys and deputies.
OPG is an executive agency of the Ministry of Justice
http://www.justice.gov.uk/about/opg.htm

HM Courts and Tribunals Service
HM Courts & Tribunals Service (HMCTS) is responsible for the administration of the criminal, civil and family courts and tribunals in England and Wales and non-devolved tribunals in Scotland and Northern Ireland. It provides for a fair, efficient and effective justice system delivered by an independent judiciary.
HMCTS is an executive agency of the Ministry of Justice
http://www.justice.gov.uk/about/hmcts/

Legal Aid Agency
The Legal Aid Agency provides both civil and criminal legal aid and advice in England and Wales. Our work is essential to the fair, effective and efficient operation of the civil and criminal justice systems. We are a delivery organisation, which commissions and procures legal aid services from providers (solicitors, barristers and the not-for-profit sector). We also make sure that people get the information, advice and legal help they need to deal with a wide range of problems. Each year the LAA helps more than 2 million people to deal with their legal problems.
LAA is an executive agency of the Ministry of Justice
http://www.justice.gov.uk/legal-aid

HM Prison Service
HM Prison Service (HMPS) keeps in custody those committed by the courts, looking after them with humanity and helping them to lead law-abiding and useful lives in custody and after release.
HMPS is an executive agency of the Ministry of Justice
http://www.justice.gov.uk/about/hmps

Executive non-departmental public body

Criminal Injuries Compensation Authority
The Criminal Injuries Compensation Authority (CICA) administers the Criminal Injuries Compensation Scheme in England, Scotland and Wales.
CICA is an executive non-departmental public body of the Ministry of Justice
http://www.justice.gov.uk/guidance/compensation-schemes/cica/

Judicial Appointments Commission
The JAC is an independent commission that selects candidates for judicial office in courts and tribunals in England and Wales, and for some tribunals whose jurisdiction extends to Scotland or Northern Ireland. They select candidates for judicial office on merit through fair and open competition from the widest range of eligible candidates.
JAC is an executive non-departmental public body of the Ministry of Justice
http://jac.judiciary.gov.uk/

Parole Board
The Parole Board is an independent body that carries out risk assessments on prisoners to determine whether they can be safely released into the community.
Parole Board is an executive non-departmental public body of the Ministry of Justice
http://www.justice.gov.uk/about/parole-board/index.htm

Youth Justice Board for England and Wales
The Youth Justice Board (YJB) oversees the youth justice system in England and Wales, ensures that custody for under-18s is safe and secure, and works to prevent offending and re-offending.
YJB is an executive non-departmental public body of the Ministry of Justice
http://www.justice.gov.uk/about/yjb/

Criminal Cases Review Commission

The Criminal Cases Review Commission (CCRC) is an independent public body that reviews possible miscarriages of justice in the criminal courts of England, Wales and Northern Ireland and refers cases to the appeal courts.

CCRC is an executive non-departmental public body of the Ministry of Justice

http://www.justice.gov.uk/about/criminal-cases-review-commission

Legal Services Board

The Legal Services Board (LSB) ensures that regulation in the legal services sector is carried out in the public interest and that the interests of consumers are placed at the heart of the system.

LSB is an executive non-departmental public body of the Ministry of Justice

http://www.legalservicesboard.org.uk/

Probation Trusts

Probation Trusts across the country supervise offenders over the age of 18 who are given a community order by the courts or are released from prison on licence. They also work with the victims of serious crimes.

Probation Trusts is an executive non-departmental public body of the Ministry of Justice

http://www.justice.gov.uk/about/probation/probation-trusts

Information Commissioner's Office

The Information Commissioner's Office (ICO) upholds information rights in the public interest, promoting openness by public bodies and data privacy for individuals.

ICO is an executive non-departmental public body of the Ministry of Justice

http://www.ico.org.uk/

Advisory non-departmental public body

Civil Justice Council

The Civil Justice Council (CJC) is responsible for overseeing and co-ordinating the modernisation of the civil justice system.

CJC is an advisory non-departmental public body of the Ministry of Justice

http://www.judiciary.gov.uk/about-the-judiciary/advisory-bodies/cjc

Law Commission

The Law Commission is a statutory independent body that keeps the law under review and recommends reform where it is needed. The aim of the Commission is to ensure that the law is fair, modern, simple and as cost-effective as possible.

Law Commission is an advisory non-departmental public body of the Ministry of Justice

http://www.justice.gov.uk/lawcommission/

Sentencing Council for England and Wales

The Sentencing Council (SC) for England and Wales promotes greater consistency in sentencing while maintaining the independence of the judiciary. The Council produces guidelines on sentencing for the judiciary and aims to increase public understanding of sentencing.

SC is an advisory non-departmental public body of the Ministry of Justice

http://sentencingcouncil.judiciary.gov.uk/

Victim's Advisory Panel

The Victim's Advisory Panel (VAP) is for victims of crime and their families to have a say in the reform of the Criminal Justice System.

VAP is an advisory non-departmental public body of the Ministry of Justice

Administrative Justice and Tribunals Council

The Administrative Justice and Tribunals Council (AJTC) oversees the administrative justice system as a whole and ensures that the relationships between the courts, tribunals, ombudsmen and alternative dispute resolution providers reflect the needs of users.

AJTC is an advisory non-departmental public body of the Ministry of Justice

http://www.justice.gov.uk/ajtc/index.htm

Advisory Committees on Justices of the Peace

ACJPs in every local authority interview candidates and make recommendations to the Lord Chancellor about who to appoint to their local benches as Justices of the Peace (magistrates).

ACJP is an advisory non-departmental public body of the Ministry of Justice http://www.justice.gov.uk/about/all

The Advisory Council on National Records and Archives
The Advisory Panel on Public Sector Information (APPSI) advises ministers on greater re-use of public sector information, helping the Office of Public Sector Information and HM Stationery Office to keep aligned with current and emerging developments in the information industry.
ACNRA is an advisory non-departmental public body of the Ministry of Justice
http://www.nationalarchives.gov.uk/advisorycouncil%5Cdefault.htm

Civil Procedure Rule Committee
The Civil Procedure Rule Committee (CPRC) makes rules of court for the Civil Division of the Court of Appeal, the High Court and the county courts.
CPRC is an advisory non-departmental public body of the Ministry of Justice
http://www.justice.gov.uk/about/moj/advisory-groups/civil-procedure-rule-committee

Family Justice Council
The Family Justice Council (FJC) helps to get better results for families in the court system, with input from 30 locally based FJCs around the country.
FJC is an advisory non-departmental public body of the Ministry of Justice
http://www.judiciary.gov.uk/about-the-judiciary/advisory-bodies/fjc

Family Procedure Rule Committee
The Family Procedure Rule Committee (FPRC) makes rules of court governing the practice and procedure to be followed in family proceedings in the High Court, county courts and magistrates' courts.
FPRC is an advisory non-departmental public body of the Ministry of Justice
http://www.justice.gov.uk/about/moj/advisory-groups/family-procedure-rule-committee

IAPDC
The Independent Advisory Panel on Deaths in Custody (IAPDC) helps to shape government policy on custody and detention by collecting, analysing and disseminating information on deaths in prisons, in or following police custody, immigration detention, or detention in hospital under the Mental Health Act.
IAPDC is an advisory non-departmental public body of the Ministry of Justice
http://iapdeathsincustody.independent.gov.uk/

Insolvency Rules Committee
The Insolvency Rules Committee (IRC) members are from the legal and accountancy professions. They consider amendments to the rules arising out of a review of secondary insolvency legislation, and give their recommendations to the Lord Chancellor.
IRC is an advisory non-departmental public body of the Ministry of Justice
http://www.insolvencydirect.bis.gov.uk/insolvencyprofessionandlegislation/irc/irc.htm

Prison Services Pay Review Body
The Prison Services Pay Review Body (PSPRB) gives independent advice on pay for governors and managers, prison officers and support grades in the England and Wales Prison Service, and equivalent posts in Northern Ireland.
PSPRB is an advisory non-departmental public body of the Ministry of Justice
http://www.ome.uk.com/Prison_Service_Pay_Review_Body.aspx

Tribunal Procedure Committee
The Tribunal Procedure Committee (TPC) makes rules governing the practice and procedure in the First-tier Tribunal and the Upper Tribunal of the Tribunals Service. These are the names given to two categories of tribunal, or specialist judicial body, which usually hear appeals against decisions made by a government department or agency.
TPC is an advisory non-departmental public body of the Ministry of Justice
http://www.justice.gov.uk/about/moj/advisory-groups/tribunal-procedure-committee

Advisory Panel on Public Sector Information
The Advisory Panel on Public Sector Information (APPSI) advises ministers on greater re-use of public sector information, helping the Office of Public Sector Information and HM Stationery Office to keep aligned with current and emerging developments in the information industry.
APPSI is an advisory non-departmental public body of the Ministry of Justice
http://www.nationalarchives.gov.uk/appsi/default.htm

Other

Her Majesty's Inspectorate of Prisons
Her Majesty's Inspectorate of Prisons for England and Wales (HMI Prisons) is an independent inspectorate which reports on conditions for and treatment of those in prison, young offender institutions and immigration detention facilities.
HM Inspectorate of Prisons works with the Ministry of Justice
http://www.justice.gov.uk/about/hmi-prisons

Her Majesty's Inspectorate of Probation
HM Inspectorate of Probation reports to the government on the effectiveness of work with adults, children and young people who have offended with an aim to reduce re-offending and protect the public.
HM Inspectorate of Probation works with the Ministry of Justice
http://www.justice.gov.uk/about/hmi-probation

Victims' Commissioner
The role of the Victims' Commissioner is to promote the interests of victims and witnesses, encourage good practice in their treatment, and regularly review the Code of Practice for Victims which sets out the services victims can expect to receive.
Victims' Commissioner works with the Ministry of Justice
http://www.justice.gov.uk/about/vc

Prisons and Probation Ombudsman
The Prisons and Probation Ombudsman (PPO) investigates complaints from prisoners, those on probation and those held in immigration removal centres. It also investigates all deaths that occur among prisoners, immigration detainees and the residents of probation hostels (Approved Premises).
PPO works with the Ministry of Justice
http://www.ppo.gov.uk/

Prisons and Probation Ombudsman
The Prisons and Probation Ombudsman (PPO) investigates complaints from prisoners, those on probation and those held in immigration removal centres. It also investigates all deaths that occur among prisoners, immigration detainees and the residents of probation hostels (Approved Premises).
PPO works with the Ministry of Justice
http://www.ppo.gov.uk/

Official Solicitor and Public Trustee
The Official Solicitor and Public Trustee (OSPT) support the work of the MOJ. They carry out separate functions, although their respective trusts, estates and deputyships are managed by the same team. The Official Solicitor provides access to the justice system for vulnerable people who may have problems understanding it due to their age or disability. The Public Trustee acts as executor or administrator of estates and as the appointed trustee of settlements.
OSPT works with the Ministry of Justice
http://www.justice.gov.uk/about/ospt

The Legal Ombudsman
The Legal Ombudsman for England and Wales is appointed by the Office for Legal Complaints to run an independent scheme that resolves complaints about lawyers in a fair and effective way, helping to drive improvements to legal services.
The Legal Ombudsman works with the Ministry of Justice
http://www.legalombudsman.org.uk/

Judicial Appointments and Conduct Ombudsman
The Judicial Appointments and Conduct Ombudsman (JACO) investigates complaints about the judicial appointments process and the handling of matters involving judicial discipline or conduct.
JACO works with the Ministry of Justice
http://www.justice.gov.uk/about/jaco

Independent Monitoring Boards of Prisons, Immigration, Removal Centres and Short Term Holding Rooms are made up of local, unpaid volunteers, working 2 to 3 days a month. They monitor day-to day life in prisons and removal centres, listening to problems of individuals and ensuring that proper standards of care and decency are maintained.
IMBPIRC works with the Ministry of Justice
http://www.justice.gov.uk/about/imb

Criminal Procedure Rule Committee

What we do
The Criminal Procedure Rules govern the way criminal cases are managed. The committee's goal is to simplify and streamline them

Northern Ireland Office

What we do
We ensure the smooth working of the devolution settlement in Northern Ireland. We represent Northern Irish interests within the UK government and we represent the UK government in Northern Ireland.
Responsibilities
We are responsible for:

- representing Northern Ireland interests within the UK government
- representing the UK government in Northern Ireland
- working in partnership with the Northern Ireland Executive (NIE) to bring about a stable, prosperous Northern Ireland
- supporting and implementing political agreements to increase stability

Priorities
In 2013 our priorities are:

- working with the NIE to rebalance the Northern Ireland economy, promoting growth, trade and encouraging inward investment
- supporting reconciliation and the NIE's objective of building a shared future for all, while acknowledging the past
- supporting democracy and taking the lead against the terrorism and violence that threatens national security
- working closely with the Irish government on matters of common interest

Who we are
The Northern Ireland Office employs around 175 staff, with offices in Belfast and London. The Crown Solicitors Office in Belfast, which provides legal services in Northern Ireland to all Whitehall departments and to other public bodies in Northern Ireland, is also part of the Northern Ireland Office.

NIO is a ministerial department, supported by 3 agencies and public bodies.

Other

Boundary Commission for Northern Ireland
The Boundary Commission for Northern Ireland (BCNI) carries out boundary reviews of parliamentary constituencies in Northern Ireland, and submits its recommendations to the government.
BCNI works with the Northern Ireland Office
http://www.boundarycommission.org.uk/

Northern Ireland Human Rights Commission
The Northern Ireland Human Rights Commission (NIHRC) ensures government and other public bodies protect the human rights of everyone in Northern Ireland. The commission has an A status accreditation from the UN and operates in full accordance with the UN Paris Principles.
NIHRC works with the Northern Ireland Office
http://www.nihrc.org/

Parades Commission for Northern Ireland
The Parades Commission for Northern Ireland (PCNI) is independent of government. It has the power to place restrictions on public processions and related protest meetings.

PCNI works with the Northern Ireland Office
http://www.paradescommission.org/

Office of the Advocate General for Scotland

What we do
The Office of the Advocate General (OAG) is the UK government's Scottish legal team. We provide legal advice, drafting and litigation services to the UK government in relation to Scotland. We also support the Advocate General in his role as a Law Officer.

Responsibilities
We are responsible for:

- providing legal advice to UK government departments on policy and legislation affecting Scotland and the Scottish devolution settlement
- representing the UK government in the courts and tribunals in Scotland
- supporting the Advocate General in his capacity as a UK Law Officer, including the exercise of statutory functions under the Scotland Act

Priorities
In 2013, our priorities are:

- advising UK government departments on the implications of their policies for Scotland and working with them to ensure UK legislation works for Scotland
- reviewing Scottish Parliament legislation and engaging with UK government departments and the Scottish Government to ensure implications of Scottish legislation are understood and competence issues are addressed
- protecting the UK government's interests in the Scottish courts and the UK Supreme Court
- taking forward legal work to support Scotland's place within the UK, including contributing to the cross-government Scotland analysis programme
- helping to ensure that devolution works, ensuring that the UK Government operates effectively for Scotland in reserved areas and facilitating co-operation between Scotland's two administrations
- ensuring that UK government Ministers achieve their objectives in Scotland, with a focus on support for the Advocate General for Scotland and the Secretary of State for Scotland

Who we are
The Office of the Advocate General consists of around 30 lawyers plus administrative staff, with offices in Victoria Quay, Edinburgh and in Dover House, London.

We have 4 divisions. The Litigation Division provides Scots law advice and support in respect of any action raised by or against a UK government department in Scotland. It also supports the Advocate General in relation to his devolution issue functions under the Scotland Act 1998 and in respect of any action raised or defended in the Scottish Courts. Involvement in Cases

The Advisory and Legislation Division provides legal advice and services to UK government departments, ensuring Scots Law and the devolution settlement are taken into account in the development of UK government policy and legislation.

The HMRC Division deals with HM Revenue & Customs' legal work in Scotland. This covers tax appeals through the tribunal system and on appeal to the higher courts, as well as a variety of other litigation for the department. The team also provides advisory services to HMRC in relation to Scottish matters, and undertakes some legislative work, notably in connection with the annual Finance Bill.

The Legal Secretariat to the Advocate General provides support to the Advocate General in his capacity as a UK Law Officer, including the exercise of statutory functions under the Scotland Act. It also supports him with his ministerial responsibilities, including supporting him as a member of Cabinet Committees and as a Member of the House of Lords.

Office of the Leader of the House of Commons

What we do
We provide support to the Leader of the House of Commons, who is responsible for planning and supervising the government's legislative programme (including the Queen's speech), and managing

government business within the House of Commons while also upholding the rights and interests of the backbench members of the House.

Responsibilities
We are responsible for:

- delivering the government's legislative programme
- managing business in the House of Commons
- reform of the House of Commons, including co-ordinating e-petitions across government and parliament
- remaining issues relating to pay, pensions and expenses for MPs following the establishment of the Independent Parliamentary Standards Authority

Priorities
Our main priorities are to:

- deliver the government's legislative programme
- respond to the Joint Committee on Parliamentary Privilege

Who we are
Our team is based in the Palace of Westminster and 1 Horse Guards Road, London.

Although resourced by Cabinet Office, the Leader and the Deputy Leader of the Commons are not Cabinet Office ministers. Together with the Leader of the House of Lords, the Chief Whips and their respective deputies in both houses, our ministers and offices are otherwise known as the Parliamentary Business Managers.

The Leader is an ex-officio member of the House of Commons Commission and the Speaker's Committee on IPSA, and as Lord Privy Seal acts as the Chair of the Board of Trustees for the Chevening Estate.

Office of the Leader of the House of Lords
What we do
We provide support to the Leader of the House of Lords. The Leader of the House is appointed by the Prime Minister, is a member of the Cabinet and is responsible for the conduct of government business in the Lords. The Leader advises the House on procedure and order, and he and his office are available to assist and advise all members of the House.
Responsibilities
We support the Leader in his parliamentary and ministerial duties, which include:

- leading the government benches in the House of Lords
- delivery of the government's business in the Lords (jointly responsible with the Lords Chief Whip)
- repeating in the Lords statements made by the Prime Minister in the Commons
- giving guidance to the House on matters of procedure and order
- taking part in formal ceremonies in the House, like the State Opening of Parliament
- Chair, Board of Trustees for Chequers and Dorneywood
- as Chancellor of the Duchy of Lancaster, responsible to the Sovereign for the administration of the Duchy (a collection of land, property and assets held in trust for the Sovereign as private income)

We also provide private office support to the Rt. Hon Lord McNally in his capacity as Deputy Leader.

Who we are
We are a small team based in the Palace of Westminster and 1 Horse Guards Road, London.

Together with the Leader of the House of Commons, the Chief Whips and their respective deputies in both houses, our ministers and offices are otherwise known as the Parliamentary Business Managers.

Scotland Office

What we do
We ensure the smooth working of the devolution settlement in Scotland. We represent Scottish interests within the UK government and we represent the UK government in Scotland.
The Scotland Office ensures that when it comes to reserved matters (the issues that the UK government deals with in Scotland), the people of Scotland's voice is heard at the highest level in UK government.

Responsibilities
We are responsible for:

- representing Scottish interests within the UK government
- representing the UK government in Scotland
- acting as guardian of the devolution settlement and delivering secondary legislation under the Scotland Act 1998
- providing constitutional advice and advice on reserved matters and other Scottish interests across government
- conducting and funding Scottish Parliament elections

Priorities
In 2013, our priorities are:

- strengthening Scotland within the UK by working with the Scottish government to implement the Scotland Act 2012 and on issues of significance to Scotland
- communicating the benefits that Scotland gains from being part of the UK and that the UK gains from having Scotland within it
- promoting a wider understanding of UK government policies in Scotland
- building strong partnerships across government, business and industry in Scotland and the UK, to help develop Scotland's global economic competitiveness and combat unemployment
- supporting the effective administration of the Boundary Commission and of Parliamentary elections in Scotland

Who we are
We are a small team with offices in Melville Crescent in Edinburgh and in Dover House in London.

We have 2 divisions. The policy division advises on all reserved matters of home, national security, social, industrial, economic, energy, and environment and transport policy for their actual or potential impact on Scotland.

The constitution and communications division is responsible for constitutional advice, the operation of the devolution settlement, and for communicating UK government policies in Scotland.

Scotland Office is a ministerial department, supported by 1 public body.

Other

Boundary Commission for Scotland
The Boundary Commission for Scotland (BCS) carries out boundary reviews of parliamentary constituencies in Scotland, and submits its recommendations to the government.
BCS works with the Scotland Office
http://www.bcomm-scotland.independent.gov.uk/

UK Export Finance

What we do
We are the UK's export credit agency, helping exporters and investors by providing credit insurance policies, political risk insurance on overseas investments and guarantees on bank loans. UK Export Finance is the operating name of the Export Credits Guarantee Department (ECGD).
Responsibilities
We work closely with exporters, banks, buyers and project sponsors and have 90 years' experience of supporting exports to, and investments in, markets across the world. We do this by providing guarantees, insurance and reinsurance against loss, taking into account the government's international policies.

We:

- insure UK exporters against non-payment by their overseas buyers
- help overseas buyers to purchase goods and services from UK exporters by guaranteeing bank loans to finance the purchases
- share credit risks with banks to help exporters raise tender and contract bonds, in accessing pre- and post-shipment working capital finance and in securing confirmations of letters of credit
- insure UK investors in overseas markets against political risks

Priorities

In 2013 our priorities will be to:

- fulfil our statutory remit to support exports
- operate within the policy and financial objectives set by the government, including international obligations
- achieve fair competition by seeking to establish a level playing field internationally, through obtaining multilateral improvements in export credit policies and practices
- recover the maximum amount of debt in respect of claims paid, taking account of the government's policy on debt forgiveness

You can read our Mission and Principles statement in full in our annual report.

Who we are

We employ around 200 staff. Our main office is in London and we are supported by an advisory non-departmental body.

UKEF is a ministerial department, supported by 1 public body.

Advisory non-departmental public body

Export Guarantees Advisory Council

What we do

We advise the Secretary of State for Business, Innovation and Skills (BIS) on UK Export Finance's operations.

What we do

We advise ministers on the operations of UK Export Finance.

Responsibilities

The Export Guarantees Advisory Council (EGAC) is a statutory body that provides advice to UK Export Finance and its ministers on the policies UK Export Finance applies when doing business including:

- environmental impacts and human rights
- anti-bribery and corruption
- sustainable lending
- disclosure (freedom of information)

Ministers have a statutory duty to consult EGAC on matters related to the provision of reinsurance by UK Export Finance to the private credit insurance market.

The council doesn't provide advice on decisions UK Export Finance makes to support individual export transactions and projects, although it does carry out reviews to understand how UK Export Finance's principles and policies are applied in practice. As appropriate, it also gives advice on how these might be further developed.

Priorities

Our main function is to provide advice on UK Export Finance's work, so our priorities reflect the work UK Export Finance has set out for 2013 to 2014.

Who we are

The council has 8 members, each representing a separate area of expertise. The members come from industry, government and academia, and are appointed by UK Export Finance's ministers.

Wales Office Swyddfa Cymru

What we do

We ensure the smooth working of the devolution settlement in Wales, representing the UK government in Wales. We also represent Welsh interests in Westminster.

Responsibilities

We are responsible for:

- the effective working partnership between government and devolved institutions

- representing Welsh interests in Westminster and supporting the Secretary of State for Wales in steering Welsh-specific legislation through the UK Parliament
- representing the UK government in Wales - our Secretary of State may attend and speak at the Welsh National Assembly

Priorities
In 2013, our priorities will be to:

- act as an advocate for Wales at the heart of the UK government and represent Welsh interests in non-devolved policy areas
- work with UK government colleagues, the Welsh government and other stakeholders to encourage economic growth and create a more balanced Welsh economy
- work with government departments and private investors to encourage inward investment, such as in new homes, electrification of railways, broadband internet coverage and a new nuclear power station
- raise awareness of all that Wales has to offer economically and help to promote Wales as a place to live, visit and work

Who we are
The Wales Office was established in 1999 and is based in both Cardiff and London:

- in London the Wales Office is in Gwydyr House on Whitehall
- in Cardiff the Wales Office is at Caspian Point in Cardiff Bay

WO is a ministerial department, supported by 1 public body.

Boundary Commission for Wales
The Boundary Commission for Wales (BCW) carries out boundary reviews of parliamentary constituencies in Wales, and submits its recommendations to the government.
BCW is an advisory non-departmental public body of the Wales Office and the Cabinet Office
http://bcomm-wales.gov.uk/

20 Non ministerial departments

Competition and Markets Authority
Crown Prosecution Service
Food Standards Agency
Forestry Commission
Works with 2 agencies and public bodies view all
Government Actuary's Department
HM Revenue & Customs
Works with 2 agencies and public bodies view all
NS&I
Office of Fair Trading
Office of Rail Regulation
Ofgem
Ofqual
Ofsted
Royal Mint
Serious Fraud Office
Supreme Court of the United Kingdom
The Charity Commission for England and Wales
The Crown Estate
The Water Services Regulation Authority
UK Statistics Authority
Works with 1 public body view all
UK Trade & Investment

334 Agencies & other public bodies

Acas
The Adjudicator's Office
Administration of Radioactive Substances Advisory Committee
Administrative Justice and Tribunals Council

Advisory Committee on Business Appointments
Advisory Committee on Clinical Excellence Awards
Advisory Committee on Conscientious Objectors
Advisory Committee on Pesticides
Advisory Committee on Releases to the Environment
Advisory Committees on Justices of the Peace
Advisory Council on Libraries
The Advisory Council on National Records and Archives
Advisory Council on the Misuse of Drugs
Advisory Group on Military Medicine
Advisory Panel on Public Sector Information
Agricultural Dwelling House Advisory Committees (x16)
Agricultural Land Tribunal
Agricultural Wages Committee (x15)
Agriculture and Horticulture Development Board
Air Accidents Investigation Branch
Airports Commission
Animal Health and Veterinary Laboratories Agency
Animals in Science Committee
Armed Forces Pay Review Body
Arts Council England
Arts and Humanities Research Council
Big Lottery Fund
Biometrics Commissioner
Biotechnology & Biological Sciences Research Council
Board of Trustees of the Royal Botanic Gardens Kew
Boundary Commission for England
Boundary Commission for Northern Ireland
Boundary Commission for Scotland
Boundary Commission for Wales
British Council
British Film Institute
British Hallmarking Council
British Library
British Museum
British Pharmacopoeia
British Transport Police Authority
Broads Authority
Building Regulations Advisory Committee
Cafcass
Capital for Enterprise Ltd
Care Quality Commission
Central Advisory Committee on Pensions and Compensation
Central Arbitration Committee
Centre for Environment, Fisheries and Aquaculture Science
Certification Office
Chevening Foundation
Civil Justice Council
Civil Nuclear Police Authority
Civil Procedure Rule Committee
Civil Service Commission
The Coal Authority
Commission on Human Medicines
Commissioner for Public Appointments
Committee on Climate Change
Committee on Mutagenicity of Chemicals in Food, Consumer Products and the Environment
Committee on Radioactive Waste Management
The Committee on Standards in Public Life
Commonwealth Scholarship Commission in the UK
Companies House
Competition Appeal Tribunal
Competition Commission
Competition Service

Construction Industry Training Board
Consumer Council for Water
Consumer Focus
Copyright Tribunal
Council for Science and Technology
Covent Garden Market Authority
Criminal Cases Review Commission
Criminal Injuries Compensation Authority
Criminal Procedure Rule Committee
Dartmoor National Park Authority
Defence Academy of the United Kingdom
Defence Nuclear Safety Committee
Defence Science and Technology Laboratory
Defence Scientific Advisory Council
Defence Sixth Form College
Defence Support Group
Defence, Press and Broadcasting Advisory Committee
Directly Operated Railways Limited
Disabled Persons Transport Advisory Committee
Disclosure and Barring Service
Drinking Water Inspectorate
Driver and Vehicle Licensing Agency
Driving Standards Agency
Economic and Social Research Council
Education Funding Agency
Engineering Construction Industry Training Board
Engineering and Physical Sciences Research Council
English Heritage
Environment Agency
Equality 2025
Equality and Human Rights Commission
Exmoor National Park Authority
Export Guarantees Advisory Council
FCO Services
Family Justice Council
Family Procedure Rule Committee
Fire Service College
Fleet Air Arm Museum
The Food and Environment Research Agency
Foreign Compensation Commission
Forensic Science Regulator
Forest Enterprise (England)
Forest Research
Fuel Poverty Advisory Group
Gambling Commission
Gangmasters Licensing Authority
Geffrye Museum
Government Communications Headquarters
Government Equalities Office
Government Estates Management
Government Procurement Service
Great Britain China Centre
Groceries Code Adjudicator
HM Courts and Tribunals Service
HM Crown Prosecution Service Inspectorate
HM Inspectorate of Constabulary
HM Inspectorate of Prisons
HM Inspectorate of Probation
HM Land Registry
HM Passport Office
HM Prison Service
Health Education England
Health Research Authority

Health and Safety Executive
Health and Social Care Information Centre
Heritage Lottery Fund
High Speed Two Limited
Higher Education Funding Council for England
Highways Agency
Homes and Communities Agency
Horniman Museum
Horserace Betting Levy Board
House of Lords Appointments Commission
Housing Ombudsman
Human Fertilisation and Embryology Authority
Human Tissue Authority
Imperial War Museum
Independent Advisory Panel on Deaths in Custody
Independent Agricultural Appeals Panel
Independent Chief Inspector of Borders and Immigration
Independent Commission for Aid Impact
Independent Living Fund
Independent Monitoring Boards of Prisons, Immigration, Removal Centres and Short Term Holding Rooms
Independent Police Complaint Commission
Independent Reconfiguration Panel
Independent Reviewer of Terrorism Legislation
Industrial Development Advisory Board
Industrial Injuries Advisory Council
Information Commissioner's Office
Insolvency Practitioners' Tribunal
Insolvency Rules Committee
The Insolvency Service
Intellectual Property Office
Intelligence Services Commissioner
Interception of Communications Commissioner
Investigatory Powers Tribunal
Joint Nature Conservation Committee
Judicial Appointments Commission
Judicial Appointments and Conduct Ombudsman
Lake District National Park Authority
Land Registration Rule Committee
Law Commission
Leasehold Advisory Service
Legal Aid Agency
The Legal Ombudsman
Legal Services Board
Local Government Ombudsman
London Thames Gateway Development Corporation
Low Pay Commission
Marine Accident Investigation Branch
Marine Management Organisation
Maritime and Coastguard Agency
Marshall Aid Commemoration Commission
The McKay Commission
Medical Research Council
Medicines and Healthcare Products Regulatory Agency
Met Office
Migration Advisory Committee
Monitor
NHS Blood and Transplant
NHS Business Services Authority
NHS England
NHS Litigation Authority
NHS Pay Review Body
NHS Trust Development Authority
The National Archives

National Army Museum
National College for Teaching and Leadership
National DNA Database Ethics Group
National Employer Advisory Board
National Employment Savings Trust (NEST) Corporation
National Forest Company
National Fraud Authority
National Gallery
National Heritage Memorial Fund
National Institute for Health and Care Excellence
National Lottery Commission
National Measurement Office
National Museum of the Royal Navy
National Museums Liverpool
National Offender Management Service
National Portrait Gallery
Natural England
Natural Environment Research Council
Natural History Museum
New Forest National Park Authority
North York Moors National Park Authority
Northern Ireland Human Rights Commission
Northern Lighthouse Board
Northumberland National Park Authority
Nuclear Decommissioning Authority
Nuclear Liabilities Financing Assurance Board
Nuclear Research Advisory Council
Ofcom
Office for Budget Responsibility
Office for Fair Access
Office for National Statistics
Office of Manpower Economics
Office of Surveillance Commissioners
The Office of the Children's Commissioner
Office of the Immigration Services Commissioner
Office of the Public Guardian
The Office of the Schools Commissioner
Official Solicitor and Public Trustee
Olympic Delivery Authority
Olympic Lottery Distributor
Ordnance Survey
Parades Commission for Northern Ireland
The Parliamentary and Health Service Ombudsman
Parole Board
Passenger Focus
Peak District National Park Authority
Pension Protection Fund Ombudsman
The Pensions Advisory Service
Pensions Ombudsman
The Pensions Regulator
Planning Inspectorate
Plant Varieties and Seeds Tribunal
Police Advisory Board for England and Wales
Police Arbitration Tribunal
Police Discipline Appeals Tribunal
Police Negotiating Board
Prison Services Pay Review Body
Prisons and Probation Ombudsman
Privy Council Office
Probation Trusts
Public Health England
Public Lending Right
Queen Elizabeth II Conference Centre

Rail Accident Investigation Branch
Railway Heritage Committee
Regulatory Policy Committee
Remploy Ltd
Review Board for Government Contracts
Review Body on Doctors' and Dentists' Remuneration
Review Body on Senior Salaries
The Reviewing Committee on the Export of Works of Art and Objects of Cultural Interest
Royal Air Force Museum
Royal Armouries Museum
Royal Marines Museum
Royal Mint Advisory Committee
Royal Museums Greenwich
Royal Navy Submarine Museum
Royal Parks
Rural Payments Agency
School Teachers' Review Body
Science Advisory Committee on the Medical Implications of Less-Lethal Weapons
Science Advisory Council
Science Museum Group
Science and Technology Facilities Council
Sea Fish Industry Authority
Secret Intelligence Service
Security Industry Authority
The Security Service (MI5)
Security Vetting Appeals Panel
Sentencing Council for England and Wales
Serious Organised Crime Agency
Service Children's Education
Service Complaints Commissioner
Service Personnel and Veterans Agency
Service Prosecuting Authority
Sir John Soane's Museum
Skills Funding Agency
Social Mobility and Child Poverty Commission
Social Security Advisory Committee
South Downs National Park Authority
Sport England
Sports Grounds Safety Authority
Standards and Testing Agency
Student Loans Company
Surveillance Camera Commissioner
Technical Advisory Board
Technology Strategy Board
The Theatres Trust
Traffic Commissioners
Treasure Valuation Committee
Treasury Solicitor's Department
Tribunal Procedure Committee
Trinity House
Trust ports
UK Anti-Doping
UK Atomic Energy Authority
UK Commission for Employment and Skills
UK Debt Management Office
UK Financial Investments Limited
UK Green Investment Bank
UK Hydrographic Office
UK Space Agency
UK Sport
Valuation Office Agency
Valuation Tribunal
Vehicle Certification Agency

Vehicle and Operator Services Agency
Veterans Advisory and Pensions Committees (x13)
Veterinary Medicines Directorate
Veterinary Products Committee
Victim's Advisory Panel
Victims' Commissioner
Victoria and Albert Museum
VisitBritain
VisitEngland
Wallace Collection
West Northamptonshire Development Corporation
Westminster Foundation for Democracy
Wilton Park
Yorkshire Dales National Park Authority
Youth Justice Board for England and Wales

12 Public corporations

Architects Registration Board
Audit Commission
BBC
BBC World Service
BRB (Residuary) Ltd
Channel 4
Civil Aviation Authority
Historic Royal Palaces
London and Continental Railways Ltd
Oil and Pipelines Agency
Pension Protection Fund
S4C

Ministers by department

Attorney General's Office
The Rt. Hon Dominic Grieve QC MP

Attorney General
Oliver Heald QC MP
Solicitor General
Cabinet Office
The Rt. Hon David Cameron MP
Minister for the Civil Service, First Lord of the Treasury, Prime Minister
The Rt. Hon Nick Clegg MP
Deputy Prime Minister and Lord President of the Council
The Rt. Hon Francis Maude MP
Minister for the Cabinet Office and Paymaster General
The Rt. Hon Oliver Letwin MP
Minister for Government Policy
The Rt. Hon David Laws MP
Minister of State for Cabinet Office
Nick Hurd MP
Minister for Civil Society
Chloe Smith MP
Minister for Political and Constitutional Reform
Jo Johnson MP
Parliamentary Secretary
Unpaid
The Rt. Hon Kenneth Clarke QC MP
Minister without Portfolio
The Rt. Hon Grant Shapps MP
Minister without Portfolio
John Hayes MP
Minister without Portfolio

Department for Transport
The Rt. Hon Patrick McLoughlin MP
Secretary of State for Transport
The Rt. Hon Simon Burns MP
Minister of State for Transport
Norman Baker MP
Parliamentary under Secretary of State for Transport
Stephen Hammond MP
Parliamentary under Secretary of State for Transport
Department for Work & Pensions
The Rt. Hon Iain Duncan Smith MP
Secretary of State for Work and Pensions
Mark Hoban MP
Minister of State for Employment
Steve Webb MP
Minister of State for Pensions
Esther McVey MP
Parliamentary under Secretary of State for Disabled People
Lord Freud
Parliamentary under Secretary of State for Welfare Reform
Unpaid
Foreign & Commonwealth Office
The Rt. Hon William Hague MP
Secretary of State for Foreign and Commonwealth Affairs, First Secretary of State
The Rt. Hon Baroness Warsi
Senior Minister of State
The Rt. Hon David Lidington MP
Minister of State for Europe
The Rt. Hon Hugo Swire MP
Minister of State at the Foreign & Commonwealth Office
Lord Green of Hurstpierpoint
Minister of State for Trade and Investment
Unpaid
Alistair Burt MP
Parliamentary under Secretary of State for Foreign and Commonwealth Affairs
Mark Simmonds MP
Parliamentary under Secretary of State for Foreign and Commonwealth Affairs
Home Office
The Rt. Hon Theresa May MP
Secretary of State for the Home Department
Mark Harper MP
Minister of State for Immigration
The Rt. Hon Damian Green MP
Minister of State for Policing and Criminal Justice
James Brokenshire MP
Parliamentary under Secretary of State for Crime and Security
Lord Taylor of Holbeach CBE
Parliamentary under Secretary State for Criminal Information
Jeremy Browne MP
Minister of State for Crime Prevention
Northern Ireland Office
The Rt. Hon Theresa Villiers MP
Secretary of State for Northern Ireland
Mike Penning MP
Minister of State for Northern Ireland
Office of the Advocate General for Scotland
The Rt. Hon Lord Wallace of Tankerness QC
HM Advocate General for Scotland
Office of the Leader of the House of Commons
The Rt. Hon Andrew Lansley CBE MP
Leader of the House of Commons and Lord Privy Seal
The Rt. Hon Tom Brake MP
Deputy Leader of the House of Commons

Unpaid

Scotland Office

The Rt. Hon Michael Moore MP
Secretary of State for Scotland

The Rt. Hon David Mundell MP
Parliamentary under Secretary of State for Scotland

The Rt. Hon Lord Wallace of Tankerness QC
Spokesperson in the House of Lords

Wales Office Swyddfa Cymru

The Rt. Hon David Jones MP
Secretary of State for Wales

Stephen Crabb MP
Parliamentary under Secretary of State for Wales
Unpaid

Baroness Randerson
Parliamentary under Secretary of State for Wales
Unpaid

UK Export Finance

The Rt. Hon Dr Vince Cable MP
Secretary of State for Business, Innovation and Skills and President of the Board of Trade

Lord Green of Hurstpierpoint
Minister of State for Trade and Investment
Unpaid

Department for Business Innovation & Skills

The Rt. Hon Dr Vince Cable MP
Secretary of State for Business, Innovation and Skills and President of the Board of Trade

The Rt. Hon David Willetts MP
Minister of State for Universities and Science

The Rt. Hon Michael Fallon MP
Minister of State for Business and Enterprise

Lord Green of Hurstpierpoint
Minister of State for Trade and Investment
Unpaid

Jo Swinson MP
Parliamentary under Secretary of State for Employment Relations and Consumer Affairs

Matthew Hancock MP
Parliamentary under Secretary of State for Skills

Viscount Younger of Leckie
Parliamentary under Secretary of State for Intellectual Property

Department for Communities and Local Government

The Rt. Hon Eric Pickles MP
Secretary of State for Communities and Local Government

The Rt. Hon Baroness Warsi
Minister of State for Faith and Communities

Mark Prisk MP
Minister of State for Housing

Nick Boles MP
Parliamentary under Secretary of State for Planning

The Rt. Hon Don Foster MP
Parliamentary under Secretary of State for Communities and Local Government

Brandon Lewis MP
Parliamentary Under Secretary of State for Communities and Local Government

Baroness Hanham. CBE
Parliamentary Under Secretary of State for Communities and Local Government

Department for Culture Media & Sport

The Rt. Hon Maria Miller MP
Secretary of State for Culture, Media and Sport, Minister for Women and Equalities

The Rt. Hon Hugh Robertson MP
Minister of State for Sport and Tourism

Ed Vaizey MP
Parliamentary under Secretary of State for Culture, Communications and Creative Industries

Jo Swinson MP
Parliamentary under Secretary of State for Women and Equalities

Helen Grant MP
Parliamentary under Secretary of State for Women and Equalities
Department for Education
The Rt. Hon Michael Gove MP
Secretary of State for Education
The Rt. Hon David Laws MP
Minister of State for Schools
Lord Nash
Parliamentary under Secretary of State for Schools
Edward Timpson MP
Parliamentary under Secretary of State for Children and Families
Elizabeth Truss MP
Parliamentary under Secretary of State for Education and Childcare
Matthew Hancock MP
Parliamentary under Secretary of State for Skills
Department for Environment Food & Rural Affairs
The Rt. Hon Owen Paterson MP
Secretary of State for Environment, Food and Rural Affairs
David Heath CBE MP
Minister of State for Agriculture and Food
Richard Benyon MP
Parliamentary under Secretary of State for Natural Environment, Water and Rural Affairs
Lord de Mauley
Parliamentary under Secretary of State for Resource Management, the Local Environment and Environmental Science Department for International Development
The Rt. Hon Justine Greening MP
Secretary of State for International Development
The Rt. Hon Alan Duncan MP
Minister of State for International Development
Lynne Featherstone MP
Parliamentary under Secretary of State for International Development
Department of Energy & Climate Change
The Rt. Hon Edward Davey MP
Secretary of State for Energy and Climate Change
The Rt. Hon Gregory Barker MP
Minister of State for Climate Change
The Rt. Hon Michael Fallon MP
Minister of State for Energy
Baroness Verma
Parliamentary under Secretary of State for Energy and Climate Change
Department of Health
The Rt. Hon Jeremy Hunt MP
Secretary of State for Health
Norman Lamb MP
Minister of State for Care and Support
Lord Howe
Parliamentary under Secretary of State for Quality
Dr Daniel Poulter MP
Parliamentary under Secretary of State for Health
Anna Soubry MP
Parliamentary under Secretary of State for Public Health
HM Treasury
The Rt. Hon George Osborne MP
Chancellor of the Exchequer
The Rt. Hon Danny Alexander MP
Chief Secretary to the Treasury
The Rt. Hon Greg Clark MP
Financial Secretary to the Treasury
David Gauke MP
Exchequer Secretary to the Treasury
Paid as a Parliamentary Secretary
Sajid Javid MP
Economic Secretary to the Treasury

Paid as a Parliamentary Secretary
Lord Paul Deighton
Commercial Secretary to the Treasury
Ministry of Defence
The Rt. Hon Philip Hammond MP
Secretary of State for Defence
The Rt. Hon Andrew Robathan MP
Minister of State for the Armed Forces
The Rt. Hon Mark Francois MP
Minister of State for Defence Personnel, Welfare and Veterans
Dr Andrew Murrison MP
Parliamentary under Secretary of State for International Security Strategy
Philip Dunne MP
Parliamentary under Secretary of State for Defence Equipment, Support and Technology
Lord Astor of Hever DL
Parliamentary under Secretary of State and the Lords Spokesman on Defence
Unpaid
Ministry of Justice
The Rt. Hon Chris Grayling MP
Lord Chancellor and Secretary of State for Justice
Lord McNally
Minister of State for Justice
The Rt. Hon Damian Green MP
Minister of State for Policing and Criminal Justice
Helen Grant MP
Minister for Victims and the Courts
Jeremy Wright MP
Minister for Prisons and Rehabilitation
Office of the Leader of the House of Lords
Lord Hill of Oareford CBE
Leader of the House of Lords and Chancellor of the Duchy of Lancaster
Lord McNally
Deputy Leader of the House of Lords

Whips
House of Commons
The Rt. Hon Sir George Young Bt MP
Chief Whip and Parliamentary Secretary to the Treasury
The Rt. Hon Alistair Carmichael MP
Deputy Chief Whip, Comptroller of HM Household
The Rt. Hon Greg Knight MP
Government Whip, Vice Chamberlain of HM Household
The Rt. Hon John Randall MP
Deputy Chief Whip, Treasurer of HM Household
Junior Lords of the Treasury
David Evennett MP
Government Whip, Lord Commissioner of HM Treasury
Unpaid
The Rt. Hon Desmond Swayne TD MP
Government Whip, Lord Commissioner of HM Treasury
Anne Milton MP
Government Whip, Lord Commissioner of HM Treasury
Robert Goodwill MP
Government Whip, Lord Commissioner of HM Treasury
Mark Lancaster TD MP
Government Whip, Lord Commissioner of HM Treasury
Stephen Crabb MP
Government Whip, Lord Commissioner of HM Treasury
Assistant Whips
Greg Hands MP
Assistant Whip
Karen Bradley MP

Assistant Whip
Jo Johnson MP
Assistant Whip
Nicky Morgan MP
Assistant Whip
Robert Syms MP
Assistant Whip
Mark Hunter MP
Assistant Whip
Jenny Willott MP
Assistant Whip
House of Lords
Baroness Anelay of St Johns
Lords Chief Whip and Captain of the Honourable Corps of Gentlemen at Arms
Lord Newby OBE
Government Deputy Chief Whip and Captain of the Queen's Bodyguard of the Yeomen of the Guard
Baronesses and Lords in Waiting
Baroness Garden of Frognal
Government Whip, Baroness in Waiting
Unpaid
Baroness Stowell of Beeston MBE
Spokesman and Whip in the House of Lords, Baroness in Waiting
Lord Ahmad of Wimbledon
Government Whip, Lord in Waiting
Lord Attlee
Government Whip, Lord in Waiting
Lord Gardiner of Kimble
Government Whip, Lord in Waiting
The Rt. Hon Lord Wallace of Saltaire
Government Whip, Lord in Waiting
Unpaid
Baroness Northover
Spokesperson in the House of Lords
Unpaid

Civil Service

The Civil Service does the practical and administrative work of government. It is co-ordinated and managed by the Prime Minister, in his role as Minister for the Civil Service.
Around half of all civil servants provide services direct to the public, including:
* paying benefits and pensions
* running employment services
* staffing prisons
* issuing driving licences

What is a policy?

A policy is a statement of what the government is trying to achieve and why. Government policy is the sum of all the individual policies – as a whole they help to define where the government stands on broad political issues.
On GOV.UK you can see all our policies and find out exactly what we are doing, who's involved, who we're working with (partner organisations) and who we've asked (consultations).

There are currently 223 policies on Inside Government. https://www.gov.uk/government/policies

Legislation

Laws go through several stages before they are passed by Parliament. The House of Commons and the House of Lords work together to make them.

They can include:

Draft legislation

White papers outline proposals for new laws. Green papers ask for public comments before the white paper is published.

Bills are proposals for new laws or changes to existing ones. Once agreed by Parliament, they have to be approved by The Queen before becoming law.

Acts of Parliament

These are bills, which have been approved by the Commons, the Lords, and The Queen. The relevant government department is responsible for putting the act into practice.

Visit www.legislation.gov.uk

Access to information

Freedom of information

The Freedom of Information Act gives you the right to ask any public sector organisation for all the recorded information it has on any subject. Anyone can make a request for information – known as a Freedom of Information (or FOI) request. There are no restrictions in your age, nationality or where you live.

Statistics

Government produces official statistics about most areas of public life. Statistics are used by people inside and outside government to make informed decisions and to measure the success of government policies and services. Find out about the legislation that governs the publication of UK national and official statistics.

https://www.gov.uk/how-national-and-official-statistics-are-assured
https://www.gov.uk/government/publications?publication_filter_option=statistics

Transparency

The government publishes information about how government works to allow you to make politicians, public services and public organisations more accountable. We are committed to publishing information about:

- how much public money has been spent on what
- the job titles of senior civil servants and how much they are paid
- how the government is doing against its objectives

Data

Putting data in people's hands can help them have more of a say in the reform of public services. On data.gov.uk you can easily find, review and use information about our country and communities - for example, to develop web applications.

Devolved government

In Scotland, Wales and Northern Ireland, devolved administrations are responsible for many domestic policy issues, and their Parliaments/Assemblies have law-making powers for those areas.

Areas the Scottish Government, Welsh Government, and the Northern Ireland Executive are responsible for, include:

- health
- education
- culture
- the environment
- transport

Local government

Councils make and carry out decisions on local services. Many parts of England have 2 tiers of local government: county councils and district, borough or city councils.

In some parts of the country, there's just one tier of local government providing all the functions, known as a 'unitary authority'. This can be a city, borough or county council – or it may just be called 'council'. As well as these, many areas also have parish or town councils.

Understand how you're council works

1. Types of council

This guide relates to councils in England. Find information about councils in Scotland, Wales and Northern Ireland.

Many parts of England have 2 tiers of local government:

- county councils
- district, borough or city councils

In some parts of the country, there's just 1 (unitary) tier of local government providing all the local services. The 3 main types are:

- unitary authorities in shire areas
London boroughs
- metropolitan boroughs
County councils

These are responsible for services across the whole of a county, like:

- education
- transport
- planning
- fire and public safety
- social care
- libraries
- waste management
- trading standards

District, borough and city councils
These cover a smaller area than county councils. They're usually responsible for services like:

- rubbish collection
- recycling
- Council Tax collections
- housing
- planning applications

Unitary authorities and London and metropolitan boroughs
In some parts of the country, 1 tier of local government provides all the local services listed above.

In London and metropolitan areas some services, like fire, police and public transport, are provided through 'joint authorities' (in London by the Greater London Authority).

Parish, community and town councils
These operate at a level below district and borough councils and in some cases, unitary authorities.

They're elected and can help on a number of local issues, like providing:

- allotments
- public clocks
- bus shelters
- community centres
- play areas and play equipment
- grants to help local organisations
- consultation on neighbourhood planning

They also have the power to issue fixed penalty fines for things like:

- litter
- graffiti
- fly posting
- dog offences

2. Decision-making
The full council (a meeting of all council members) is responsible for all decisions. But in practice, most of the work is given to smaller groups of councillors or council officers (paid staff).

Every council must publish:

- details of when key decisions will be taken
- papers of meetings – at least 5 working days beforehand
- minutes of meetings – showing the decisions that were made

You can view council meeting agendas, minutes and reports on your council's website.

You can also attend most council meetings, although usually you won't be able to speak at them.

Mayors

Many councils have a civic mayor or chairman of the council. They carry out ceremonial duties and chair meetings, but can't make decisions about council business.

Some councils have an elected mayor. They're responsible for the day-to-day running of local services.

Councils can have both elected and civic mayors.

3. Spending and accounts

Many local councils provide information on their websites to show how they spend their budget.

You can view details of:

- payments for goods and services over £500
- contracts and tenders over £500

Looking at annual accounts

Every year councils must open their detailed financial accounts to the public for 20 working days.

This allows you to check any spending under £500 without having to make a freedom of information request.

Your council must publish on its website and in the local press details of when you can check its accounts.

4. Local councillors and elections

Local councillors are elected for 4-year terms by the local community to represent its views.

You can contact your local councillor online or by going to an advice surgery.
http://www.writetothem.com/

When local elections are held

Elections to councils are normally held on the first Thursday in May.

Some councils elect all of their councillors at the same time. Other councils elect half or a third of their councillors at each election.

You can find out more about local council elections from the Local Government Boundary Commission for England.
http://www.lgbce.org.uk/records-and-resources/local-authorities-in-england

Declaring interests

All local councillors have to declare any interests, gifts or hospitality they get that could influence decisions they make.

Your local council must publish details of these. You can usually access them on your council's website or at the town hall.

5. Make a complaint

If you feel that a council service hasn't been properly delivered, you can make an official complaint.

- Complain to the council service provider.
- If you're still not happy, complain to your council's complaints officer.

- If this doesn't resolve the issue, you may be able to get the Local Government Ombudsman to look into it.
  http://www.lgo.org.uk/

The Ombudsman considers complaints if you've suffered because of:

- the way a council service has been given
- how a decision has been made

The Ombudsman usually only considers your complaint once it's been through your local council's complaints procedure.

Local Government Ombudsman

0300 061 0614

Parliament
Parliament is separate from government. Made up of the House of Commons and the House of Lords, its role is to:
- look at what the government is doing
- debate issues and pass new laws
- set taxes

There are 650 elected MPs in the House of Commons

How Parliament works

Parliament's role

What Parliament does in its role in UK politics, and its relationship with Government, the Crown and Europe?

Parliament is an essential part of UK politics. Its main roles are:

- Examining and challenging the work of the government (scrutiny)

- Debating and passing all laws (legislation)

- Enabling the government to raise taxes

The two-House system

The business of Parliament takes place in two Houses: the House of Commons and the House of Lords.

The two-House system

The business of Parliament takes place in two Houses: the House of Commons and the House of Lords. Their work is similar: making laws (legislation), checking the work of the government (scrutiny), and debating current issues. The House of Commons is also responsible for granting money to the government through approving Bills that raise taxes. Generally, the decisions made in one House have to be approved by the other. In this way the two-chamber system acts as a check and balance for both Houses.

The Commons

The Commons is publicly elected. The party with the largest number of members in the Commons forms the government.

Members of the Commons (MPs) debate the big political issues of the day and proposals for new laws. It is one of the key places where government ministers, like the Prime Minister and the Chancellor, and the principal figures of the main political parties, work.

The Commons alone is responsible for making decisions on financial Bills, such as proposed new taxes. The Lords can consider these Bills but cannot block or amend them.

The Lords

The House of Lords is the second chamber of the UK Parliament, it complements the work of the House of Commons. It makes laws, holds government to account and investigates policy issues. Its membership is mostly appointed and includes experts in many fields.

Checking the work of government
Parliament examines and challenges the work of government.

Parliament examines and challenges the work of the government. Both the House of Commons and the House of Lords use similar methods of scrutiny, although the procedures vary. The principal methods are questioning government ministers, debating and the investigative work of committees. The government can publicly respond to explain and justify policies and decisions.

Questions

Questions to government ministers may be answered orally or in writing. Ministers from each government department attend the Commons on a rota basis to answer oral questions. The Prime Minister answers questions every Wednesday. In the Lords, the House questions government ministers at the start of each day's business, but there is no set days for government departments.

Debates

Debates in the Commons look at the creation and amendment of laws as well as national and international issues and can be on any subject. Votes are often taken to see whether a majority of Members either support or reject any discussed laws or proposals.

In the Lords, one day a week is set aside for general debates and short debates take place on most days (lasting one and a half-hours). There are no votes on such debates. The House of Lords also check the work of government by scrutinising legislation.

Committees

Committees of smaller groups of MPs and/or Lords look at specific policy issues or legislation in detail. Different committees have different roles ranging from offering advice, to producing reports or altering legislation. Both Houses have permanent and temporary committees. MPs and Lords also work together in Joint Select Committees. The government issues responses to most committee reports.

Legislation

Parliament is responsible for approving new laws (legislation).

Legislation

Parliament is responsible for approving new laws (legislation). The government introduces most plans for new laws, or changes to existing laws - but they can originate from an MP, Lord or even a member of the public or private group. Before they can become law, both the House of Commons and House of Lords must debate and vote on the proposals.

Introducing legislation

Bills normally introduce new laws. Bills that deal with more political or controversial issues usually begin in the Commons.

Defeating and delaying legislation

To become law the text of a Bill must be agreed by both Houses. Either House can vote down a Bill in which case it will normally not become law - but there are exceptions. The Commons can pass the same Bill in two successive years, in which case it can become law without the agreement of the Lords. Bills, which are only about money (raising taxes or authorising government expenditure), are not opposed in the Lords and may only be delayed for a month.

Royal Assent

The reigning monarch has to approve all new laws - called the Royal Assent - but this is a formality as in practice it is not withheld. Royal Assent was last withheld in 1708 when Queen Anne refused a Bill to settle the Militia in Scotland.

When a Bill is given Royal Assent it becomes an Act of Parliament. It is then the responsibility of the relevant government department to implement that law (e.g., the Home Office will deal with new Acts relating to immigration).

Debate

Both Houses of Parliament hold debates in which Members discuss government policy, proposed legislation and current issues.

Debate

Both Houses of Parliament hold debates in which Members discuss government policy, proposed new laws and current issues.

Debates are designed to assist MPs and Lords to reach an informed decision on a subject. Votes are often held to conclude a debate, which may involve then passing or rejecting a proposed new law (legislation) or simply registering their opinion on a subject. All debates are recorded in a publication called 'Hansard' which is available online or in print.

Debates - General

A similar system for debates applies across the Commons and Lords. Subjects are introduced as a proposal, or motion, by Members, then debated according to strict sets of rules.

Why does Parliament have debates?

Debates are an opportunity for MPs and Lords to discuss government policy, proposed new laws and current issues. It allows MPs to voice the concerns and interests of their constituents, and Members of the House of Lords can speak about issues brought to their attention by the public.

Debates are designed to assist MPs and Lords to reach an informed decision on a subject. This decision is then often expressed in a vote (called a 'division'), for or against.

Debates in the Commons

Commons debates are often lively, with MPs intervening on each other's speeches to support or challenge what they are saying. It is a dynamic style of discussion, in which MPs generally respond to the points made by other speakers rather than reading out formal, set-piece speeches.

However, rules still govern debates. MPs have a right to be heard without overwhelming background noise, and unparliamentary language is not allowed.

Debates in the Lords

The main role of the House of Lords is to debate and revise major legislation, but Lords also take part in general debates and discuss subjects of topical interest - like a new report, or a matter of public concern.

The Lords regulate themselves and the order of business in the House. Therefore, there can be greater flexibility amongst its Members to examine an issue for longer than is typical in the Commons.

Rules and customs

The origins of Parliament go back to the 13th century, so there are many rules about how it runs.

Rules and customs

The origins of Parliament go back to the 13th century, and there are many rules and customs that affect how it runs. Some of these are written down and are called 'Standing Orders'. Other rules are set out in resolutions of the House. However, much of how Parliament does its business is not determined by rules but has become established through continued use over the centuries - this is sometimes known as 'custom and practice'.

Standing Orders

Standing Orders are written rules under which Parliament conducts its business. They regulate the way Members behave, Bills are processed and debates are organised. Some Standing Orders are temporary and only last until the end of a session or a parliament. There are around 150 standing orders relating to parliamentary business and public Bills, and about 250 relating to private business.

Read the Standing Orders:

House of Commons - Public Business
House of Commons - Private Business
House of Lords - Public Business
House of Lords - Private Business
Companion to the Standing Orders and Guide to the Proceedings of the House of Lords
Custom and practice

Much of parliamentary procedure is not written into the Standing Orders but exist as the custom and practice of Parliament. Some stem from Speaker's rulings in the House of Commons chamber, other procedures are followed because that's the way things have been done in the past, so a precedent has been set. An example of a well known practice is of Bills being 'read' three times in both Houses, this is not in the Standing Orders.

Traditions of Parliament

A number of traditions are involved in the working of Parliament.

Traditions of Parliament

A number of traditions are involved in the working of Parliament. Below are some examples.

Dragging the Speaker of the House of Commons

When a new Speaker of the House of Commons is elected, the successful candidate is physically dragged to the Chair by other MPs.

This custom has its roots in the Speaker's function to communicate the Commons' opinions to the monarch. Historically, if the monarch didn't agree with the message being communicated then the early death of the Speaker could follow. Therefore, as you can imagine, previous Speakers required some gentle persuasion to accept the post.

Voting

When MPs vote in the Commons they say 'aye' or 'no'. In the Lords, Members vote saying 'content' or 'not content'.

Prayers

Each sitting in both Houses begins with prayers that follow the Christian faith. In the Commons the Speaker's Chaplain usually reads the prayers. In the Lords a senior bishop (Lord Spiritual) who sits in the Lords usually reads the prayers.

Catching the Speaker's eye

To participate in a debate in the House of Commons or at question time, MPs have to be called by the Speaker. MPs usually rise or half-rise from their seats in a bid to get the Speaker's attention - this is known as 'catching the Speaker's eye'.

The Woolsack in the House of Lords

The Woolsack is the seat of the Lord Speaker in the House of Lords Chamber. The Woolsack is a large, wool-stuffed cushion or seat covered with red cloth.

The Lord Speaker on the Woolsack

The Lord Speaker presides over debates in the House of Lords, but does not control them like the Speaker in the Commons, as Members of the Lords regulate their own discussions.

If a Deputy Speaker presides in the absence of the Lord Speaker, then that individual uses the Woolsack.

When the House of Lords is sitting, the Mace is placed on the rear of the Woolsack, behind the Lord Speaker.

Judges' Woolsack

In front of the Woolsack in the House of Lords Chamber is a larger cushion known as the Judges' Woolsack. During the State Opening of Parliament, the Judges' Woolsack is occupied by senior judges. This is a reminder of mediaeval Parliaments, when judges attended to offer legal advice. During normal sittings of the House, any Member of the Lords may sit on it.

Parliament and government

Parliament and government both play a part in forming the laws of the United Kingdom.

Parliament and government

Parliament and government both play a part in forming the laws of the United Kingdom. They are separate institutions that work closely together, so it's easy to mix-up exactly what each one is responsible for.

Government

The government runs the country. It has responsibility for developing and implementing policy and for drafting laws. It is also known as the Executive.

Parliament

Parliament is the highest legislative authority in the UK. It has responsibility for checking the work of government and examining, debating and approving new laws. It is also known as the Legislature.

Forming a government

The political party that wins the most seats in a general election forms the new government, led by their party leader - who becomes Prime Minister. The Prime Minister appoints ministers, including the Cabinet, who often work in a government department, and run and develop public services and policies.

Ministers and MPs

Government ministers are chosen from MPs and Lords in Parliament. Your MP may be a member of the party forming the current Government, but it doesn't necessarily mean they are working 'in government'. Ministers must regularly respond to oral and written questions from MPs and Lords.

Scrutiny of the government

Parliament checks the work of the government on behalf of UK citizens through investigative select committees and by asking government ministers questions. The House of Commons also has to approve proposals for government taxes and spending.

Confidence motion

The government needs to retain the confidence of a majority in the House of Commons. If the House votes to indicate that it has no confidence in the government, either by defeating the government on a confidence motion or by defeating a policy that the government has indicated is a 'matter of confidence', then a General Election would be called if a confidence motion in the new government was not passed within 14 days of the original no confidence motion.

Government Bills

Each year the government informs Parliament of its plans for new legislation in the Queen's Speech. New legislation is usually introduced in the form of a Bill that must be debated and approved by Parliament before it can become an Act of Parliament - the government needs the support of the majority of the House of Commons to function.

Parliament and Crown

Along with the House of Commons and the House of Lords, the Crown is an integral part of the institution of Parliament.

Parliament and Crown

Along with the House of Commons and the House of Lords, the Crown is an integral part of the institution of Parliament. The Queen plays a constitutional role in opening and dissolving Parliament and approving Bills before they become laws.

Parliament

The highest legislative authority in the United Kingdom. Made up of the House of Commons, House of Lords and the Queen (who is the UK's current hereditary monarch).

Crown

This is another way of referring to the monarchy - which is the oldest part of the system of government in this country. Time has reduced the power of the monarchy, and today it is broadly ceremonial. The current UK monarch is Queen Elizabeth II.

Appointing a government

The day after a general election the Queen invites the leader of the party that won the most seats in the House of Commons to become Prime Minister and to form a government.

Opening and dissolving Parliament

The Crown opens Parliament through the State Opening (marking the beginning of the parliamentary year). The Crown only dissolves Parliament before a general election under conditions laid out in the Fixed Term Parliament Act 2011 (dissolution).

Queen's Speech

The Crown informs Parliament of the government's policy ideas and plans for new legislation in a speech delivered from the throne in the House of Lords. Although the Queen makes the speech the government draws up the content.

Royal Assent

When a Bill has been approved by a majority in the House of Commons and the House of Lords it is formally agreed to by the Crown. This is known as the Royal Assent. This turns a Bill into an Act of Parliament, allowing it to become law in the UK.

Devolved Parliaments and Assemblies

UK devolution created a national Parliament in Scotland, a national Assembly in Wales and a national Assembly in Northern Ireland.

Devolved Parliaments and Assemblies

UK devolution created a national Parliament in Scotland, a national Assembly in Wales and a national Assembly in Northern Ireland. This process transferred varying levels of power from the UK Parliament to the UK's nations - but kept authority over the devolved institutions in the UK Parliament itself.

Scotland, Wales and Northern Ireland all held successful referendums on devolution in the late 1990s. This led to the establishment of separate Parliaments or Assemblies and the democratic election of officials.

Devolved and reserved powers

Devolved powers are decisions that Parliament controlled in the past, but are now taken by the separate bodies, e.g., the Scottish Parliament. This could include matters like education or health. Reserved powers are those decisions that remain with Parliament in Westminster.

In each case, the legislation establishing the separate bodies determined which powers were devolved and which were reserved.

Transfer of powers

The Scottish Parliament and the National Assembly for Wales took responsibility for their devolved powers on 1 July 1999, the Northern Ireland Assembly followed on 2 December 1999. The Northern Ireland Assembly was suspended at midnight on 14 October 2002. Power was restored to the Northern Ireland Assembly on 8 May 2007

Europe

The UK is one of 27 member states of the European Union and is subject to European Union (EU) legislation.

The UK is one of 27 member states of the European Union and is subject to European Union (EU) legislation. UK government ministers are involved in deciding this legislation and should not agree to proposals before Parliament has examined them.

What is Parliament's role in Europe?

Scrutinising EU draft legislation and other EU documents.

Changing UK law to reflect agreed EU legislation and treaties.

Holding the government to account on its EU policies and negotiating positions in the EU institutions.

Can the European Union change the law in the UK?

The EU has the authority to apply legislation in the UK but actually putting it into action may require Parliament to pass new or amended legislation.

The Scrutiny Reserve Resolutions

The Scrutiny Reserve Resolutions provide that no government minister should agree in the Council of Ministers or the European Council to a proposal that is still 'subject to scrutiny' by Parliament - and if they do, they have to explain their reasons.

The UK Parliament receives copies of EU documents, together with an Explanatory Memorandum (EM) prepared by the relevant government department. Documents are considered by the Scrutiny Committees in both the Commons and the Lords.

The Commons committee

In the Commons, the European Scrutiny Committee considers all EU documents and reports its opinion on the legal and political importance of each one. The committee may decide that no further scrutiny is required, or it may request further information from the government or recommend the document for debate in a European Legislation Committee or in the Commons chamber.

The Lords committee

The Lords examines proposals for EU legislation through the European Union Select Committee and there is close co-ordination with Commons committees. The Lords look at fewer EU documents but carry out detailed reviews on subjects selected for their general importance. These reviews are reported either just for information or to recommend a debate in the Lords.

More information can be found through the House of Commons Library Briefing: The European Union: a guide to terminology, procedures and sources

Parliamentary sovereignty

Parliamentary sovereignty is a principle of the UK constitution. It makes Parliament the supreme legal authority in the UK, which can create or end any law.

Parliamentary sovereignty

Parliamentary sovereignty is a principle of the UK constitution. It makes Parliament the supreme legal authority in the UK, which can create or end any law. Generally, the courts cannot overrule its legislation and no Parliament can pass laws that future Parliaments cannot change. Parliamentary sovereignty is the most important part of the UK constitution.

Parliamentary sovereignty and the UK constitution

People often refer to the UK having an 'unwritten constitution' but that's not strictly true. It may not exist in a single text, like in the USA or Germany, but large parts of it are written down, much of it in the laws passed in Parliament - known as statute law.

Therefore, the UK constitution is often described as 'partly written and wholly uncodified'. (Uncodified means that the UK does not have a single, written constitution.)

Developments affecting parliamentary sovereignty

Over the years, Parliament has passed laws that limit the application of parliamentary sovereignty. These laws reflect political developments both within and outside the UK.

They include:

The devolution of power to bodies like the Scottish Parliament and Welsh Assembly.
The Human Rights Act 1998.
The UK's entry to the European Union in 1972.
The decision to establish a UK Supreme Court in 2009, which ends the House of Lords function as the UK's final court of appeal.
These developments do not fundamentally undermine the principle of parliamentary sovereignty, since, in theory at least, Parliament could repeal any of the laws implementing these changes.

Guides to Parliament
Find out more about the work of Parliament, its history and traditions.

Guides to Parliament

Parliament is made up of two distinct Houses; the House of Commons and the House of Lords. Each House has its own administration to support it, including two separate public information offices.

House of Commons Information Office publications

Guides to People, Events and Places

Learn more about parliamentary office holders such as the Commons Speaker, famous events like the Budget and places including the House of Commons Chamber.

The House of Commons Information Office has produced a series of guides on the People, Events and Places that explain the work of Parliament.

People

The House of Commons Information Office answers enquiries on the work, history and membership of the House of Commons. It also produces a range of publications about the House which are available for free in hard copy on request.

Guides to People, Events and Places

Read short, informative descriptions of the parliamentary estate, state occasions and the principal office holders in the House of Commons.

Brief Guides

Browse our extended descriptions about the House of Commons, its history and membership.

Easy Read Guides

Information on MPs and the House of Commons in an easy read format

Foreign Language Guides
Read about the role of an MP and our guides to Parliament in a range of foreign languages.

House of Lords Information Office publications

The House of Lords Information Office acts as a central service for answering queries from Members, staff, the press and the public. The illustrated 'The work of the House of Lords' describes the work of the House with examples drawn from the previous session.

Lords briefing papers

Guides to business, including Welsh and foreign language versions

Parliament and Constitution Centre

The Parliament and Constitution Centre provides a focus for the House of Commons Library's work on Parliament and the Constitution.

This includes a number of background papers explaining in detail aspects of parliamentary procedure and practice.

House of Commons Background Papers
Houses of Parliament Shop

The Houses of Parliament Shop provides access to the full range of parliamentary and related publications as soon as they are available.

Guides to People, Events and Places

Learn more about parliamentary office holders such as the Commons Speaker, famous events like the Budget and places including the House of Commons Chamber.

The House of Commons Information Office has produced a series of guides on the People, Events and Places that explain the work of Parliament.

People

The great offices of state

The role of Chancellor is known as one of the 'four great offices of state'; the others are the Prime Minister, the Foreign Secretary and the Home Secretary.

The role of the Chancellor of the Exchequer

The Chancellor of the Exchequer is the government's chief financial minister. The Chancellor is responsible for raising government revenue through taxation or borrowing. Raising revenue enables the Government to put its policies into practice. The Chancellor controls all spending made by government departments.
The current Chancellor of the Exchequer is the Rt. Hon George Osborne MP.

The Chancellor and the Treasury

The Chancellor of the Exchequer also holds the title of 'Second Lord of the Treasury' and is responsible for the work of Her Majesty's Treasury. The Prime Minister holds the title 'First Lord of the Treasury' but the Chancellor is the most senior figure in the Treasury. Because the Treasury controls overall spending by government departments it has great influence over delivery of the government's policies.

The Budget

One of the Chancellor's most important responsibilities is presenting the annual Budget to the House of Commons. The Chancellor makes a statement in the Commons Chamber on the nation's finances and the Government's proposals for changes to taxation, giving the reasons why change is necessary. The Budget statement is followed by a debate on the measures announced by the Chancellor.

New measures or those that require a change in the law become part of the Finance Bill, which is then considered by the House of Commons. The House of Commons is the only body that can raise taxation for the whole of the United Kingdom. The Budget and the Finance Bill take place every year because income tax and corporation taxes have to be renewed by legislation annually.
Since 1997, the Chancellor has also delivered an annual Pre-Budget Report (PBR) to the House of Commons, usually in November or December. This report updates the House on financial matters since the previous Budget. The PBR may also outline forthcoming measures to be announced in the next Budget.

11 Downing Street

11 Downing Street has been the Chancellor of the Exchequer's official residence since 1828. Its front door is regularly featured in Budget day photo calls when the Chancellor is photographed holding up the distinctive red box containing his speech before going to the House of Commons to make the Budget statement.

Origins of the role

Historically, the Exchequer was responsible for collecting and administering royal revenues and was overseen by a Treasurer and a Chancellor. During the 13th century under the reign of Henry III, the official title of Chancellor of the Exchequer was recognised, becoming an officer of the court. The role of Chancellor in its modern form emerged in the 18th century with the establishment of the offices of Second Lord Commissioner of the Treasury and First Lord of the Treasury. In the 18th and early 19th centuries it was common for the Prime Minister to also serve as the Chancellor of the Exchequer. The last Prime Minister to hold the offices of First Lord of the Treasury and Chancellor of the Exchequer at the same time was William Ewart Gladstone in 1882.

Who is the Leader of the House of Commons?

The Leader of the House of Commons is a Government Minister and a member of the Cabinet. His main role is organising government business in the Commons and working closely with the government's Chief Whip. The Leader of the Commons represents the House of Commons within the Government.
The current Leader of the House of Commons is Rt. Hon Andrew Lansley CBE MP.

Parliamentary business

The Leader plans and supervises the Government's legislative programme in the House of Commons. This ensures that the Government can implement the policies it was elected to carry out. When the House is sitting, the Leader makes a statement each Thursday to announce the business for the following week.
This is followed by questions from MPs about the future timetable or issues relating to procedure and practice in the Commons. The Leader also introduces any debates concerning the House.

House of Commons and Government

It is the Leader's job to represent the interests and rights of the House of Commons within Government. As a member of the House of Commons Commission, they also act as the Government's representative in the House. The Commission is responsible for the administration and services of the House, it is chaired by the Speaker and its membership is drawn from senior MPs.

Cabinet matters

The Leader is involved in a number of Cabinet committees. They chair the Legislative Programme Committee which determines the content of the Queen's Speech, monitors legislation's progress in the House and considers the parliamentary handling of Government bills. The Leader also sits on the Ministerial Committee on the Constitution, a Cabinet committee which meets to consider constitutional affairs and citizenship. The Leader can deputise for the Prime Minister, either at Prime Minister's Questions or for formal duties, but usually the Deputy Prime Minister carries out this function.

Historic role

The first Leader of the House was Robert Walpole in 1721. He held the position in addition to being Prime Minister, First Lord of the Treasury and Chancellor of the Exchequer. Historically, the position of Leader of the House was usually held by the Prime Minister. Today the Leader also holds the position of Lord Privy Seal.

Leaders in other Parliaments

There are variants on the role of Leader in other Commonwealth parliaments. In Canada, the position of Government House Leader has existed as a full time position since 1968 and is usually combined with another full-time Cabinet role. There is also a Leader of the House in Australia, again normally combined with another office. New Zealand has a Leader, often combined with the role of Deputy Prime Minister. The South African Parliament has a Leader of Government Business whose responsibilities include programming national executive business. The role of Leader in these countries has not developed the association with parliamentary modernisation as the position has in the United Kingdom, nor is there an equivalent to the House of Commons Commission.

The Prime Minister's role

The Prime Minister (PM) is head of the Government of the United Kingdom. The official title is 'First Lord of the Treasury'. The PM has overall responsibility for the government's policies and, as head of the Government, is also responsible for the civil service and government agencies. The PM selects members of the Cabinet, the main decision-making body in government. Cabinet members are usually the Secretaries of State of government departments, plus other invited Ministers and Peers. The Cabinet meets each Tuesday.

The current Prime Minister is the Rt. Hon David Cameron MP.

The Prime Minister and Parliament

In the House of Commons the PM's duties are to make formal statements, answer questions from MPs and take part in debates. Prime Minister's Questions last 30 minutes and takes place every Wednesday at noon when the House is sitting. The PM sits on the Government frontbench on the Speaker's right, near the despatch box in the House of Commons. Since 2002, the PM has appeared before the Liaison Committee twice a year to answer questions on international and domestic affairs. The Liaison Committee is made up of the Chairs of the House of Commons Select Committees. These sessions usually last up to two and a half-hours The PM does not receive prior notice of the questions, although they are usually based on a limited number of themes. The Prime Minister is a sitting MP with a constituency role just like any other MP.

History

The first PM is generally agreed to have been Sir Robert Walpole who held the office from 1720 to 1742. He held the title First Lord of the Treasury and was also Chancellor of the Exchequer. The term 'Prime Minister' was not an official title at that time and was only formally recognised in 1905. David Cameron is the 53rd Prime Minister. Margaret Thatcher was the first female PM, holding the office from 1979 to 1990. Walpole holds the record for the longest period of unbroken service in office, lasting 20 years and 314 days. The youngest PM was William Pitt the Younger who was 24 when he first took office in 1783. The oldest PM was William Ewart Gladstone who was 82 when appointed to his final period in office in 1892. Other notable PMs includes Spencer Perceval, the only British PM to be assassinated. In May 1812, while in the House of Commons lobby Perceval was shot by John Bellingham, a debt-ridden merchant who blamed the government for his predicament and wanted revenge. Bellingham was later tried and hanged for Perceval's murder.

Number 10

The Prime Minister's residence in London has been Number 10 Downing Street since 1730 when it was presented by King George II as a gift to Sir Robert Walpole. Walpole refused the property as a personal gift and requested that it be made available to First Lords of the Treasury in their official capacity. Since then most PMs have used it as their official residence, although its state of repair meant that some early PMs preferred to live in their own private homes. Behind the famous black door, Number 10 is bigger than it looks. Over the years, adjoining buildings have been incorporated and extensive renovations have taken place. The PM has use of a flat in Number 10 and other rooms are used for official meetings and receptions. Margaret Thatcher described it as 'living above the shop'. The current PM and his family live in the larger flat above 11 Downing Street. The facade of Number 10 was cleaned in the 1950s, revealing it to be built of yellow brick, its black appearance was due to 200 years of London pollution. The cleaned bricks were painted black to retain their familiar appearance.

Serjeant at Arms

Who is the Serjeant at Arms?

The Serjeant at Arms is responsible for the security of the House of Commons. This includes the Chamber, the public galleries, committee rooms and other buildings on the parliamentary estate. The post of Serjeant at Arms originated in the 13th century and has evolved over time to its present form while retaining some ceremonial duties.

The current Serjeant at Arms, Lawrence Ward, was appointed in May 2012. The Serjeant's team includes a Deputy Serjeant, Assistant Serjeant and Associate Sergeants.
Other offices under the Serjeant's authority include the Admission Order Office, the Doorkeepers and the Pass Office. The parliamentary official responsible for security in the House of Lords is Black Rod. The Serjeant and Black Rod work together to ensure the security of the Houses of Parliament and its outbuildings.

Access and security

The Serjeant must balance access to Parliament with security. The Serjeant is responsible for access to the public gallery of the main and Westminster Hall debating chambers, where visitors can watch debates, and for public access to select committee hearings.

Members of Parliament meet many groups and individuals at the House of Commons to learn about their concerns or discuss their views. Access for these visitors are also facilitated by the Serjeant.

Mass lobbies and large groups sometimes come to Parliament to express their views or to attend meetings.

The Serjeant liases with the Metropolitan Police when large numbers are expected to ensure public order is maintained and Parliament remains secure.

Ceremonial duties and dress

The Serjeant at Arms' ceremonial duties includes escorting the Speaker on the procession from his state apartments to the Chamber before each sitting of the House. The Serjeant at Arms carries the Mace, which is an emblem of office and a symbol of the House of Commons' authority. It is placed on the table in front of the Speaker's Chair in the Chamber. The House can only sit and debate if the Mace is present. The official court dress of the Serjeant at Arms was established in the late 18th century and consists of black wool suit and patent leather shoes. Some changes were made when the first female Serjeant at Arms was appointed in 2008. On special occasions, a lace collar and cuffs are worn. For the Speaker's procession, the Serjeant wears white gloves, a sword, scabbard and sword sling. The Serjeant still wears the sword in the Chamber.

In the Chamber either the Serjeant or one of the Serjeant's team sits in the Commons Chamber while the House is sitting.

They are responsible for security in the Chamber, which includes removing anyone causing a disturbance in the public gallery. The Serjeant can also remove MPs from the Chamber if they have refused to leave after being asked to by the Speaker. The Serjeant also oversees access to the parliamentary press gallery, supplying passes to broadcasters and journalists who work in the Palace of Westminster or those who need access to report on a specialist interest.

Speaker of the House of Commons

Who is the Speaker?

The Speaker is the highest authority in the House of Commons, chairing debates, keeping order and calling Members of Parliament (MPs) to speak. The Speaker also represents the Commons to the Sovereign and the House of Lords, and chairs the House of Commons Commission.

The Speaker is elected to the post by other MPs and is politically impartial. When elected the Speaker resigns from their political party and remains separate from political issues, even in retirement.

The current Speaker is John Bercow, MP for Buckingham. He was elected using a secret ballot system, the first time such a procedure has been used to elect a Speaker

What does the Speaker do?

During debates the Speaker keeps order in the House, ensures that its rules are kept and decides which MPs will speak. The Speaker also decides which amendments to a motion or a bill are debated. In the Chamber, if an MP alleges dishonourable behaviour by another, the Speaker may request that they withdraw their remark.

If an MP misbehaves, the Speaker can suspend them for a day or ask the House for a longer period. This is known as 'Naming' a Member. The Speaker can also suspend a sitting in the case of serious general disorder in the Chamber. The Speaker usually sits in the Chamber for the first two hours of each sitting day, for an hour each evening and occasionally

at other times. When the Speaker is not in the Chamber, debates are chaired by one of three Deputy Speakers. The Speaker no longer wears the traditional outfit of knee breeches, silk stockings and a full-bottomed wig. Instead, on normal sitting days, the Speaker wears a suit and black robe. On state occasions, the Speaker wears a black satin damask robe trimmed with gold.

Speakers and general elections

The Speaker still stands in general elections, but by convention, is unopposed by the major political parties, who will not field a candidate. This includes the party for which they were originally an MP. During a general election, the Speaker does not campaign on any political issues but simply stands as 'the Speaker seeking re-election'. As a sitting MP, the Speaker has the same responsibilities to their constituents as any other MP.

The Speaker's procession

Before every sitting of the House, the Speaker leaves his official residence at the Westminster Bridge end of the Palace of Westminster preceded by a Doorkeeper and the Serjeant at Arms who carries the Mace. The Trainbearer, Chaplain and Speaker's Secretary follow behind.

This formal procession walks along the Library Corridor, through the Lower Waiting Hall and Central and Members' Lobbies to the Chamber. The present route was adopted during the Second World War when the Commons used the House of Lords Chamber after their own was destroyed in a bombing raid. It is still used in preference to the shorter pre-war route as it allows visitors in Central Lobby to witness the procession.

Historically, the role of Speaker could be dangerous. This may be one reason for the Speaker's formal procession and entourage.

Wider role

The Speaker acts as spokesman for the House on ceremonial and formal occasions, including presenting addresses of congratulation to the Queen on her Silver Jubilee in 1977, Golden Jubilee in 2002, and Diamond Jubilee in 2012.

Today these formal occasions are usually happy events but in past centuries a Speaker might have been called upon to deliver unpopular messages to the Sovereign, for example, the reasons why the Commons had disagreed to raising a tax for the royal revenues.

A perilous office

The position of Speaker has not been without danger in times gone by. Since the appointment of the first Speaker in 1377, nine of his successors are known to have died violent deaths, of which seven were beheaded.

Speakers Conferences

These conferences are convened by the Speaker on the invitation of the Prime Minister to examine issues within the electoral system. The most recent, in 2008/09 examined the representation of women, ethnic minorities and disabled people in the House of Commons

Events

The Budget

What is the Budget?
The Budget is an annual event when the Chancellor of the Exchequer makes a statement to the House of Commons on the nation's finances and the Government's proposals for changes to taxation. The reasons for changes are explained in the Chancellor's speech. The statement is followed by a debate on the proposals and Members of Parliament (MPs) vote on whether they should become laws.

Why have a Budget and Finance Bill every year?

The House of Commons is the only tax raising body for the UK as a whole. The Chancellor requires the House of Commons to approve his changes by passing a Finance Bill each year. The Budget and the Finance Bill are annual events because income tax, corporation tax and advanced corporation tax are annual taxes. They have to be renewed by legislation each year. Most UK taxes including all indirect taxes, petroleum revenue tax and taxes on capital are, by contrast, 'permanent'.

Is the Budget always delivered on the same day of the week?

Often, the Budget is delivered on a Tuesday or a Wednesday, though it can take place on any day. There may simply be a preference for the early part of the week and to accommodate MPs with seats outside London, who cannot always be in the House on Mondays.

Between 1964 and 1997 only one Budget did not take place on a Tuesday. Gordon Brown's first budget in 1997 was held on a Wednesday but while he reverted to Tuesday for the following three budgets, his last six were on a Wednesday. George Osborne's first budget took place on a Tuesday and his second on a Wednesday.

What happens after the Chancellor's Budget speech?

Traditionally, the Leader of the Opposition, rather than the Shadow Chancellor replies to the Budget speech. This is usually followed by four days of debate on the Budget Resolutions (the basic parts of the Budget that renew annual taxes, such as income tax), covering different policy areas such as health, education and defence. These debates are chaired by the Chairman of Ways and Means (the Deputy Speaker), rather than the Speaker.

Follow the Budget debates online

It is possible to follow the debates for the Budget online on Parliament Live or by reading the debates in Hansard. Both are available on Parliament's website. The Finance Bill's papers are also available online.

Despatch box drink

By tradition, the Chancellor, unlike Ministers at the despatch box at any other time of the year, may drink alcohol during their Budget speech if they wish. The current Chancellor George Osborne chose to drink water, as did the previous Chancellor Alistair Darling. Other Chancellors have chosen mineral water (Gordon Brown), whisky (Kenneth Clarke), spritzer (Nigel Lawson), gin and tonic (Geoffrey Howe), brandy and water (Benjamin Disraeli) and sherry and beaten egg (William Ewart Gladstone).

The Budget box

The distinctive 'Budget box', which Chancellors used to carry their speech from 11 Downing Street to the House of Commons, was in use for over one hundred consecutive years. The wooden box was handcrafted for William Ewart Gladstone in about 1860. It was lined in black satin and covered in scarlet leather. Lord Callaghan was the first Chancellor to break with tradition in 1965 when he used a new box. In July 1997, Gordon Brown became the second Chancellor to use a new box for the Budget. George Osborne used the Gladstone box for his first budget in 2010 but used a new box in 2011.

The long and the short of it

The longest Budget speech was by William Ewart Gladstone on 18 April 1853. It lasted four hours and forty-five minutes. Benjamin Disraeli made the shortest speech at forty-five minutes on 4 April 1867.

Origins of the term

The word 'budget' comes from an old French word 'bougette' which means 'little bag

Debates

What is a debate?

Debates are an opportunity for MPs to discuss government policy, proposed new laws and current issues. They allow MPs to voice the concerns and interests of their constituents. Debates are designed to assist MPs to reach an informed decision on a subject. Debates take place in the House of Commons Chamber and the Grand Committee Room of Westminster Hall.

Members take it in turns to speak on the subject concerned and the discussion is strictly controlled by a set of rules called the 'Standing Orders'. The Speaker chair debates in the Chamber and ensures these rules are followed and order is maintained. At the end of the debate, the House comes to a decision, if necessary by means of a vote. In Parliament, this is called a division.

Debates and the Speaker

During a debate, the Speaker, or Deputy Speaker, calls MPs in turn to give their opinion on an issue. MPs must get the Speaker's attention (called 'catching the Speaker's eye') and usually stand, or half-rise from their seat to do so. They may also write in advance to indicate their wish to speak but this gives no guarantee that they will be called.

MPs address their speeches to the Speaker, or Deputy. Normally MPs will speak only once in a debate, although they may intervene with a brief comment on another Member's speech.

Style of debate

The style of debate in the House differs from some overseas legislatures, where set-piece speeches from a desk or podium are more common.

In the Commons, MPs listen to speeches and intervene with opinions, expressions of approval or disapproval, or humour. It is the job of the Speaker to ensure that MPs observe the courtesies of debate while still allowing vigorous debate to take place and forthright opinions to be expressed.

Adjournment debates

The last half-hour of each sitting day in the Chamber is allocated for an adjournment debate. A backbench MP is chosen by ballot (except on Thursdays when the Speaker selects from among those unsuccessful in the ballot). The subject is often one of particular interest to the MP's constituency. A Minister attends the debate to reply to the points raised.

Westminster Hall debates

Some debates take place in the Grand Committee Room, referred to as Westminster Hall. These debates were inaugurated in 1999 in a specially converted room off the main hall.

The room is arranged in an elongated horseshoe shape rather than the opposing benches of the Commons Chamber. This is to reflect the non-partisan nature of the debates in Westminster Hall. Private Members' adjournment debates and select committee report debates are held here

Topical debates

Following recommendations made by the Modernisation Committee in 2007, debates on topical issues raised by Members take place in the Commons every week. They can focus on issues of regional, national or international importance. Topical debates were introduced, as a trial but became a permanent feature of parliamentary business in 2008.

Will the honourable Member...?

During debates in the House, there are certain conventions MPs must follow. For example, MPs are not referred to by name. The following terms of address are used instead:

> the honourable Member for (constituency)
> my honourable friend (if in the same party)
> the honourable Member opposite (if in a different party)
> Right Honourable (for Privy Counsellors)
> the Secretary of State or the Minister (for Ministers)

The Speaker and Deputy Speakers are referred to as 'Mr (or Madam) Speaker' and 'Mr (or Madam) Deputy Speaker'

HANSARD

The full text of debates and oral and written questions for any date since November 1988 is available in Hansard on www.parliament.uk.

Text from Hansard 1803-2005 is available from the Hansard Digitisation Project on http://hansard.millbanksystems.com.

Divisions

What is a division?

A 'division' is the parliamentary term for a vote in the House of Commons. When a division is called, Members of Parliament (MPs) register their vote for or against issues by physically going into one of two rooms on either side of the Commons Chamber. These rooms are called the 'division lobbies' and the procedure is known as 'dividing the House'.

Voting

When a vote is held, the Speaker asks the MPs present in the Chamber to call out whether they agree or not with the question posed. The Speaker will then judge whether there is a clear result. If this cannot be determined, the Speaker calls a division by announcing 'clear the lobbies'.

Division bells

MPs do not have to participate in a debate to be able to vote and may be elsewhere on the parliamentary estate. They are notified that a division is taking place by division bells ringing throughout Parliament and its surrounding premises. These bells have a loud and distinctive ring. When the bells ring, MPs have eight minutes to reach the division lobbies before the lobby doors are locked. In addition, TV screens across the estate display announcements that a division is taking place. These screens are known as 'annuciators' and provide a specialised information feed on the business of the House.

Division lobbies and tellers

During a division, MPs divide into either the Aye lobby or the No lobby. As they pass through the lobbies, the MPs have their names recorded by clerks and are counted by four tellers. The tellers are MPs appointed by each side of the House. Once the lobbies are empty, the results are written down and given to the senior teller. The tellers line up in front of the Table of the House before the Speaker. The teller standing nearest the Opposition despatch box announces the numbers. The written results are then passed to the Speaker who reads the figures again and announces the result. The whole process takes about fifteen minutes.

Tied votes

If the vote is tied – which is very unusual – the Speaker has the casting vote, taking certain principles into account. These principles are that the Speaker should vote for further discussion where possible; that if no further discussion is possible, decisions should not be taken except by a majority and that a casting vote on an amendment to a bill should leave the bill in its existing form

Deferred divisions

In the Commons, instead of holding divisions immediately after the end of a debate, MPs can vote on a series of motions using ballot papers at a convenient time (currently from 12.30pm on Wednesdays). These are known as deferred divisions. Deferred divisions can be used with motions on statutory instruments and on certain types of motion, which are not subject to amendment. Certain types of legislation, such as proceedings on bills, may not be subject to deferred divisions.

The division list

The division list records the way MPs vote and is usually available to the public the following day in Hansard and on Parliament's website.

Why aren't divisions electronic?

Plans to introduce electronic or mechanical voting systems in Parliament have been considered but no single alternative has gained great support. Physically congregating in the division lobbies also gives MPs a good opportunity to conduct business with each other and discuss matters of interest with Ministers in an informal setting.

Abstention

MPs cannot register an abstention but may choose to remain seated in the Chamber during a division to signify their abstention.

Nodding through

If an MP is within the Parliamentary estate but too ill to reach a lobby their vote may be 'nodded through', i.e. added to the voting total in their absence.

Pairing

Pairing is an arrangement between two MPs of opposing parties that allows them to miss occasional votes, with the agreement of their party Whips. MPs are generally only allowed to pair on votes that are not three-line whips. (divisions of the highest importance

Making Laws

Parliament and legislation

One of Parliament's main responsibilities is to scrutinise proposed bills for new laws or changes to existing laws. It is the role of Members of Parliament (MPs) and Members of the House of Lords to examine each bill before it is either approved and becomes an Act, or is rejected. Usually, a bill passes through these stages in one parliamentary session (generally running from November to November). Exceptions can be made to 'carry-over' bills to the next session. Bills can start in either the House of Commons or the House of Lords and must be approved by both Houses before becoming law.

Where do these bills come from?

Most bills that become Acts originate from the Government. Before a government bill is presented to Parliament it is drafted by a team of specialist lawyers. This may take place after a consultation period with the public or after a government policy statement. It is also possible for MPs and Members of the House of Lords to present bills for Parliament to consider.

How bills are considered by Parliament

There is a formal set of stages by which each House scrutinises, challenges and amends (changes) a bill. When both Houses agree on the text, it is sent for Royal Assent and becomes law.

First and Second readings in the Commons and Lords are essentially the same. There is no debate at First reading and at Second reading there is a debate on the general principles of the bill. Government bills are rarely defeated at this stage, but many Private Members' Bills do not progress beyond this point. When a bill has passed its Second reading, it is considered clause by clause in committee and amendments can be made to the text. In the Commons this is often delegated to a Public Bill Committee. In the Lords it usually takes place in Committee of the Whole House in the Lords Chamber. The amended bill is then considered in Report. This stage is similar in both Houses and allows all Members to speak, vote and propose amendments. Third reading in the Commons usually takes place immediately after Report stage and is normally a short one hour debate where no further changes can be made to the bill. Third reading in the Lords can take longer and further changes can be made.

An agreed text

A bill that begins in the Commons is changed, agreed and reprinted before being sent to the Lords where it is further changed, agreed and reprinted.

Changes made by the Lords are sent back to the Commons for consideration. The Commons can agree, reject or amend those changes before sending these back to the Lords. This process continues until the text is agreed or until the end of the Session, in which case the process starts from the beginning in the following Session.

Royal Assent

Bills must receive Royal Assent before becoming Acts. When Royal Assent is given, an announcement is made in both Houses. Legislation may come into force immediately, after a set period or after a commencement order by a government minister.

Other types of bill

Private Members' Bills are initiated by backbench MPs. These are public bills and can be on any issue. Few become law because of time constraints in Parliament. They can also be presented by Peers in the House of Lords.

Private bills are promoted by individuals or organisations outside Parliament (e.g. local authorities or companies) to obtain powers over and above existing public acts.

Recent procedural changes allow public bills to be published in draft for pre-legislative scrutiny, meaning MPs can examine proposed bills before they are introduced in the House. Most of t these draft bills are government bills.

The Parliament Acts

The Parliament acts of 1911 and 1949 are used to limit the powers of the House of Lords to delay the progress of Commons bills.

Following a Bill

Each stage of a bill is recorded in Hansard, Parliament's Official Report

Select Committee Enquiries

What is a select committee?

A select committee is a cross-party group of MPs or Lords who come together to look at a particular subject and make recommendations on how things might be improved. Select committees are established by both the House of Commons and the House of Lords and have powers to summon witnesses and papers as evidence, as part of their inquiries

The membership of select committees is normally comprised of backbench MPs who are appointed to the committee for the whole Parliament (the time between two General Elections). Since 2010 the majority of select committee chairs have been elected by their fellow MPs. House of Commons select committees have been used for many centuries for many different purposes, including investigating a subject rather than simply debating it. The most prominent of Commons committees are those that shadow government departments and contribute to the close scrutiny that government policy receives in Parliament.

Other select committees report on the procedures and administration of the House itself. There is also a Backbench Business Committee, which can schedule business in the Commons Chamber and in Westminster Hall at times set aside for non-government business. House of Lords select committees focus on subject areas, rather than specific government departments – for example, the Science and Technology Committee investigates a wide range of policy issues relating to science, health and medicine, food and the environment. As in the House of Commons, other committees focus on administrative matters.

Some issues require parliamentary scrutiny, and require a committee membership from both Houses e.g. the Joint Committee on Human Rights and the Joint Committee on Statutory Instruments.

Setting up a select committee inquiry

At any one time, a committee may be conducting several inquiries into different issues. When a subject is chosen, it is announced in a press release with a call for evidence from interested parties (although anyone can submit relevant information).

Select committee meetings and support

In committee meetings MPs sit around a horseshoe shaped table. This is a less adversarial layout than the chambers and encourages committees to act in a more collaborative way. Committee staff provide administrative support, gather and analyse evidence, advise the committee on questions or lines of inquiry and help in drafting reports.

Evidence and reports

Once written evidence is received and analysed, it may be supplemented by oral evidence from key witnesses. Oral evidence sessions provide committee members with the opportunity to follow-up on points raised by written submissions and to ask in-depth questions. Evidence sessions are normally held in public. Transcripts are usually published on the Parliament website soon after the session. Study visits may be conducted both in the UK and abroad so committee members can gain first-hand knowledge of the issues. After written and oral evidence has been provided, a report will be prepared by the committee. The text of the report and recommendations made are generally agreed by consensus, although sometimes a vote is required. Once agreed, the report is published and made available on the Internet.

After the report

Government departments are expected to respond to reports from departmental select committees within 60 days. Occasionally, committees then publish a further report addressing the Government response. Some committees follow up reports at later dates, asking Ministers to give further evidence as policy develops or the situation changes. Commons committees can recommend their report for debate in the House. These usually take place in Westminster Hall but three days are available each session for reports to be debated in the Commons Chamber. House of Lords committee reports can be debated in the Lords Chamber.

Select committee enquiries

Details of committee inquiries are on the Internet at: www.parliament.uk/business/committees Select committee inquiries A–Z: www.parliament.uk/business/committees/inquiries-a-z

Places

Big Ben

A brief history

Following the Great Fire of 1834 that destroyed most of the Palace of Westminster, the architect Charles Barry won a competition held to choose a design for the new building. The Astronomer Royal, Sir George Airy, judged another competition to build a clock for inclusion in Barry's design. Although the clock is commonly referred to as Big Ben, Big Ben is in fact the Great Bell, which sounds the hour. Edmund Denison, an amateur horologist, designed the Great Clock and the clockmaker Edward Dent constructed it. The Great Clock was installed in 1859 and started on 31 May. The Great Bell, Big Ben, began striking on 11 July 1859.

The Elizabeth Tower

In 2012, the Clock Tower was renamed the Elizabeth Tower in recognition of HM The Queen's Diamond Jubilee. The Speaker unveiled a plaque to mark the name change on 12 September 2012.
The outside of the tower is covered with Anston stone from Yorkshire. Inside, Caen stone from Normandy is used. The spire is covered with cast iron plates

Although no longer accessible, there are rooms in the tower which were used in the past to detain MPs or peers for breach of conduct. They were last used in 1880 when Charles Bradlaugh MP, an atheist, refused to take the oath of allegiance to Queen Victoria on the Bible.

The Great Clock

The Great Clock is accurate to within one second. Weights, including pre-decimal pennies, sit on a shelf on the pendulum rod. Adding or removing weight on the pendulum regulates the clock.

So fine is the balance that adding one penny will cause the clock to gain two-fifths of a second in 24 hours. Denison invented the "Double Three-Legged Gravity Escapement" which is crucial to the clock's accuracy. The first strike on Big Ben, the hour bell, indicates the hour. A microphone enables the BBC to broadcast the Westminster chimes world-wide. Beneath each clock dial a Latin inscription reads: "O Lord, make safe our Queen Victoria the First". Above the belfry is the Ayrton Light named after Acton Smee Ayrton, First Commissioner of Works. It was installed in 1885 and it is lit whenever either House is sitting after dark.

Big Ben – the Great Bell

Big Ben is thought to be named after Sir Benjamin Hall, Chief Commissioner of Works at the time the bell was installed. The first bell, cast in 1856 at Stockton-on-Tees, was brought to London by rail and sea. During tests in New Palace Yard a fatal crack appeared. The bell was broken up and a second bell was cast at the Whitechapel Bell Foundry. After successful tests this bell was hauled sideways up a shaft inside the Tower. After a few months the new bell also cracked and was silent for four years. It was restored to full voice in 1863 when the bell was turned by a quarter turn and a lighter hammer was installed.

Facts and figures

The Elizabeth Tower is over 96m high and 12m square. There are 334 steps to the belfry and another 59 to the Ayrton Light. The clock dials, framed in cast iron and glazed with 312 separate pieces of opal glass, are 7m in diameter. The centre of each dial is 55m from the ground. The hour hands are made of gunmetal, each 2.7m long and weighing about 300kg including counterweights. The minute hands are made of copper sheet 4.2m long. They weigh 100kg, including counterweights, and travel a distance equalling 190 kilometres (120 miles) a year. The clock mechanism weighs about 5 tonnes. The pendulum is 4.4m long overall and weighs 310kg. The pendulum bob weighs 203kg and the three-clock weight a total of nearly 2.5 tonnes. Big Ben, the bell, measures 2.7m in diameter, 2.2m in height, and weighs 13.7 tonnes. The four-quarter bells weigh between 1 and 4 tonnes each. The hammer, which strikes Big Ben, weighs 200kg.

Broadcasting the Chimes
The BBC first broadcast the Westminster Chimes on New Year's Eve 1923.

Energy Efficiency
The clock dials were originally lit by gas. Today, energy efficient electric bulbs are used, each with a life of 60,000 hours.

The Westminster Chimes
Big Ben (note E natural) and the four-quarter bells (G sharp, F sharp, E and B), sound the Westminster Chimes. The chimes are set to the following lines: "All through this hour, Lord be my Guide. And by thy power, no foot shall slide".

The House of Commons Chamber

The Chamber

The House of Commons Chamber is where Members of Parliament (MPs) debate and vote on important issues. The main business of the House takes place here and can involve MPs putting questions to government ministers, debating issues of national importance and passing legislation.

The Speaker's Chair and the Table of the House provide a focal point in the Chamber at its north end. There are green leather benches on either side where MPs sit: looking towards the Speaker's Chair the government sit on the left and the opposition parties on the right. The front benches are reserved for government ministers and opposition spokespeople. Only MPs are allowed to sit on the benches in the Chamber.

Ministers and the Official Opposition's shadow ministers stand at the despatch boxes to address the House. The Mace, a ceremonial staff of office representing the authority of House of Commons, is placed on the Table of the House when it is sitting.

Visiting the Chamber

The public gallery of the Chamber is accessible when the House is sitting, via the Cromwell Green Visitor Entrance. Visitors watch proceedings from behind a security screen installed in 2006 Sound is provided through a speaker system. UK residents can ask their MP to arrange a tour of Parliament, which includes walking through the Chamber.

Wartime damage

During the Second World War, on 10 May 1941, a bombing raid destroyed the House of Commons Chamber. MPs used the House of Lords Chamber until the Commons was rebuilt. The new Chamber, designed by Sir Giles Gilbert Scott, was used for the first time on 26 October 1950.

Reporting from the Chamber

The Press Gallery is located above and behind the Speaker's Chair. In 1803, Speaker Abbot recognised the need to protect the right of reporters to be in the gallery. His successors have strongly defended that right and access for accredited journalists have been guaranteed ever since. The Press Gallery now represents more than 300 newspapers, wire service, radio, television and Internet journalists who work at Westminster.

Broadcasting from the Chamber

The BBC is required by its Licence and Agreement to "broadcast an impartial account day by day, prepared by professional reporters, of the proceedings of both Houses of Parliament". This requirement has been met by the *Today in Parliament* radio programme since October 1945. Sound recordings of proceedings in the Chamber began in 1978

In 1990, after a trial period, the House of Commons agreed that its proceedings should also be televised. Today, BBC Parliament offers live unedited coverage of the House of Commons on cable, digital satellite and Freeview. BBC Parliament also offers 'recorded as live' coverage of the House of Lords; extensive coverage of select and standing committees and full live coverage of the main political party conferences as well as proceedings in devolved assemblies. BBC 2, BBC News Channel and Sky News show Prime Minister's Questions live, along with some ministerial statements and committee evidence, extending coverage to other important debates such as the Budget. In addition to this, most channels use brief extracts of parliamentary material in news bulletins and current affairs programmes. Live and archived coverage of Parliament's proceedings taking place in public, including debates and committee meetings of both Houses is also available on the Internet at www.parliamentlive.tv

Traditions in the chamber

MPs are not allowed to speak in the space between two red lines running along the length of the Chamber. It has been claimed these lines are traditionally two swords' lengths apart to prevent MPs duelling although there is no evidence to support this. St Stephen's Chapel the original debating chambers for the House of Commons was Saint Stephen's Chapel in the Palace of Westminster given by King Edward VI in 1547.

Parliament and The House of Commons Parliament and democracy

Parliament is made up of three parts: The House of Commons, the House of Lords and the Sovereign.

In the House of Commons, Members of Parliament (MPs) are elected as part of the democratic process. Following a general election, the political party with the most MPs forms the Government. Members of the House of Lords are mostly appointed by the Sovereign on the recommendation of the Prime Minister; some are internally elected. A small number of Church of England archbishops and bishops are also Members. The Sovereign fulfils a formal and ceremonial role, approving Royal Assent for bills and attending the State Opening of Parliament.

Parliament and Government

Parliament and Government are separate institutions. They work closely together but have distinct roles.

The Government is responsible for running the country, implementing policy and drafting laws. Parliament is responsible for checking the Government's work making and amending laws and representing the people. After a general election, the party leader who commands a majority in the House of Commons is asked to form a Government by the Sovereign and is appointed Prime Minister. This MP is usually the leader of the largest political party. The Prime Minister recommends ministers for formal appointment by the Sovereign Ministers run their government departments and propose new legislation by presenting bills to Parliament. The main business for debate in Parliament is, in general, decided by the party whips (often referred to as *the usual channels*) though this is dominated in the Commons by the government whips. This ensures that the Government can implement the policies it was elected to carry out. Roles of the House of Commons

Scrutinising Government

The House of Commons scrutinises government policies to ensure that the Government is working for the benefit of those living in the UK. This scrutiny includes „. MPs questioning government ministers either in the House or through written parliamentary questions. This process helps to inform MPs of the work of Government and to hold ministers to account.

Select committees, which 'shadow' government departments and carry out inquiries into issues of concern.

The Government is required to provide witnesses and evidence for inquiries and must respond to committee recommendations. MPs debating issues in the House and questioning ministers when they make statements.

Proposing and amending legislation

Parliament is responsible for making laws. Most legislation comes from the Government but proposals can originate from an MP, a Lord, a member of the public or a private group. The House of Commons and House of Lords must agree the text of any proposed legislation before it can become law.

Representing the people

The UK is divided into areas, called constituencies, each of which elects a single MP to represent them in Parliament. All residents of a constituency can contact the local MP about issues that affect them or that are being considered by Parliament. It does not matter whether they voted for the MP or even if they are entitled to vote at all.

Taxation

As the democratically elected part of Parliament, the House of Commons has the right to raise taxes. This provides the Government with money to deliver its policies. The Chancellor of the Exchequer presents the Budget to the House annually and the House passes a Finance Act to approve the taxes.

Opposition Days

Opposition days allow the opposition parties in the House of Commons to determine the topic for debate rather than the Government. There are usually about 20 opposition days in a parliamentary session, with the Official Opposition party being allocated 17 days.

The Right to Vote

UK citizens over the age of 18 can vote in parliamentary elections.

Parliament the Institution

Parliament's evolution

Parliament, as a political institution, has developed over hundreds of years. During this period, the two distinct Houses, Commons and Lords have emerged and the balance of power between Parliament and the monarchy has changed dramatically.

Origins of Parliament – King's councils

The origins of Parliament go back to the 12th century, when King's councils were held involving barons and archbishops. They discussed politics and were involved in taxation and judgments. The balance of power lying with the monarch.

Over time, these councils took a more formal role and saw knights representing each county. This was the beginning of a Commons element in Parliament. The first known official use of the term 'Parliament' was in 1236. The word Parliament derives from the French word parler, meaning to talk and discuss things.

Two Houses

By the 14th century two distinct Houses, the Commons and the Lords, had developed. The Commons involved representatives from counties, towns and cities. The first spokesman to be termed Speaker in the official record was Thomas Hungerford. The Lords membership was made up of the nobility and clergy, known as the Lords Temporal and the Lords Spiritual

The rise of the Commons

In 1414, it was agreed that the King and the Lords should not change the wording of any bills submitted by the Commons without its agreement and that no bill should become an Act without Commons assent.

By the mid-15th century, the Commons was in control of granting funds to the King and was on an equal footing with the Lords regarding the creation and amendment of statutes.

The Reformation Parliament

Parliament was still subject to being summoned by the King. During Henry VIII's reign, Parliament passed laws, which transferred religious authority from the Pope to the King with the formation of the Church of England. Henry VIII realised that royal power was at its strongest when it was expressed through parliamentary statute.

Civil war and the Restoration

The reign of Charles I, beginning in 1625, saw civil war break out between supporters of Parliament and the monarchy. In 1649, Charles I was tried in Westminster Hall and executed. A Commonwealth led by Oliver Cromwell was established and a series of Parliaments were elected using different constitutional rules. In 1660, the monarchy was restored under King Charles II.

Parliament's position was strengthened when the Bill of Rights was agreed in 1689. This established Parliament's authority over the monarch. From this date, Parliament would be responsible for passing or repealing all laws.

Parliament and the home nations

The 1707 Act of Union between England and Scotland saw the nations' individual Parliaments replaced by the new Parliament of Great Britain. After the 1800 Act of Union with Ireland, the Dublin Parliament was abolished and Irish MPs and Lords were represented in the Westminster Parliament.

Extending the vote

In the 19th century, the Reform Acts of 1832, 1867 and 1884 extended the number of men eligible to vote creating a more democratic, representative Parliament. However, women were still excluded from voting and did not gain the right to vote until 1918 after the suffragette campaigns and the impact of the First World War.

Parliament Acts - 1911 and 1949

The Parliament Acts of 1911 and 1949 increased the authority of the Commons over the Lords when passing new laws. The Acts removed the powers of the Lords to amend any Bills concerning money and reduced the amount of time they could delay a bill.

Parliament Live

Parliament Live video and audio on www.parliament. uk carries live and archived coverage of all UK Parliament proceedings taking place in public, including select and general committees of both Houses. The material is available from an on-demand archive going back to 1 July 2009.

Westminster Hall

Over 900 years of history...

Westminster Hall is the oldest remaining part of the original Palace of Westminster and has great historical and architectural importance. It has witnessed many events during its 900-year history, including fire, dramatic legal trials and coronation banquets. It has even been a shopping arcade and has housed law courts. Today it is used for ceremonial addresses and public exhibitions.

Building the Hall

The Hall was commissioned in 1097 under William II (Rufus), the son of William the Conqueror, and was completed two years later. At the time, the Hall was by far the largest hall in England, and probably in Europe, measuring 73m by 20m, covering a floor area of 1547m.
The Hall's walls were built two metres thick. Inside, there was an arcade with large arches and windows. Above the windows was a chequer-work pattern of light and dark stones. The Hall's inside walls were plastered and painted with decorative hangings draped from the arcade.

The hammer-beam roof

The magnificent hammer-beam roof of Westminster Hall is the largest medieval timber roof in Northern Europe. Measuring 20.7 by 73.2m, the roof was commissioned in 1393 by Richard II and is a masterpiece of design.

The design work was undertaken by the King's chief mason Henry Yevele and by carpenter Hugh Herland. Great oak beams provided horizontal support and the walls were strengthened by massive buttresses. Wooden arches joined to the beams met centrally across a span of 18m or more.

Craftsmen then built the roof with its weight borne by the beams, which were in turn supported by the buttressed walls. Richard II commissioned other additions to the Hall, including angels carved on beams and sculptures of England's kings since Edward the Confessor complete with gilded crowns and painted robes.

A royal palace

The Hall played an important role in royal life through the centuries. Feasts and entertainment's were held there with masques, music, dancing and jousting taking place in front of hundreds of guests.

Between 1189 and 1821, the Hall was the traditional venue for coronation banquets for newly crowned monarchs. Richard III's coronation banquet was attended by 3000 guests with galleries specially built to accommodate them. The King's champion rode through the Hall on horseback, challenging anyone to deny the King's right to succeed. On becoming King in 1830, William IV chose not to hold a coronation banquet in the Hall on the grounds of expense and the tradition ended.

The Hall in danger

In 1834, a fire started in the House of Lords and spread northwards towards the Hall, destroying existing buildings in its path and threatening the Hall's wooden roof. The Prime Minister, Lord Melbourne, quickly directed efforts to douse the roof with water, saving the Hall although much of the Palace's other buildings were lost in May 1941, on the last day of the blitz, both the House of Commons Chamber and Westminster Hall were hit by incendiary bombs. A decision was made once again to concentrate efforts on saving the medieval Hall at the cost of the Chamber, which was completely destroyed.

Trials in Westminster Hall

The Hall has witnessed many high-profile legal trials, including Sir William Wallace the Scottish patriot, Sir Thomas More adviser to Henry VIII, Guy Fawkes and the Gunpowder Plot conspirators, all of who were sentenced to death. The most famous trial held in the Hall was the trial of Charles I who was sentenced to death there on 27 January 1649. The Royal Courts of Justice were based in Westminster Hall until moving to the building they currently occupy on The Strand in 1882. Alongside the law courts, there were shops selling legal paraphernalia, wigs, pens and stationery.

Lying in State

The Hall has been used for the lying-in-state of monarchs and great parliamentarians, including George V, Queen Elizabeth the Queen Mother, William Ewart Gladstone and Sir Winston Churchill.

Beheaded

Oliver Cromwell's head was impaled on a spike on Westminster Hall's roof after his body was exhumed and decapitated in 1661 by Charles II's supporters, following the restoration of the monarchy. It remained there for at least 20 years.

Elections and voting

Voting systems in the UK

The House of Commons, devolved assemblies and mayors in the UK are elected using different voting systems. The House of Commons and the House of Lords use a variety of voting systems for internal elections.

Voting systems

Voting systems, also known as electoral systems, are the method by which we elect representatives. A voting system determines the rules on how parties and candidates are elected.

A number of different voting systems are used to elect mayors and representatives to the House of Commons, Scottish Parliament, National Assembly for Wales, Northern Ireland Assembly, European Parliament and UK local authorities.

First-past-the-post

First-past-the-post is used to elect MPs to the House of Commons and for local elections in England and Wales.

Under first-past-the-post, the UK or local authority is divided into numerous voting areas, i.e. constituencies or wards. At a general or local election, voters put a cross (X) next to their preferred candidate on a ballot paper.

Ballot papers are then counted and the candidate that has received the most votes is elected to represent the constituency or ward.

Alternative Vote (AV)

The Alternative Vote is used to elect the majority of chairs of select committees in the House of Commons. The AV is also used for the election of the Lord Speaker and by-elections for hereditary peers.

Under AV, voters rank candidates in order of preference by marking 1, 2, 3 and so on next to names of candidates on a ballot paper. A voter can rank as many or as few candidates as they like or just vote for one candidate.

Ballot papers are then counted by using the first preference votes (i.e. those with a number 1 marked next to their name). If a candidate receives more than 50 per cent of the first preference votes then they are elected.

If no candidate reaches this 50 per cent threshold, then the candidate with the fewest first preference votes is eliminated. Their second preference votes are then reallocated to the remaining candidates. If after this stage one candidate has more votes than the other remaining candidates put together, that candidate is elected.

If not, the process of elimination and reallocation of preference votes is repeated until one candidate has more votes than the other remaining candidates put together, and is then elected.

Supplementary Vote (SV)

The Supplementary Vote system is used to elect the Mayor of London and other elected mayors in England and Wales.

The SV system is very similar to the AV system. Under SV, voters are limited to a first and second preference choice. A voter marks a cross in one column for their first preference candidate and another cross in a second column for their second preference (if they wish to do so).

The ballot papers are counted and if a candidate received more than 50 per cent of the first preference votes on the first count, then they are elected.

If no candidate reaches the 50 per cent threshold, the two candidates with the highest number of votes are retained and the other candidates are eliminated. The second preferences on the ballot papers of the eliminated candidates are counted and any cast for the two remaining candidates are transferred. The candidate with the most votes at the end of this process is elected.

Single Transferable Vote (STV)

The Single Transferable Vote system is used to elect the Deputy Speakers in the House of Commons. STV is also used for electing the Northern Ireland Assembly, local elections in Scotland and Northern Ireland and European Parliament elections in Northern Ireland.

Multi-member constituencies are required for STV, which means constituencies, are normally larger but elect several representatives rather than just one.

Under STV, voters rank candidates in order of preference by marking 1, 2, 3 and so on next to the names of candidates on a ballot paper. A voter can rank as many or as few candidates as they like or just vote for one candidate.

Each candidate needs a minimum number of votes to be elected. This number is calculated according to the number of seats and votes cast and are called a quota. The first preference votes for each candidate are added up and any candidate who has achieved this quota is elected.

If a candidate has more votes than are needed to fill the quota, that candidate's surplus votes are transferred to the remaining candidates. Votes that would have gone to the winner instead go to the second preference listed on those ballot papers.

If candidates do not meet the quota, the candidate with the fewest first preference votes is eliminated and the second preference votes are transferred to other candidates. These processes are repeated until all the seats are filled.

Additional Member System (AMS)

The Additional Member System is used to elect the Scottish Parliament, the National Assembly for Wales and the London Assembly.

Under AMS, voters are given two votes; one for an individual candidate and one for a party. Individual candidates are elected to single-member constituencies using first-past-the-post (or the second ballot or alternative vote). Under the second, party vote, representatives (additional members) are elected proportionally to a larger region.

The percentage of votes obtained by the parties in the party vote (second ballot) determines the overall number of representatives including those elected for the single member constituencies after taking into account the seats gained in each region by each party in the first ballot.

Closed Party List

The Closed Party List system is used to elect Members of the European Parliament, with the exception of Northern Ireland, which uses Single Transferable Vote.

A voter marks a cross on the ballot paper next to the party's name they wish to support. Once the ballot papers have been counted, each party gets the number of seats proportionate to the number of votes it has received in each constituency.

Multi-member constituencies are required for the Closed Party List which means constituencies are normally larger but elect several representatives rather than just one.

As voters choose parties rather than candidates, it is for the parties to determine the order in which candidates appear on the list and are then elected.

General elections

When Parliament is dissolved every seat in the House of Commons becomes vacant and a general election is held. Each constituency in the UK elects one MP (Member of Parliament) to a seat in the House of Commons. The political party that wins a majority of seats in the House of Commons usually forms the Government.

How often are general elections held?

The date of the next general election is set at 7 May 2015 after the Fixed Term Parliament Act was passed on 15 September 2011.

The act provides for general elections to be held on the first Thursday in May every five years. There are two provisions that trigger an election other than at five year intervals.

A motion of no confidence is passed in Her Majesty's Government by a simple majority and 14 days elapses without the House passing a confidence motion in any new Government formed. A motion for a general election is agreed by two thirds of the total number of seats in the Commons including vacant seats (currently 434 out of 650) Previous to this act, the duration of a Parliament was set at five years, although many were dissolved before that, at the request of the Prime Minister to the Queen.

How does it work?

MPs are elected from a choice of candidates by a simple majority system in which each person casts one vote. The candidate with the most votes then becomes the MP for that constituency.

Candidates may be from a political party registered with the Electoral Commission or they may stand as an 'Independent' rather than represent a registered party.

Where do people vote?

Most voting takes place in polling stations but anyone eligible to vote can apply for a postal vote. British citizens living abroad are also entitled to a postal vote as long as they have been living abroad for less than 15 years.

Last general election

The last general election in the UK took place on 6 May 2010:

No single party won an overall majority at the 2010 General Election, for the first time in the UK since February 1974. The Conservatives won the most seats, 305, gaining 96compared with notional 2005 general election results on the new constituency boundaries.
Labour lost 90 seats, leaving them with 258, while the Liberal Democrats were down five on 57. *General Election 2010* provides a summary of the results of the General Election held on 6 May 2010. It provides a first analysis of voting. The data for vote's cast and electorates have been checked with local authority returning officers. A detailed paper with more in-depth analysis, including regional and constituency analysis will follow.

By-elections

A by-election takes place when a seat in the House of Commons becomes vacant between general elections.

Reasons for by-elections

A seat becomes vacant during the lifetime of a Parliament either when an MP resigns from Parliament, for example to take up a job, which by law cannot be done by an MP, or because an MP has died. The law also allows a seat to be declared vacant because of a Member's bankruptcy, mental illness or conviction for a serious criminal offence.

A by-election does not automatically take place if an MP changes political party.

Until a new MP is elected, constituency matters are handled by an MP of the same party in a neighbouring constituency.

'Moving the Writ'

Traditionally the Chief Whip of the political party whose MP held the vacant seat will begin the procedure for a by-election. This is known as 'moving the Writ' and takes the form of a motion in the House of Commons.

By-election timetable

A new Writ is moved within three months of the vacancy occurring. There have been a few instances of seats remaining vacant longer than six months before a by-election was called. Seats have also been left vacant towards the end of a Parliament to be filled at the general election.

If there are several vacant seats then a number of by-elections can take place on the same day.

Parliamentary constituencies

The UK is currently divided into 650 parliamentary constituencies, each of which is represented by one MP in the House of Commons. Although constituencies vary widely in area, the average number of voters in each constituency is approximately 68,175.

Constituency breakdown

There are currently 533 constituencies in England, 59 in Scotland, 40 in Wales and 18 in Northern Ireland.

Boundary Commissions

Constituency boundaries were kept under review by four permanent Boundary Commissions, one each for England, Scotland, Wales and Northern Ireland. The Commissions made reports at regular intervals recommending any necessary changes due to population change or changes in local government boundaries.

What is my constituency?

You can find out what constituency you are in, and the MP who represents that constituency, by using the Find your MP service.

Swearing in and the parliamentary oath

Members of both Houses of Parliament are required by law to take an oath of allegiance to the Crown before they take their seats in Parliament after a general election or by-election and after the death of the monarch. Any MP or Member of the House of Lords who objects to swearing an oath can makes a solemn affirmation instead. This process is known as swearing in.

Until the oath or affirmation is taken, an MP may not receive a salary, take their seat, and speak in debates or vote. They could also be fined £500 and – more important – have their seat declared vacant "as if they were dead" if they attempt to do so.

Similar restrictions apply to Members of the Lords: they may not sit, vote or receive allowances until they take the oath or affirmation.

Wording of the oaths

The wording of the oaths and the way the oaths are taken in both Houses was established in the Oaths Act 1978.

An MP takes the oath by holding the sacred text in his or her uplifted hand and says the words:

I (name of Member) swear by Almighty God that I will be faithful and bear true allegiance to Her Majesty Queen Elizabeth, her heirs and successors, according to law. So help me God.
The Act also permits the oath to be taken in the Scottish manner, with uplifted hand but not holding the sacred text. Members who want to do so may also take the oath as prescribed in the Promissory Oaths Act 1868, by kissing the book and using the words:

I (name of Member) do swear that I will be faithful and bear true allegiance to Her Majesty Queen Elizabeth, her heirs and successors, according to law. So help me God.
Alternatively, Members may under the Oaths Act 1978 make a solemn affirmation instead of taking an oath, using the words:

I (name of Member) do solemnly, sincerely, and truly declare and affirm, that I will be faithful and bear true allegiance to Her Majesty Queen Elizabeth, her heirs and successors, according to law.
Texts of the oath and affirmation in Braille are available for use by Members of both Houses with impaired sight.

The oath/affirmation must be made/taken initially in English, but Members of both Houses may, if they wish, to follow this with an oath or affirmation in Welsh, Scottish Gaelic or Cornish. Oath/affirmation cards in these languages are available at the time of swearing-in.

Welsh wording

Yr wyf yn addo, trwy gymorth y Goruchaf, y byddaf yn ffyddlon ac yn wir deyrngar i'w Mawrhydi, y Frenhines Elizabeth, ei hetifeddion a'i holynwyr, yn ôl y Ddeddf, yn wyneb Duw.
Scottish Gaelic wording

Tha mi a' mionnachadh air DIA UILECHUMHACHDACH gum bi mi dìleas agus daingeann d'a Mòrachd, a' Bhan-Rìgh Ealasaid, a h-Oighrean agus ladsan a thig na h-Aite, a'rèir an Lagha. DIA gam chuideachadh.
Cornish wording

Me a le gans Dew Ollgallojak del vedhaf len ha perthy omryans gwyr dhe Hy Braster an Vyternes Elisabet, hy Erys ha Sewyoryon, herwyth an laha. Ytho Dew re'm gweressa.
A new Parliament

After a general election, the new Parliament is opened by the Royal Commission in the House of Lords, in the presence of Members of both Houses, after which the House of Commons meets to elect a Speaker and the Lords commences oath taking.

Taking the oath in the House of Commons

At the start of a new Parliament, all MPs (whether or not they have been MPs in the past) must take the oath of allegiance or make a solemn affirmation.

After the Commons Speaker has taken the oath, MPs come forward one by one to swear or affirm at the despatch box. MPs take the oath/affirm in order of seniority:

- Father of the House (the longest continuous serving Member)
- Cabinet Ministers
- Shadow Cabinet Ministers
- Privy Counsellors
- Other Ministers
- Other Members in order of seniority (by the Parliament of first entry or, for those with broken service, that of most recent entry)

The Principal Clerk of the Table Office at the despatch box offers a choice of affirmation or oath cards to read. If the MP wishes to swear on a sacred text, that will be provided. At the Table are:

- the New Testament
- the Old Testament (in English and Hebrew, or in Hebrew)
- the Koran
- the Granth
- the Welsh Bible
- the Gaelic Bible

Those books which may not be handled by non-believers are kept in slip-cases.

The MP takes the oath or affirms, then moves along the Table to the Clerk Assistant and signs the Test Roll, a parchment book headed by the oath and affirmation which is kept by the Clerk of the House of Commons.

Finally, the MP is introduced to the Commons Speaker by the Clerk of the House. After shaking the Speaker's hand, the MP goes behind the Speaker's Chair, where staff will take a signature for recognition purposes and ask how the MP wishes to be known in House documents.

The initial period of swearing in lasts for about two hours. Most MPs are sworn on the first day, although the House of Commons will also meet for swearing-in on following days.

Taking the oath in the House of Lords

The swearing in procedure for taking the oath is similar in the House of Lords. Immediately after the Royal Commission for the opening of Parliament, Members of the Lords present their writs of summons at the Table of the House and take the oath or subscribe to the affirmation.

Members are also required to sign an undertaking to abide by the House of Lords Code of Conduct as part of the swearing in procedure for the new 2010 Parliament. This implements a new Code of Conduct, agreed by the House on 30 November 2009.

State Opening

After the initial swearing in process most MPs and Members of the Lords are able to sit and vote in each House. Any remaining MPs or Members of the Lords can take the oath at later sittings.

When the majority of MPs and Members of the Lords have been sworn in, both Houses of Parliament are ready to hear the Queen's Speech at the State Opening starting the business of the session.

Seniority of MPs

If two or more MPs enter the House at the same election their seniority is determined by the date and/or time they took the oath. This matters when questions of seniority between them arise, for example when deciding who might become Father of the House many years later.

By-elections and MPs

MPs who have been elected at a by-election are accompanied from the bar of the House by two sponsors. The new Member will have collected a certificate relating to his or her election from the Public Bill Office to hand to the Clerk of the House before taking the oath or making the affirmation.

Related information:

The requirement to take an oath dates back to the Reformation and the Supremacy of the Crown Act 1562. The current wording of the oath was established in the Promissory Oaths Act 1868.

Any MP or Member of the House of Lords, who objects to swearing an oath can, instead, makes a solemn affirmation, under the terms of the Oaths Act 1978. MPs who have not sworn in may not receive salaries, take their seats, and speak in debates or vote.

Charles Bradlaugh was elected to Parliament in 1880. An atheist, he asked to be allowed to affirm rather than take an oath. This was refused; fellow MPs objected and stated that, as an atheist, he was not competent to take an oath. In a subsequent Parliament he took his seat without taking the oath, voted three times and was fined £1,500.

Permission to substitute a solemn affirmation for an oath was eventually granted by the Oaths Act 1888.

Daily business

The business of both Houses follows a similar daily pattern. An example of the main business in each House is set out below.

Prayers

Sittings in both Houses begin with prayers. These follow the Christian faith and there is currently no multi-faith element. Attendance is voluntary.

The practice of prayers is believed to have started in about 1558, and was common practice by 1567. The present form of prayers probably dates from the reign of Charles II. Members of the public are not allowed into the public galleries during prayers.

In the Commons

The Speaker's Chaplain usually reads the prayers. The form of the main prayer is as follows:

"Lord, the God of righteousness and truth, grant to our Queen and her government, to Members of Parliament and all in positions of responsibility, the guidance of your Spirit. May they never lead the nation wrongly through love of power, desire to please, or unworthy ideals but laying aside all private interests and prejudices keep in mind their responsibility to seek to improve the condition of all mankind; so may your kingdom come and your name be hallowed.

Amen."

In the Lords

A senior Bishop (Lord Spiritual) who sits in the Lords usually reads the prayers. Prayers are read at the beginning of each sitting. The text of the Prayers read in the House of Lords is printed in the Companion to the Standing Orders.
Read the Lords' Prayers for the Parliament

Custom and practice

MPs and Peers stand for prayers facing the wall behind them. It is thought this practice developed due to the difficulty Members would historically have faced of kneeling to pray while wearing a sword.

Question Time Commons chamber

Question Time is an opportunity for MPs and Members of the House of Lords to question government ministers about matters for which they are responsible.

These questions are asked at the start of business in both chambers and are known as 'oral questions'. The Prime Minister answers questions in the Commons every Wednesday.

House of Commons

Question Time takes place for an hour, Monday to Thursday, after prayers. Each government department answers questions according to a rota called the Order of Oral Questions. The questions asked must relate to the responsibilities of the government department concerned.

House of Lords

Question Time (Oral Questions) takes place at the beginning of the day's business for up to 30 minutes on Mondays to Thursdays. Lords questions are to the Government as a whole, not to particular government departments (as they are in the Commons).

Notice of questions in the Commons

Commons oral questions are tabled by MPs at least three days in advance of Question Time. The questions are then printed in the Commons Questions Book. The order in which the questions are asked is determined randomly by a computer.

MPs who are called by the Speaker to ask their question do not read it out, but simply call out its number. When the government minister has replied, the MP can ask another question (known as a supplementary) and other MPs may also be called to ask supplementary questions. The Minister must reply to each in turn. Supplementary questions must be on the same subject as the original question.

The last 15 minutes (for those departments with a 60 minute question time) or 10 minutes (for those departments with a 40 minute question time) of question time is reserved for 'topical questions'.

During the 'topical questions' slot, MPs can ask supplementary questions on any subject relating to the department's responsibilities.

Notice of questions in the Lords

Lords Oral Questions can be tabled anywhere between 1 month and 24 hours in advance. The questions are printed in the Lords Order Paper. Slots are reserved for 'topical questions', tabled two days in advance.

Prime Minister's Question Time

The Prime Minister answers questions from MPs in the Commons for half an hour every Wednesday from Midday.

The session normally starts with a routine question from an MP about the Prime Minister's engagements. This is known as an 'open question' and means that the MP can then ask a supplementary question on any subject.

Following the answer, the MP then raises a particular issue, often one of current political significance. The Leader of the Opposition then follows up on this or another topic, they are permitted to ask a total of six questions. The Leader of the Opposition is the only MP who is allowed to come back with further questions.

Most MPs will table the same question about engagements and if they do, only their names will appear on the question book. After the first engagements question has been asked, any other MPs who have tabled the same question are simply called to ask an untabled, supplementary question. This means, in theory, that the Prime Minister will not know what questions will be asked of him. However, the Prime Minister will be extensively briefed by government departments in anticipation of likely subjects he could be asked about.

Table or Tabling: When MPs or Members of the Lords hand in questions, amendments to Bills or notices of motions, or when a document is formally placed before either House.

Urgent Questions

If something has happened which an MP believes requires an immediate answer from a Government Minister, they may apply to ask an urgent question. If the Speaker (or in the House of Lords the Lord Speaker) agrees that the matter is urgent and important, the question will be asked at the end of question time.

Applications for urgent questions must be submitted to the speaker to receive an oral answer on the same day. Relevant interests must also be declared. The relevant Government department will be asked to provide a background briefing on the issue for the speaker.

Urgent questions are asked straight after question time on Monday to Thursday. If an urgent question is asked on a sitting Friday then the question will be asked at 11am.

Ministerial statements

After Question Time (and any urgent questions that may have been allowed) a government minister may make an oral statement to the House. Notice of statements is not usually given until the day they are to be made.

House of Commons

Oral statements are made after Question Time (or at 11am on a Friday). The statements usually relate to matters of policy or government actions.

A business statement announces the future business of the Commons and usually takes place on Thursdays at 11.30am.

At the end of a statement MPs can respond or question the government minister on its contents.

House of Lords

Commons statements will sometimes be repeated in the Lords at an appropriate time to fit in with the main business.

Personal statements

Other statements are occasionally made, for example, by an MP who has resigned as a Minister or wishes to correct an error in a statement they have made to the House of Commons. These statements can only be made with permission of the Speaker.

In the House of Lords a Peer can make a short personal statement in order to correct information given in a speech by them or to reply to claims made about them in the House.

Read ministerial statements

Ministerial statements are published in Hansard, the edited record of what was said in Parliament.
Read Hansard

Urgent question: If something has happened which a Member believes requires an immediate answer from a government minister, he may apply to ask an urgent question. If the Speaker (or in the House of Lords, the Lord Speaker) agrees that the matter is urgent and important, the question will be asked at the end of Question Time.

Read Hansard

Read Questions and debates going back to 1988. Older editions of Hansard are held by the Parliamentary Archives.

Application for emergency debates

An emergency debate is a debate called at short notice in the House of Commons on a matter that should have urgent consideration. An MP may apply to the Speaker for an emergency debate under the rules of Standing Order No. 24.

Members may seek an emergency debate from the Speaker on Mondays to Thursdays during sitting time. If the Speaker has given the member leave they will have three minutes to make a speech after question time. The Speaker then decides whether to submit the application to the House.

The House will have to agree that the debate takes place. If the House agrees the debate will take place on a future day, it is usually the next sitting day. The motion to be debated will be "That the House has considered the matter of [Topic]"

Applications for emergency debates in the House of Commons since May 2012

MP	Debate Title	Date	Decision of the House	Proposal for debate
Peter Bone	Wellingborough Prison	17.06.12	Declined	c854
Tim Farron	West Coast Main Line	03.09.12	Declined	c69
Caroline Nokes	The closure of the Ford assembly plant at Swaythling	29.10.12	Declined	c52
Jeremy Lefroy	mid Staffordshire NHS Foundation Trust special administrator	05.03.13	Declined	c863
David Cameron	Royal Charter on Press Conduct	18.03.13	Agreed	c630

Main business (Debates)

The main business in both chambers often takes the form of a debate. This includes debates on legislation, general topics of interest or issues selected by the major parties.

What is a debate?

A debate is a formal discussion on a Bill or topic of interest or importance.

A typical debate takes the following form:

A Member introduces a subject (known as moving a motion); e.g., 'I beg to move, That the Bill be now read a Second time'.

The Speaker in the Commons or Lord Speaker in the Lords proposes a question, which repeats the terms of the motion; e.g., 'The Question is, That the Bill be now read a second time'.

The motion is debated.

The original question is repeated and the House comes to a decision - if necessary by means of a vote (division).

Members take it in turns to speak on the subject concerned and the discussion is strictly controlled by a set of rules called the 'Standing Orders'.

Debates in the Commons - The Speaker

In the Commons, an MP called the 'Speaker' chairs debates and calls MPs in turn to give their opinion on an issue. MPs must get the Speaker's attention (called 'catching the Speaker's eye') and usually stand, or half-rise from their seat to do so. They may also write in advance to indicate their wish to speak, although this gives no guarantee.

MPs address their speeches to the Speaker or their deputy, using notes only. Normally MPs will speak only once in a debate, although they may 'intervene' with a brief comment on another member's speech. MPs who introduced the subject of debate (called 'tabling a motion') have the right to reply to speeches.

Debates in the Lords - The Lord Speaker

The Lord Speaker chairs debates in the House of Lords but does not call it to order (as the Commons Speaker does) because the Lords manage debates themselves.

Lords address their speeches to the other Members, not the Lord Speaker. Members normally speak only once, except to give clarification or by special leave.

Divisions

At the end of a debate the question (i.e., the motion that is the subject of the debate) is put to see if Members agree or not. The question may be decided either with or without formal voting or by a simple majority vote.

Transcripts of debates

Public debates and results of divisions in the chamber and committees of both Houses are published in Hansard. (Read Hansard)

Will the Honourable Member...?

In the House of Commons MPs are not referred to by name. The following terms of address are used instead:

The Speaker and Deputy Speakers are referred to as 'Mr (or Madam) Speaker' and 'Mr (or Madam) Deputy Speaker'.

And that's just in the Commons. The House of Lords has a whole set of different addresses.

You can't say that!

Language and expressions used in the chambers must conform to a number of rules. Members may not:

- accuse other Members of lying
- use abusive or insulting language
- refer to the alleged views of members of the royal family;
- refer to matters before a court of law (except when discussing legislation)

How do you address a Lord?

Members of the House of Lords have a number of different titles. Find out the correct title to use in your correspondence.

(Please note, in all instances 'XXX' should be replaced with the Member's surname.)

Lord Speaker
Beginning of letter ... Dear Lord Speaker
End of letter ... Yours sincerely
Envelope ... The Rt. Hon. the Baroness D'Souza CMG, Lord Speaker

Baron (Lord)
Beginning of letter ... Dear Lord XXX
End of letter ... Yours sincerely
Envelope ... The (Rt. Hon. the) Lord XXX

Baroness
Beginning of letter ... Dear Lady XXX
End of letter ... Yours sincerely
Envelope ... The (Rt. Hon. the) Baroness XXX

Countess
Beginning of letter ... Dear Lady XXX
End of letter ... Yours sincerely
Envelope ... The Countess (of) XXX

Duke
Beginning of letter ... Dear Duke of XXX
End of letter ... Yours sincerely
Envelope ... His Grace the Duke of XXX

Earl
Beginning of letter ... Dear Lord XXX
End of letter ... Yours sincerely
Envelope ... The (Rt. Hon. the) Earl (of) XXX

Lady
Beginning of letter ... Dear Lady XXX
End of letter ... Yours sincerely
Envelope ... The (Rt. Hon. the) Lady XXX

Marquess
Beginning of letter ... Dear Lord XXX
End of letter ... Yours sincerely
Envelope ... The Most Hon. the Marquess of XXX

Viscount
Beginning of letter ... Dear Lord XXX
End of letter ... Yours sincerely
Envelope .. The (Rt. Hon. the) Viscount XXX

Archbishop
Beginning of letter ... Dear Archbishop
End of letter ... Yours sincerely
Envelope ... The Most Rev. and the Rt. Hon. the Archbishop of XXX

Bishops
Beginning of letter ... Dear Lord Bishop
End of letter ... Yours sincerely
Envelope ... The Rt. Rev. the Lord Bishop of XXX

Divisions

Members of both Houses register their vote for or against issues by physically going into two different areas either side of their debating chambers. This is known as 'dividing the House', while the areas concerned are 'division lobbies'. Therefore, a vote is called a 'division'.

Votes

When a vote is held the Speaker in the Commons - or Lord Speaker in the Lords - asks Members to call out whether they agree or not. The Speaker will then judge whether there is a clear result. If this cannot be determined, the Speaker or Lord Speaker calls a division by announcing 'clear the lobbies' (in the Commons) or 'clear the bar' (in the Lords).

Division bells

Members do not have to participate in a debate to be able to vote, and may be elsewhere in the parliamentary estate. To notify Members that a division is taking place, division bells located throughout the Parliamentary estate and surrounding premises ring and TV screens with a specialised feed (called the 'annunciator service') display that a division is taking place.

There are different division bells for the Commons and Lords, and Members only vote in the divisions specific to their House. When the division bells ring Members have eight minutes to vote before the doors to the division lobbies are locked.

Division lobbies

During a division, Members literally divide into two separate areas. These are called the Aye and No lobbies in the Commons and the Contents and Not Contents lobbies in the Lords. As they pass through the lobbies, the Members have their names recorded by clerks and are counted by tellers. Once the lobbies are empty the Speaker (Commons) or the Lord Speaker (Lords) announces the result of the division. The whole process takes about fifteen minutes.

Tied votes

If the vote is tied - which is very unusual - in the Commons the Speaker has the casting vote. The Speaker casts his vote according to what was done in similar circumstances in the past. Where possible the issue should remain open for further discussion and no final decision should be made by a casting vote.

In the Lords, the Lord Speaker does not have a casting vote. Instead, the tied vote is resolved according to established rules (called the Standing Orders).

Deferred divisions

In the Commons, MPs can vote on a series of motions using ballot papers at a convenient time (currently from 12.30pm on Wednesdays) instead of holding divisions immediately at the end of a debate. These are known as deferred divisions.

Deferred divisions can be used with motions on statutory instruments and on certain types of motion, which are not subject to amendment.

The Division List

The Division List records the way in which Members voted and is usually available to the public the following day in Hansard and on the Parliament website.

Nodding through:

If a Member is within the Parliamentary estate but too ill to reach a lobby his vote may be 'nodded through', i.e., added to the voting total in their absence.

Why aren't divisions electronic?

Plans to introduce electronic or mechanical voting systems in Parliament have been considered but no single alternative gained great support. Also, physically congregating in the voting lobbies gives the Members a good opportunity to talk and conduct business with each other in an informal setting.

Adjournment debates

An adjournment debate is simply a way in the Commons of having a general debate without requiring the House to vote.

There are several different types of adjournment debate. Some allow the Commons to hold a general open-ended debate on a subject or a government policy without reaching a formal decision about it. Others provide an opportunity for backbench MPs to raise constituency issues or other matters relating to government administration or policy - and to obtain a response from a government minister.

In the Commons chamber

There is a half-hour adjournment debate at the end of each day's sitting. Members apply for an adjournment debate to the Speakers Office. Subject matters of adjournment debates are varied; examples include debates on defence issues, pensions and combating benefit fraud. The Speaker chooses Thursday's subject; for other days, MPs are selected by ballot.

At the end of the day's business, which is normally 10pm on Mondays and Tuesdays, 7pm on Wednesdays, 6pm on Thursdays and 2.30pm on Fridays, the Speaker calls a government whip to move 'That this House do now adjourn'.

The MP who tabled the relevant adjournment debate is called to speak and a Minister will reply. The MP has no right of response, but can intervene in the Minister's speech if he or she is willing to allow it (called 'giving way').

In Westminster Hall

At sittings in Westminster Hall on Tuesdays and Wednesdays there are two one-and-a-half hour debates and three half-hour debates. The one-and-a-half hour debates are intended to be more general involving a number of MPs.

Each government department is available to respond to debates only every other week, according to a rota

Applications are made to the Speaker's Office and MPs are selected by ballot on Wednesday mornings.

Successful applications, and the dates and times they will be debated are listed on the parliamentary website.

Members will not be granted more than one debate in the same week or two debates in successive weeks.

Motions for the adjournment

General debates are often held on what is called 'a motion for the adjournment'. In practice this means that a motion is put forward that the House should adjourn (the day's business is finished) - but it's not actually answered.

Instead, the MP who tabled the adjournment debate starts to make their speech on the subject and a government minister responds to it. At the end of the half-hour debate the motion for the adjournment of the House is put forward again and agreed to - signalling the end of the day's business.

In the Lords chamber

The House of Lords do not have adjournment debates as such but their Questions for Short Debate have a similar purpose.

These questions allow for a short debate that lasts for up to one-and-a-half hours (or one hour if taken in the dinner break).

British residents and overseas visitors can watch debates, including Prime Minister's Questions, from the public galleries in both Chambers.

Read adjournment debates

Transcripts of 'End of Day' adjournment debates are at the end of the 'Debates' section of Hansard. Transcripts of the adjournment debates held in Westminster Hall are in the 'Westminster Hall' section of Hansard.

What are Early day motions?

Early day motions (EDMs) are formal motions submitted for debate in the House of Commons. However, very few EDMs are actually debated.

How are EDMs used?

EDMs are used for reasons such as publicising the views of individual MPs, drawing attention to specific events or campaigns, and demonstrating the extent of parliamentary support for a particular cause or point of view.

Do they get debated?

Although there is very little prospect of EDMs being debated, many attract a great deal of public interest and frequently receive media coverage.

Do they have to comply with a format?

EDMs have a strict format. Each one has a short title, like 'Internet Gambling', and a sentence no longer than 250 words detailing the motion.

What are the rules?

Other than following the above format, EDMs must abide by certain rules about their subject matter. The main ones are:

EDMs may only criticise other MPs, Lords, judges or members of the royal family if that is the main subject of the motion

- no reference should be made to matters before the courts

- no unparliamentary language or irony should be used

- titles must be purely descriptive

Types of EDMs

EDMs against statutory instruments (are known as 'prayer') - generally the only type of EDM that leads to a debate.

Internal party groups - put forward by party members to express a different view on an issue to the official party position.

All-party EDMs - usually promote an issue, such as animal welfare, across party divides. Generally, only all party EDMs attract a large number of signatures.

Critical - occasionally EDMs are tabled criticising another Member of the House, or a member of the House of Lords.

Promotion - of an outside campaign or report (often by the voluntary sector).

Constituency issue - drawing attention to and commenting on.

Commenting on deficiencies in other parties' policies - often by government MPs, as they can't criticise the Opposition at question time.

Signatures

In an average session only six or seven EDMs reach over two hundred signatures. Around seventy or eighty get over one hundred signatures. The majority will attract only one or two signatures.

An EDM is not likely to be debated even if it gains a large number of signatures.

Who will not sign?

The following people in Parliament normally will not sign EDMs:

Ministers and government whips

Parliamentary Private Secretaries

The Speaker and his deputies

Tracing EDMs

EDMs dating back to the 1989-90 session of Parliament can be traced using the EDM database. It records the full title and text of EDMs and signatures of supporting MPs.

EDMs database

For Early Day Motions prior to 1989-90, enquirers should contact the Parliamentary Archives.

Archive Enquiry Services

We can answer simple enquiries over the telephone, but most enquiries should be sent to us by post, fax or e-mail.

If you are telephoning to make a searchroom booking, please also give us your e-mail address if you have one, so we can confirm your appointment by e-mail.

We cannot undertake detailed research for users but we can provide advice about the scope of the records for particular topics. Our Reprographic Service can also supply copies of readily identifiable material, by post or e-mail. We aim to answer all enquiries within 10 working days.

Please ensure you have consulted the following before you send your enquiry:

- Frequently Asked Questions
- Planning Your Visit
- Catalogue

E-mail: archives@parliament.uk
Phone +44 (0)20 7219 3074
Fax +44 (0)20 7219 2570
Post: Parliamentary Archives, Houses of Parliament, London, SW1A 0PW, United Kingdom

Early Day Motions (EDMs) are formal motions submitted for debate in the House of Commons. The EDM database contains up-to-date information on the latest EDMs and signatures added to existing EDMs.

Statutory instrument: This is a type of delegated or secondary legislation. Delegated legislation allows the government to make changes to a law without needing to pass a completely new Act of Parliament.

Most popular EDM

The record for most signatures on an EDM was set in the 2001-02 session. Malcolm Savidge's EDM on the need to avoid conflict between India and Pakistan attracted 502 signatures. Previously the record was 482 signatures for an EDM on service pensions tabled in 1964 by Sir Robert Cary.

Written answers

In addition to oral questions, MPs and Peers can ask government ministers questions for written answer. These are often used to obtain detailed information about policies and statistics on the activities of government departments.

'Ordinary' questions

In the House of Commons 'ordinary' questions do not have to be answered on a specific date. An MP will date a written question for two days after they have tabled it (i.e., submitted it for answer via the Table Office).

The convention is that the MP can expect it to be answered within seven days of the question being tabled. However, there is no parliamentary rule that states ordinary written questions have to be answered by a certain date.
Read Commons questions for written answer

House of Lords written questions

All House of Lords written questions follow a similar procedure. Lords enter questions on the Order Paper via the Table Office. Lords may table up to six questions each day and can expect an answer within 14 days.
Read Lords questions for written answer

'Named day' questions

'Named day' questions only occur in the House of Commons. The MP tabling the question specifies the date on which they should receive an answer. The MP must give a minimum of two days' notice for these types of question. MPs may not table more than five-named day questions on a single day.

Questions originally tabled for oral answer that do not get answered at oral question time are submitted to the government department as named day questions.

Answers

Answers are sent directly to the MP or Lord and printed in Hansard along with the original question.
Read written answers in Hansard

'Will write' answers

Occasionally Commons questions are answered in Hansard with 'I will write to the Hon Member...' The subsequent letters are not published in Commons Hansard but placed in the House of Commons Library for MPs' use (but the House of Commons Information Office can supply copies of these).
Contact the House of Commons Information Office

Written Ministerial Statements

Until 2002 the government often used written answers to make statements but these are now published separately.

Table or Tabling: When MPs or Peers hand in questions, amendments to Bills or notices of motions; or when a document is formally placed before either House.

Did you know?

Written questions account for the vast majority of parliamentary questions. For example, of the 27,391 answers printed in Commons Hansard in the 2009-10 session, 25,467 of them were written answers.

Written ministerial statements

Government ministers can make written statements to Parliament as well as oral ones. Oral statements often address major incidents, policies and actions. Written ministerial statements are normally used to put the day-to-day business of government on the official record and in the public domain.

History of written statements

Until 2002 the government mainly used written answers to make statements - by getting a backbench MP to table a written question drafted by the government department. The need for these 'arranged' or 'planted' questions was removed in October 2002 when a new system allowing written statements to be printed independently in their own section in Hansard was introduced in the Commons. The Lords did the same in January 2004.

Content of written statements

Written ministerial statements are often used to provide or announce:

Detailed information and statistics from the government

The publication of reports by government agencies

Findings of reviews and inquiries and the government's response

Financial and statistical information

Procurement issues

Procedure and policy initiatives of government departments

Access to written statements

A list of daily written ministerial statements is printed in the Order Paper. Where the government has indicated that it will make a written ministerial statement on a future day this is recorded in Future Business.
Today's scheduled written ministerial statements

Once they are received by Parliament, they will be published on the parliamentary website.

Did you know?

There were over 1300 written ministerial statements in the House of Commons in each of the first two parliamentary years they were used (2002-03 and 2003-04).

Read written ministerial statements
Read current and past written ministerial statements in Hansard.

Hansard

Hansard is an edited record of what was said in Parliament. It also includes votes, written ministerial statements and written answers to parliamentary questions. The report is published daily covering the preceding day, and is followed by weekly and final versions.

Transcribing and publishing

Members' words are recorded by Hansard reporters and then edited to remove repetitions and obvious mistakes but without taking away from the meaning. Reports of the latest proceedings are published online and updated during the day. The Commons and Lords have separate reports.

The text of Daily Debates in the Commons and Lords are published online the following morning by 6am and is also available in hard copy. Weekly and bound final versions follow, proof-read to eliminate any errors that may have occurred in the original.

Today in the Commons and Lords

When the Commons and Lords are sitting, the reports of the latest proceedings are published about three hours after the live event and updated during the sitting. The following day this becomes the Official Report (Hansard).

Judgments

The House of Lords was the UK's highest Court of Appeal until 30 July 2009. From 1 October 2009, the Supreme Court of the United Kingdom assumed jurisdiction on points of law for all civil law cases in the UK and all criminal cases in England and Wales and Northern Ireland.

Access to judgments since 1996

All judgments of the Law Lords since 14 November 1996 to 30 July 2009 are available on the Parliament website. They are available in browsable html and print-friendly PDF formats.

House of Lords judgments: archive

Access to judgments prior to 1996

Access to judgments prior to 1996 can be arranged through the Parliamentary Archives. The Archives holds appeal cases and other records of the House of Lords acting in its judicial capacity, dating from 1621. Parliamentary Archives

Other judgments

The archived House of Lords judgments are the only case law that Parliament holds. For any other court decision you will need to use a legal information service such as the British and Irish Legal Information Institute (BAILII), which is free to access. British and Irish Legal Information Institute (BAILII)

Making laws

One of Parliament's main roles is debating and passing laws.

Why are new laws needed?

One of Parliament's main roles is debating and passing statute law (legislation).

New laws

The Government introduces most plans for new laws, with many included in the Queen's Speech at the opening of each session of Parliament, and changes to existing laws. However, new laws can originate from an MP or a Lord.

Emergency issues such as the threat of terrorism, pressure on the Government to update old laws and case law in the courts, interpreting, clarifying and re-applying established principles of statute law, all contribute to the need for new laws.

Who is consulted about changes to the law?

Before draft laws, known as Bills, are introduced into Parliament, there is often consultation or discussion with interested parties such as professional bodies, voluntary organisations and pressure groups.

White and Green Papers

Proposals for legislative changes may be contained in government White Papers. These may be preceded by consultation papers, sometimes called Green Papers, which set out government proposals that are still taking shape and seek comments from the public. There is no requirement for White or Green papers to be introduced before a Bill is introduced into Parliament.

Draft Bills and pre-legislative scrutiny

A Draft Bill is a Bill that is published to enable consultation and pre-legislative scrutiny before a Bill is formally introduced into either the House of Commons or House of Lords.

A Draft Bill is considered, often by a departmental select committee in the Commons or by a joint committee of Lords and Members of the Commons. This allows MPs and Members of the Lords to have early influence on the Bill. This process is known as pre-legislative scrutiny.

Do all Bills apply to the whole of the UK?

Some Bills apply to the whole of the UK.

However, Bills may apply to one or more constituent parts - for example, only to England and Wales. Law-making powers in some subjects rest with the Scottish Parliament, the Welsh Assembly and the Northern Ireland Assembly, rather than the UK Parliament.

International and EU legislation

Sometimes new laws are also needed to ensure that the UK complies with international or EU legislation.

Queen's Speech

The Queen's Speech is read by the Queen from the Throne in the House of Lords at the State Opening of Parliament.

It is drawn up by the Government, and contains an outline of the Government's proposed legislative programme and policies for the new parliamentary session.

Draft Bills

Draft Bills are issued for consultation before being formally introduced to Parliament. This allows proposed changes to be made before the Bill's formal introduction. Almost all Draft Bills are Government Bills. Government departments produce Draft Bills and issue them to interested parties. MPs and Lords can also consider them in committees.

Why are there Draft Bills?

The practice of publishing Draft Bills has become more frequent in recent years. It allows examination and amendments to be made to texts and made more easily - before their formal introduction to Parliament as a Bill proper.

Parliament's role in Draft Bills

Most Draft Bills are examined either by select committees in the Commons or Lords or by a joint committee of both Houses. Draft Bills considered by Parliament are available on this website.

Government's role in Draft Bills

The consultation process on Draft Bills may involve the government issuing a paper for public discussion and response. The best-known examples of this are White and Green Papers.

Although not formal definitions, Green Papers usually put forward ideas for future government policy that are open to public discussion and consultation. White Papers generally state more definite intentions for government policy.

Government Bill: This is a term for a type of Public Bill, introduced by government ministers.

Scrutiny Unit

The Scrutiny Unit forms part of the Committee Office in the House of Commons. It provides specialist expertise to select committees, especially (but not exclusively) on Draft Bills.

The Scrutiny Unit forms part of the Committee Office in the House of Commons and exists to strengthen the scrutiny function of the House.

It provides specialist expertise to select committees, especially (but not exclusively) on financial matters and on draft bills.

The Scrutiny Unit has a staff of around 14 including lawyers, accountants, an economist and a statistician, as well as House of Commons Clerks and a small team of administrative staff.

Further information is available at About the Scrutiny Unit and at Reports and Publications.

Bills

A Bill is a proposal for a new law, or a proposal to change an existing law that is presented for debate before Parliament.

Bills are introduced in either the House of Commons or House of Lords for examination, discussion and amendment.

When both Houses have agreed on the content of a Bill it is then presented to the reigning monarch for approval (known as Royal Assent).

Once Royal Assent is given a Bill becomes an Act of Parliament and is law.

Different types of Bills can be introduced by:

- The government
- Individual MPs or Lords
- Private individuals or organisations
- There are three different types of Bill: Public, Private and Hybrid Bills. There is also another kind of Public Bill called Private Members' Bills.

More on Public Bills
Public Bills
Public Bills change the law as it applies to the general population and are the most common type of Bill introduced in Parliament. Government ministers propose the majority of Public Bills, those put forward by other MPs or Lords are known as Private Members' Bills.

Introduction of Public Bills

Public Bills are introduced in either House and go through a number of set stages that generally involve Members of both Houses examining the Bill.

Bills that are largely financial, or involve the public's money - like new taxes or public spending - are always introduced in the Commons.

When a Public Bill becomes law

Once passed into law, a Public Bill becomes an Act of Parliament. The conditions of Public Bills apply to the general public, such as a change to the national speed limit on motorways.

Voicing opposition to a Public Bill

Members of the public who want to voice their objections to Public Bills can do so by:

- writing to their MP or a Lord
- writing to the government department responsible for the Bill
- lobbying Parliament
- submitting evidence to the relevant Public Bill Committee

More on Private Members' Bills

Private Members' Bills
Private Members' Bills are Public Bills introduced by MPs and Lords who are not government ministers. As with other Public Bills their purpose is to change the law as it applies to the general population. A minority of Private Members' Bills become law but, by creating publicity around an issue, they may affect legislation indirectly.

Introducing Private Members' Bills

Like other Public Bills, Private Members' Bills can be introduced in either House and must go through the same set stages. However, as less time is allocated to these Bills, it's less likely that they will proceed through all the stages.

Find out more about the stages of a Bill

To introduce a Bill a Member needs to provide its short title (by which it is known) and its long title (which describes briefly what it does). Complete texts are not necessary and some Private Members' Bills are never published in full.

There are three ways of introducing Private Members' Bills in the House of Commons: the Ballot, the Ten Minute Rules and Presentation.

The Ballot

Ballot Bills have the best chance of becoming law, as they get priority for the limited amount of debating time available. The names of Members applying for a Bill is drawn in a ballot held on the second sitting Thursday of a parliamentary session. The draw for the 2013-14 ballot was announced in reverse order. Normally, the first seven ballots Bills are most likely to get a day's debate.

Result of the Private Members' Bill ballot: session 2013-14
The first reading (formal presentation - no debate) of ballot bills takes place on the fifth sitting Wednesday of a parliamentary session.

Ten Minute Rule

Ten-Minute Rule Bills are often an opportunity for Members to voice an opinion on a subject or aspect of existing legislation, rather than a serious attempt to get a Bill passed.

Members make speeches of no more than ten minutes outlining their position, which another Member may oppose in a similar short statement. It is a good opportunity to raise the profile of an issue and to see whether it has support among other Members.

Presentation

Any Member may introduce a Bill in this way as long as he or she has previously given notice of their intention to do so. Members formally introduce the title of the Bill but do not speak in support of it - they rarely become laws.

Private Members' Bills from the Lords

Private Members' Bills introduced in the Lords go through the same stages as any other Public Bill. Once completed, and if an MP supports the Bill, it continues in the Commons. Lords Private Members' Bills are treated like other Private Members' Bills, but do not have priority over Bills introduced in the Commons. They are therefore unlikely to have much, if any, time devoted to them.

Time for consideration of Private Members' Bills in the Commons

Private Members' Bills have precedence over government business on thirteen Fridays in each session under standing order 14 (9).

More on Private Bills

Private Bills
Private Bills are usually promoted by organisations, like local authorities or private companies, to give themselves powers beyond, or in conflict with, the general law. Private Bills only change the law as it applies to specific individuals or organisations, rather than the general public. Groups or individuals potentially affected by these changes can petition Parliament against the proposed Bill and present their objections to committees of MPs and Lords.

How Private Bills start

Bills can start in either House. The formal stages of Private Bills are broadly the same as Public Bills.

Letting the public know

Parliament requires that Private Bills are publicised through newspaper adverts, official gazettes of local areas, and in writing to all interested parties. People directly affected by a Private Bill - for example, residents near a proposed site for a new cemetery - should also be informed.

Petitioning against Private Bills

Any group or individual directly affected by a Bill's proposals can object to it through petitions, examined and considered by committees of MPs and of Lords. Further details on drafting a petition are available from the Private Bill Offices in the Commons and Lords.

More on Hybrid Bills

Hybrid Bills
Hybrid Bills mix the characteristics of Public and Private Bills. The changes to the law proposed by a Hybrid Bill would affect the general public but would also have a significant impact for specific individuals or groups. The Bill passed concerning the construction of the Channel Tunnel was an example of a Hybrid Bill.

Channel Tunnel and Crossrail Bills

Hybrid Bills often propose works of national importance but in a specific area of the UK. Examples would be the Channel Tunnel Bills passed in the 1970s and 1980s that affected the South East of the UK, and the Crossrail Bill to build a new east to west rail link through central London passed in 2008.

Who decides what is a Hybrid Bill?

The Public Bill Offices decide whether a Bill falls into the Hybrid category. Both Houses debate these Bills and they go through a longer parliamentary process than Public Bills.

Petitioning against Hybrid Bills

Opponents to Hybrid Bills may submit petitions and certain individuals and groups can state their case before a select committee.

You can access the amendments that have been tabled in relation to a particular Bill as well as view what happened to each amendment on the bills individual WebPages found in Bills before Parliament. You can access the amendments through 'Bill documents' or through the 'Public Bill Committee' proceedings.

Bills before Parliament

We carry a full list of Bills before Parliament with complete texts, amendments and all proceedings. You can follow the progress of legislation on this site by accessing our Bills and Legislation section.

Bills v Acts

A Bill is not an Act of Parliament. This is what a Bill becomes if approved by a majority in the House of Commons and the House of Lords, and formally agreed to by the reigning monarch (known as Royal Assent). An Act of Parliament is a law, enforced in all areas of the UK where it is applicable.

Once a Bill becomes an Act of Parliament, it is the responsibility of the appropriate government department to implement it. For example, the Department for Transport would enforce a new law concerning speeding.

Access to current Bills and Acts

Texts of Bills are available on the Bills pages of the Parliament website.

Bills before Parliament

Texts of Acts of Parliament going back to 1988 are hosted on Legislation.gov.uk (National Archives) website. legislation.gov.uk

Access to earlier Bills and Acts

Earlier Bills and Acts that are not available on the Parliament or Legislation.gov.uk website are held in hardcopy by the Parliamentary Archives.

Parliamentary Archives

If you wish to conduct your own research and trace earlier Acts of Parliament, a guide to useful external services and reference texts is available.

Passage of a Bill

A Bill can start in the House of Commons or the House of Lords and must be approved in the same form by both Houses before becoming an Act of Parliament (law).

The Bill has to go through all five stages in the House of Commons before it can go to the House of Lords.
Acts

An Act of Parliament creates a new law or changes an existing law. An Act is a Bill approved by both the House of Commons and the House of Lords and formally agreed to by the reigning monarch (known as Royal Assent). Once implemented, an Act is law and applies to the UK as a whole or to specific areas of the country.

Putting the Act into force

An Act may come into force immediately, on a specific starting date, or in stages.

The practical implementation of an Act is the responsibility of the appropriate government department, not Parliament. For example, laws relating to transport issues would come under the administration of the Department for Transport.

Parliament or its committees may investigate how the government implements the Act and would consider any future Bills that amended or replaced it.

Changes to Acts

Future changes to the law happen through the passing of another Act or delegated legislation. An Act can also be repealed so that its provisions no longer apply. Parliamentary committees examine UK laws and recommend the removal of out of date legislation.

Finding the text of Acts

Looking for the text of an Act? The first question you need to answer is do you need the text of the Act in the form it was passed by Parliament or are you looking for a revised version of the Act incorporating any changes that have been made by subsequent legislation?

Text of Acts as passed

Texts of Acts of Parliament as originally passed by Parliament since 1800 are available on the Legislation.gov.uk website. The Parliamentary Archives has copies of original Acts from 1497.

Acts of Parliament

Full texts of all Public General Acts as passed since 1988 and all Private Acts since 1991 are available on the Legislation.gov.uk website.

Bills v Acts

A Bill is not an Act of Parliament. This is what a Bill becomes if approved by a majority in the House of Commons and the House of Lords, and formally agreed to by the reigning monarch (known as Royal Assent). An Act of Parliament is a law, enforced in all areas of the UK where it is applicable.

Delegated legislation

Delegated or secondary legislation is usually concerned with detailed changes to the law made under powers from an existing Act of Parliament. Statutory instruments form the majority of delegated legislation but it can also include Rules or Codes of Practice.

What delegated legislation does?

Delegated legislation allows the Government to make changes to a law without needing to push through a completely new Act of Parliament. The original Act (also known as primary legislation) would have provisions that allow for future delegated legislation to alter the law to differing degrees.

These changes range from the technical, like altering the level of a fine, to fleshing out Acts with greater detail; often an Act contains only a broad framework of its purpose and more complex content is added through delegated legislation.

Statutory instruments

Statutory instruments (SIs) are a type of delegated legislation. Approximately 3000 SIs are issued each year, making up the bulk of delegated legislation. About two-thirds of SIs are not actively considered before Parliament and simply become law on a specified date in the future.

SIs are normally drafted by the legal office of the relevant government department. Consultations often take place with interested bodies and parties.

House of Commons Background Paper: Statutory Instruments

The House of Lords Delegated Powers Scrutiny Committee

The Delegated Powers Scrutiny Committee (established in 1992) keeps under constant review the extent to which legislative powers are delegated by Parliament to government ministers, and examines all Bills with delegating powers which allow SIs to be made before they begin their passage through the House.

There is an informal understanding in the Lords that, when the Delegated Powers Committee has approved provisions in a Bill for delegated powers, the form of those powers should not normally be the subject of debate during the Bill's subsequent passage.

The House of Commons has no equivalent committee.

The House of Lords Secondary Legislation Scrutiny Committee (formerly the Merits Committee)

Established in 2003, the Lords Secondary Legislation Scrutiny Committee considers every negative and affirmative SI (or draft SI) laid before Parliament - about 1200 per year - with a view to determining whether the special attention of the House should be drawn to it on any of the following grounds that it:

- is politically or legally important or gives rise to issues of public policy likely to be of interest to the House

- may be inappropriate in view of the changed circumstances since the passage of the parent Act

- may inappropriately implement EU legislation

- may imperfectly achieve its policy objectives

The Secondary Legislation Scrutiny Committee reports every week, normally considering SIs written 12-15 days of being laid before the House.

Like the Delegated Powers and Regulatory Reform Committee, the Secondary Legislation Scrutiny Committee's role is to advise the House of Lords, and it is for the House to decide whether or not to act on the Committee's conclusions.

The House of Commons has no equivalent committee.

Affirmative and negative SIs
There are two types of procedure for Statutory Instrument (SI):

Affirmative procedure: Both Houses of Parliament must expressly approve them

Negative procedure: become laws without a debate or a vote but may be annulled by a resolution of either House of Parliament

In both cases, Parliaments room for manoeuvre is limited. Parliament can accept or reject an SI but cannot amend it.

The Parliament Acts

The powers of the House of Lords are limited by a combination of law and convention.

The Parliament Acts, although rarely used, provide a way of solving disagreement between the Commons and the Lords.

Parliament Acts: background

Until the early years of the 20th century, the House of Lords had the power to veto (stop) legislation.

However, this arrangement was put under pressure when the House of Lords refused to pass David Lloyd-George's 'people's budget' of 1909. Eventually, the budget was passed after a general election in 1910; a second general election was then fought on the issue of reform of the House of Lords.

Parliament Act 1911

The result was the Parliament Act 1911, which removed from the House of Lords the power to veto a Bill, except one to extend the lifetime of a Parliament. Instead, the Lords could delay a Bill by up to two years. The Act also reduced the maximum lifespan of a Parliament from seven years to five years.

Parliament Act 1949

The Parliament Act 1949 further reduced the Lords' delaying powers to one year.

The Parliament Acts define the powers of the Lords in relation to Public Bills as follows.

Money Bills

Money Bills (Bills designed to raise money through taxes or spend public money) start in the Commons and must receive Royal Assent no later than a month after being introduced in the Lords, even if the Lords has not passed them. The Lords cannot amend Money Bills.

Other Commons Bills

Most other Commons Bills can be held up by the Lords if they disagree with them for about a year but ultimately the elected House of Commons can reintroduce them in the following session and pass them without the consent of the Lords.

Bills not subject to the Parliament Acts

Bills prolonging the length of a Parliament beyond five years

Private Bills

Bills sent up to the Lords less than a month before the end of a session

Bills which start in the Lords

The Salisbury Convention

The Salisbury Convention ensures that Government Bills can get through the Lords when the Government of the day has no majority in the Lords.

In practice, it means that the Lords do not vote down a Government Bill mentioned in an election manifesto.

House of Commons Library briefings

The House of Commons Library produces briefing papers to inform MPs of key issues. The papers contain factual information and a range of opinions on each subject, and aim to be politically impartial. The Library has published briefing papers on the Parliament Acts and conventions on the relationship between the House of Commons and House of Lords.

Commons Library standard note: The Parliament Acts

Commons Library standard note: Conventions on the relationship between the House of Commons and House of Lords

Salisbury Convention: ensures that Government Bills included in the election manifesto can get through the Lords when the Government of the day has no majority in the Lords. (Also known as the Salisbury Doctrine.)

Acts passed into law without consent of the Lords

Since 1949 the following Acts have been passed into law without the consent of the House of Lords:

- War Crimes Act 1991
- European Parliamentary Elections Act 1999
- Sexual Offences (Amendment) Act 2000

- Hunting Act 2004

Committees

Much of the work of the House of Commons and the House of Lords takes place in committees, made up of around 10 to 50 MPs or Lords. These committees examine issues in detail, from government policy and proposed new laws, to wider topics like the economy.

Select Committees

Select Committees work in both Houses. They check and report on areas ranging from the work of government departments to economic affairs. The results of these inquiries are public and many require a response from the government.

Differences between the two Houses

House of Commons Select Committees are largely concerned with examining the work of government departments. Committees in the House of Lords concentrate on four main areas: Europe, science, economics, and the UK constitution.

Commons Select Committees

There is a Commons Select Committee for each government department, examining three aspects: spending, policies and administration.

These departmental committees have a minimum of 11 members, who decide upon the line of inquiry and then gather written and oral evidence. Findings are reported to the Commons, printed, and published on the Parliament website. The government then usually has 60 days to reply to the committee's recommendations.

Some Select Committees have a role that crosses departmental boundaries such as the Public Accounts or Environmental Audit Committees. Depending on the issue under consideration they can look at any or all of the government departments.

Other Commons Committees are involved in a range of on-going investigations, like administration of the House itself or allegations about the conduct of individual MPs.

Following the adoption by the House of recommendations from the Reform of the House of Commons Committee (which was chaired by the former MP, Dr Tony Wright);

- the majority of Select Committee Chairs are now elected by their fellow MPs. This applies to departmental committees and the Environmental Audit, Political and Constitutional Reform, Procedure, Public Administration and Public Accounts committees.

- a Backbench Business Committee has been established with the ability to schedule business in the Commons Chamber and in Westminster Hall on days, or parts of days, set aside for non-government business.

Lords Select Committees

Lords Select Committees do not shadow the work of government departments. Their investigations look into specialist subjects, taking advantage of the Lords' expertise and the greater amount of time (compared to MPs) available to them to examine issues.

There are currently five major Lords Select Committees:

- the European Union Committee

- the Science and Technology Committee

- the Communications Committee

- the Constitution Committee

- the Economic Affairs Committee

These five committees are re-appointed at the beginning of a new session. Each one runs inquiries and reports on issues within their specific areas. Occasionally, other committees are set up to look at issues outside of the five main groups.

Joint Committees

Joint Committees are committees consisting of MPs and Lords. They have similar powers to Select Committees. Some are set up on a permanent basis, like the Joint Committee on Human Rights. Other appointments are for specific purposes, such as examining draft proposals for Bills on subjects ranging from gambling to stem cell research.

How they work

In Joint Committees, Members from both Houses meet and work as one committee, and appoint a single chairman who can be an MP or Lord.

Joint Committees operate like Select Committees. They may conduct an ongoing examination of a particular area (such as human rights) or of a specific matter, such as Draft Bills or House of Lords reform. Reports are available to the public in printed and online formats.

Major Joint Committees

Two Joint Committees meet on a regular basis: Human Rights, which meets to consider human rights issues in the UK; and Statutory Instruments, which meets to scrutinise delegated legislation.

Other Joint Committees

Committees such as those on Consolidation Bills and Tax Law Rewrite Bills meet as Bills are referred to them. Joint Committees on specific topics, like those set up to consider draft Bills and other issues, stop meeting once they have fully reported.

General Committees (including Public Bill Committees)

The main role of General Committees is to consider proposed legislation in detail. This committee system allows faster processing of Bills and is unique to the House of Commons; the Lords meet as a whole House in this function. The committees reflect the political makeup of the House. The government always has a majority.

Committees on Bills

A Public or Private Bill Committee is appointed for each Bill that goes through Parliament. Depending on its complexity, the consideration of a Bill can take a few minutes to a few months.

The Lords meet as a whole House in this function (in the debating chamber) or as a Grand Committee away from the chamber. Proceedings in a Grand Committee are the same as Committees of the whole House with an important exception: motions must be passed unanimously, so a dissenting voice from one Member could block an amendment to a Bill.

Naming Public Bill Committees

Each Public Bill Committee is named after the Bill it considers. For example, a committee considering a Bill titled the Climate Bill would be called the Climate Bill Committee.

How they work

Each committee is assigned a chairman and debate Bills as they would do in the Commons chamber, with broadly the same rules of debate applying. Public Bill Committees, unlike the Standing Committees they replace, have the power to take written and oral evidence from officials and experts outside of Parliament. This is intended to give Committee members more information on which to make their decisions.

The minimum number of Members in a committee is 16 and the maximum is about 50. The proportion of Members in a Public Bill Committee mirrors the political parties' strengths in the Commons, so there is always a government majority.

Reports

Public Bill Committees examine each Bill line by line. Once a committee has finished looking at a Bill, it reports its conclusions and any amendments made to the Commons, where Members debate the Bill further.

The Bill is printed again with the amendments made by the Public Bill Committee; this is publicly available in printed and online formats.

Although the Lords do not meet in Public Bill Committees, they have a report stage to allow further consideration of Bills.

Other General Committees

Additional General Committees exist to debate matters in specific areas, such as the Scottish Grand Committee, the Welsh Grand Committee, the Northern Ireland Grand Committee; committees on Delegated Legislation and European documents.

Grand Committees

Grand Committees give MPs the opportunity to debate issues affecting their region. The Committees function in a similar way to the Commons Chamber, with ministerial statements and an opportunity to question the Ministers. Every MP representing a constituency in the region is entitled to attend Grand Committee meetings.

Welsh Grand Committee

The Welsh Grand Committee consists of the 40 Welsh MPs, and currently up to 5 others. It debates issues relevant to Wales, such as the effects on Wales of the Government's programme announced in the Queen's Speech.

Scottish Grand Committee

The Scottish Grand Committee includes all 72 Scottish MPs. It may meet anywhere in Scotland as well as Westminster. Traditionally it considered the principles of Scottish Bills which were referred to it at second reading. However, UK Parliament Bills relating only to Scotland are rare since the establishment of the Scottish Parliament. It also takes questions and statements and debates other matters concerning Scotland. However, there have been no meetings of the Committee in the last few years.

Northern Ireland Grand Committee

The Northern Ireland Grand Committee includes each of the 18 MPs in Northern Ireland, together with up to 25 other MPs. It debates matters relating specifically to Northern Ireland.

Grand Committees: House of Lords

Most Bills, which are not committed to a Committee of the Whole House in the Lords, are instead sent to a Grand Committee. The proceedings are identical to those in a Committee of the Whole House except that voting is not allowed. This means that all decisions must be made unanimously. Any Member of the House of Lords may attend a Grand Committee.

Regional Grand Committees

Regional Grand Committees were established in November 2008 but Standing Orders that set up these committees expired in April 2010. Regions of the UK that were covered by a Regional Grand Committee included:

- East Midlands
- East of England
- North East
- North West
- South East
- South West
- West Midlands
- Yorkshire and the Humber

Parliamentary occasions

Addresses to Members of Parliament

State visits or visits by other leading figures are often marked by a speech given to Members of both Houses of Parliament.

Aung San Suu Kyi address 2012

Nobel peace prize-winner and newly elected parliamentarian Aung San Suu Kyi addressed members of both Houses in Westminster Hall on Thursday 21 June during her visit to the UK.

State Visit of the President of the USA 2011

As part of his State visit to the UK on 24-26 May 2011, President Barack Obama addressed Members of both Houses on Wednesday 25 May.

Papal address 2010

On Friday 17 September 2010, as part of his official visit to the UK, Pope Benedict XVI addressed an audience of invited guests in Westminster Hall that included Members of both Houses of Parliament, diplomats and representatives of civic society.

Recent addresses

The Prime Minister of Canada, Stephen Harper, gave an address to Members of both Houses of Parliament on 13 June 2013 in the Queen's Robing Room, as part of his visit to the UK. He was the first Canadian Prime Minister to address UK parliamentarians in the Palace of Westminster since William Lyon Mackenzie King on May 11, 1944.

On 1 November 2012, President Yudhoyono of Indonesia addressed Members of both Houses. The Amir of Kuwait, His Highness Sheikh Sabah Al-Ahmad Al-Jaber Al-Sabah, also gave an address on 29 November 2012.

Other notable addresses

On 15 May 2007, Bertie Ahern, Taoiseach of Ireland, addressed 500 Members of Parliament in the Royal Gallery to commemorate the restoration of devolution in Northern Ireland. It was the first time that an Irish Prime Minister had addressed Members of both Houses.

Nelson Mandela, François Mitterand, Mikhail Gorbachev, Bill Clinton and the Dalai Lama are among those who have all given addresses to MPs and Members of the Lords.

Commons Library notes: Speeches to Members of both Houses of Parliament
Can I attend an address?

The public cannot gain access to addresses made to Members of Parliament. However, details about addresses will be posted on this webpage.

The Budget

Every year the Chancellor of the Exchequer makes a major speech to the House of Commons on the state of the national finances and the Government's proposals for changes to taxation. This statement is known as the Budget.

When is the Budget?

The Budget usually takes place in March or April. There has to be a Budget every year because some taxes, such as income tax and corporation tax, are annual taxes (not permanent), so they must be renewed each year.

In election years, after a change of Government, a Budget will usually be introduced by the incoming Chancellor of the Exchequer, whether or not the outgoing Chancellor has already delivered one.

What's in the Budget?

The Budget speech usually includes:

- a review of how the UK economy is performing

- forecasts of how the UK economy will perform in the future

- details of any changes to taxation.

The Chancellor's statement is followed by several days' debate.

Budget Resolutions

Tax measures announced in the Budget, known as the Budget Resolutions, can be approved by the House of Commons to come into effect in law immediately. But the decisions to agree the resolutions themselves are taken at the end of the debate on the Budget.

Finance Bill

The Finance Bill is the Bill presented to Parliament each year which enacts the Chancellor of the Exchequer's Budget proposals for taxation.

Once the House of Commons has agreed the Budget Resolutions, the Bill starts its passage through Parliament in the same way as any other Bill.

The House of Lords has a very limited role in respect of Finance Bills. Many Finance Bills are classed as Money Bills, which the Lords may not reject and can only delay for a month.

Pre-Budget Report

Since 1997, the Chancellor of the Exchequer has presented an annual pre-Budget report. This usually takes place in November/December. The pre-Budget report speech to the House of Commons usually includes:

- a report of progress since the previous Budget

- an update on the state of the UK economy

- details of any proposed changes to taxation.

The term "budget"

The term "budget" derives from the word 'bougette', which is French for a little bag; a word which was in use in the eighteenth century.

It was customary to bring the statement on financial policy to the House of Commons in a leather bag. The modern equivalent of the bag is the red despatch box, which was first used by William Ewart Gladstone in about 1860.

Budget record holders

The longest continuous Budget speech was delivered by William Ewart Gladstone in 1853 and was 4 hours and 45 minutes. Benjamin Disraeli's speech in 1852 lasted 5 hours but included a break.

The shortest Budget speech was delivered by Benjamin Disraeli in 1867 and lasted 45 minutes.

With twelve Budget speeches, William Ewart Gladstone holds the record for delivering more Budget speeches than any other Chancellor of the Exchequer.

Budget tipples

The Chancellor of the Exchequer is allowed to drink alcohol during his Budget speech.

Chancellors over the years have chosen water (Gordon Brown), whisky (Kenneth Clarke), gin and tonic (Geoffrey Howe), brandy and water (Benjamin Disraeli), sherry and beaten egg (Gladstone) and spritzer (Nigel Lawson).

Calendar of sittings

Each five year Parliament is divided into sessions. These have usually begun in November with the State Opening of Parliament and have finished the following November. In 2010, however, the Leader of the House announced the Government's intention to move towards five 12-month sessions over a Parliament, beginning and ending in the spring.

Written ministerial statement: Parliamentary Sessions

When does Parliament usually meet?

Although there is no definitive timetable for a parliamentary session, the following recess dates have been announced when the Commons and Lords will not be sitting:

FAQs: Recess dates

House of Commons recess dates

What are the House of Commons recess dates for the current session (2013-14)?

Recess dates 2013-14 (Note: All recess dates are provisional)

State Opening: 8 May 2013 (2013-14)

Prorogation: 25 April 2013 (2012-13)

Recess

House rises

House returns

Whitsun	21 May 2013	3 June 2013
Summer	18 July 2013	2 September 2013
Conference	13 September 2013	8 October 2013
November	12 November 2013	18 November 2013
Christmas	19 December 2013	6 January 2014

Parliament does not sit all year round. During periods called recesses, Members can carry out their other duties.

Recess dates are announced in the House of Commons by the Leader of the House of Commons. The exact pattern of recesses can change and is normally slightly different for the two Houses.

The Leader of the House of Commons has only announced recess dates up to January 2014. This page will be updated within one working day when further announcements have been made. This page was last updated on 30 April 2013.

Short and long sessions

Often the sessions immediately before or after a general election are shorter or longer than usual. For example, following the 2010 general election the session started on 25 May 2010 and ended on 1 May 2012.

What do MPs and Lords do when Parliament is not sitting?

When Parliament is not sitting, MPs work in their constituencies. This work includes holding advice sessions (known as surgeries), dealing with constituency casework and correspondence, and attending local events.

What MPs do?

The UK public elects Members of Parliament (MPs) to represent their interests and concerns in the House of Commons. MPs are involved in considering and proposing new laws, and can use their position to ask government ministers questions about current issues.

MPs split their time between working in Parliament itself, working in the constituency that elected them and working for their political party. Some MPs from the governing party (or parties) become government ministers with specific responsibilities in certain areas, such as Health or Defence.

Working in Parliament

When Parliament is sitting (meeting), MPs generally spend their time working in the House of Commons. This can include raising issues affecting their constituents, attending debates and voting on new laws. Most MPs are also members of committees, which look at issues in detail, from government policy and new laws, to wider topics like human rights.

Working in their constituency

In their constituency, MPs often hold a 'surgery' in their office, where local people can come along to discuss any matters that concern them. MPs also attend functions, visit schools and businesses and generally try to meet as many people as possible. This gives MPs further insight and context into issues they may discuss when they return to Westminster.

Members of the Lords do not represent constituencies. Many Lords hold additional jobs outside Parliament which they can devote more time to during recess.

What Lords do?

What individual Lords do?

The Lords work in Parliament's second Chamber - the House of Lords - and complement and operate alongside the business of the House of Commons. It is one of the busiest second chambers in the world. The expertise of its Members and flexibility to scrutinise an issue in depth means the Lords makes a significant contribution to Parliament's work. The UK public does not elect Members of the Lords.

Making laws

Making laws takes up the bulk of the House of Lords time, and Members are involved throughout the process of proposing, revising and amending legislation. Some Bills introduced by the Government begin in the Lords to spread the workload between the two Houses.

Checking the work of Government

Lords check the work of the Government by questioning and debating decisions made by Ministers and Government Departments.

Specialist committees

There are permanent committees investigating work relating to Europe, science and technology, economics, communications and the constitution. Occasionally one-off committees are set up to deal with issues outside these areas.

State Opening of Parliament

The State Opening of Parliament marks the formal start of the parliamentary year and the Queen's Speech sets out the government's agenda for the coming session, outlining proposed policies and legislation. It is the only regular occasion when the three constituent parts of Parliament – the Sovereign, the House of Lords and the House of Commons – meet.

When is State Opening?

State Opening happens on the first day of a new parliamentary session or shortly after a general election.

The Fixed Term Parliament Act, which sets out new rules on the timing of general elections, received royal assent (became law) on 15 September 2011. This means that the next general election will be on 7 May 2015. There will be a state opening soon after this date.

What happens during State Opening?

State Opening is the main ceremonial event of the parliamentary calendar, attracting large crowds and a significant television and online audience. It begins with the Queen's procession from Buckingham Palace to Westminster, escorted by the Household Cavalry.

The Queen arrives at Sovereign's Entrance and proceeds to the Robing Room. Wearing the Imperial State Crown and the Robe of State, she leads the Royal Procession through the Royal Gallery, packed with 600 guests, to the chamber of the House of Lords.

The House of Lords official known as 'Black Rod' is sent to summon the Commons. The doors to the Commons chamber are shut in his face: a practice dating back to the Civil War, symbolising the Commons' independence from the monarchy. Black Rod strikes the door three times before it is opened. Members of the House of Commons then follow Black Rod and the Commons Speaker to the Lords chamber, standing at the opposite end to the Throne, known as the Bar of the House, to listen to the speech.

The Queen's Speech

The Queen's Speech is delivered by the Queen from the Throne in the House of Lords. Although the Queen reads the Speech, it is written by the government. It contains an outline of its policies and proposed legislation for the new parliamentary session.

After the Queen's Speech

When the Queen leaves, a new parliamentary session starts and Parliament gets back to work. Members of both Houses debate the content of the speech and agree an 'Address in Reply to Her Majesty's Gracious Speech'. Each House continues the debate over the planned legislative programme for several days, looking at different subject areas. The Queen's Speech is voted on by the Commons, but no vote is taken in the Lords.

History of State Opening

Traditions surrounding State Opening and the delivery of a speech by the monarch can be traced back as far as the 16th century. The current ceremony dates from the opening of the rebuilt Palace of Westminster in 1852 after the fire of 1834.

Sessions and parliaments

What is the difference between a parliament and a session?

A parliament can last a maximum of five years and runs from one general election to the next. Due to the Fixed Term Parliament Act 2011 the date of the next general election is 7 May 2015.

A session of Parliament runs from the State Opening of Parliament, in the past this has usually been in November through to the following November. However, in 2010 the Leader of the House announced the Government's intention to move towards five 12-month sessions over a Parliament, beginning and ending in the spring.

Prorogation

Prorogation marks the end of a parliamentary session. It is the formal name given to the period between the end of a session of Parliament and the State Opening of Parliament that begins the next session. The parliamentary session may also be prorogued when Parliament is dissolved and a general election called.

How is prorogation marked?

The Queen formally prorogues Parliament on the advice of the Privy Council.

Prorogation usually takes the form of an announcement, on behalf of the Queen, read in the House of Lords. As with the State Opening, it is made to both Houses and the Speaker of the House of Commons and MPs attend the Lords Chamber to listen to the speech.

The same announcement is then read out by the Speaker in the Commons. Following this both the House of Commons and House of Lords are officially prorogued and will not meet again until the State Opening of Parliament.

Prorogation announcement

The prorogation announcement sets out the major Bills which have been passed during that session and also describes other measures which have been taken by the Government.

Prorogation: what happens to Bills still in progress?

Prorogation brings to an end nearly all parliamentary business.

However, Public Bills may be carried over from one session to the next, subject to agreement. The first Bill to be treated in this way was the Financial Services and Markets Bill in session 1998-99.

Prorogation: what happens to questions for Government Departments

Motions (including early day motions) lapse when the House becomes prorogued, questions which have not been answered fall, nothing more will happen with them. If they have not been answered then they will stay unanswered. No motions or questions can be tabled during a prorogation. On the occasions when Departments are unable to answer questions substantively before prorogation, Ministers provide a standard answer worded as follows: 'It has not proved possible to respond to the [Right] Hon Member in the time available before Prorogation.

Prorogation (pro-ro-ga-tion): Term for the formal end of the parliamentary year.

Recall of Parliament

During times when the House of Commons is not sitting, the Speaker can, if asked by the Government, decide to recall the House of Commons. The House of Lords is usually recalled by the Lord Speaker at the same time as the House of Commons.

Recall of Parliament

Both Houses of Parliament were last recalled on 10 April 2013 for tributes to be paid to former Prime Minister, Baroness Thatcher, following her death. Parliament was previously recalled on 11 August 2011 to debate public disorder.

Government's role

When the House is not sitting, for example at the weekend, or during a recess, the Government can ask the Speaker to recall the House of Commons. They might do this because of events of major national importance.

In the past, the Commons has been recalled because of events such as the invasion of the Falkland Islands in 1982 or the terrorist attacks in the USA in 2001.

Speaker's role

When the Speaker of the House of Commons receives a request from the Government to recall the House of Commons, he must decide whether it is in the public interest to agree to that request.

If the Speaker agrees to the request, he will then decide what day or days the House should sit during the recall.

The Speaker cannot decide to recall the House of Commons without being asked to do so by the Government.

Recall of the House of Lords

The Lord Speaker has the power to recall the House of Lords following consultation with the Government. The House of Lords is usually recalled at the same time as the House of Commons.

Recall of Parliament

If there is an important development during a recess period, the House of Commons and House of Lords may be recalled. Below is a list that goes back to 1948 with links to Hansard.

Latest / Last Recall information

Wednesday 10 April 2013

The House of Commons and House of Lords have been recalled for tributes to be paid to Baroness Thatcher.

Thursday 11 August 2011

The House of Commons and the House of Lords were recalled on Thursday 11 August 2011 at 11.30am and 12.00pm respectively. There was a statement on civil disorder followed by a statement on the global economy. In the House of Commons these were followed by a debate on civil disorder.

Civil Disorder (Commons)
Civil Disorder (Lords)

Wednesday 20 July 2011

The House of Commons was recalled on Wednesday 20 July 2011 at 11.30am. There was a statement on public confidence in the media and police followed by a debate on the same subject.

Public Confidence in the Media and Police
Tuesday 24 September 2002

The House of Commons and the House of Lords were both recalled on Tuesday 24 September 2002 at 11.30am. There was a statement on Iraq and weapons of mass destruction followed by a debate on the same subject.

Iraq and Weapons of Mass Destruction (Commons)
Iraq and Weapons of Mass Destruction (Lords)
Wednesday 3 April 2002

The House of Commons and the House of Lords were both recalled on Wednesday 3 April 2002 at 11.30am. Both Houses moved a humble address expressing sympathies and condolences on the death of Her Majesty Queen Elizabeth, the Queen Mother.

Death of Her Majesty Queen Elizabeth The Queen Mother (Commons)
Her Majesty Queen Elizabeth The Queen Mother (Lords)
Friday 14 September, 4 & 8 October 2001

The House of Commons and the House of Lords were both recalled on Friday 14th September 2001 at 9.30am. There was a statement on international terrorism and attacks in the USA followed by a debate on the same subject. There were further statements and debates on the 4th & 8th October 2001.

International Terrorism and Attacks in the USA (Commons - 14.09.01)
US Terrorist Attacks (Lords - 14.09.01)
Coalition against International Terrorism (Commons -14.10.01)
US Terrorist Attacks: Developments (Lords - 04.10.01)
Coalition against International Terrorism (Commons - 8.10.01)
Coalition against International Terrorism (Lords - 08.10.01)
Recalls of Parliament from 1948

Date of Sitting of the House	*Reason for Recall*
Wed 2 Sept 1998	Omagh bomb and pass the Criminal Justice (Terrorism and Conspiricy) Bill
Thu 3 Sept 1998	Omagh bomb and pass the Criminal Justice (Terrorism and Conspiricy) Bill
Wed 31 May 1995	Bosnia
Thu 24 Sept 1992	Economic Policy
Fri 25 Sept 1992	United Nations operations - Yugoslavia, Iraq, Somalia
Thu 6 Sept 1990	Kuwait invasion
Fri 7 Sept 1990	Kuwait Invasion
Sat 3 April 1982	Falkland Islands
Wed 14 April 1982	Falkland Islands
Mon 3 June 1974	Northern Ireland
Tue 4 June 1974	Northern Ireland
Wed 9 Jan 1974	Fuel - state of emergency
Thu 10 Jan 1974	Fuel - three day working week
Wed 22 Sept 1971	Northern Ireland
Thu 23 Sept 1971	Northern Ireland
Tue 26 May 1970 until	Prorogation followed by dissolution - 1970 General Election
Fri 29 May 1970	Prorogation followed by dissolution - 1970 General Election
Mon 26 Aug 1968	Czechoslovakia
Tue 27 Aug 1968	Czechoslovakia, Nigeria
Tue 16 Jan 1968	Government public expenditure cuts
Tue 17 Oct 1961 until	Berlin Crisis
Mon 23 Oct 1961	Berlin Crisis
Fri 18 Sept 1959	Prorogation followed by dissolution - 1959 General Election
Wed 12 Sept 1956 and	Suez Crisis
Thu 13 Sept 1956 and	Suez Crisis
Fri 14 Sept 1956	Suez Crisis
Thu 4 Oct 1951	Prorogation followed by dissolution - 1951 General Election
Tue 12 Sept 1950 until	Korean War
Tue 19 Sept 1950	Korean War
Tue 27 Sept 1949 and	Devaluation of Sterling
Wed 28 Sept 1949 and	Devaluation of Sterling
Thu 29 Sept 1949	Devaluation of Sterling

House of Lords recalls

Recalls of the House of Lords this list sets out previous recall dates for the House of Lords going back to 1931

Lord Chancellor's breakfast

The start of the legal year is marked with a religious service in Westminster Abbey in which judges arrive from the Royal Courts of Justice followed by a reception at the Houses of Parliament, hosted by the Lord Chancellor.

History

The ceremony in Westminster Abbey has roots in the religious practice of judges praying for guidance at the beginning of the legal term. The custom dates back to the Middle Ages when the High Court was held in Westminster Hall and judges would walk over to Westminster Abbey for the service.

Before the Reformation, during the 16th century, anyone taking communion was required to fast for some hours beforehand. Afterwards it became customary for the Lord Chancellor to offer the judges something to eat before they went into the High Court - hence 'breakfast'.

Present day

Today, judges still keep to the traditional ceremony but instead of the two-mile walk from the Royal Courts of Justice to Westminster Abbey, the judges now travel by car for the service conducted by the Dean of Westminster.

After the service, the Lord Chancellor entertains those present at a breakfast - a light buffet - to which the fully robed guests proceed, on foot, from Westminster Abbey to the Houses of Parliament. The breakfast is held in Westminster Hall, or the Royal Gallery.

Service and guest list

The religious service includes prayers, hymns, anthems and psalms, with both the Lord Chancellor and the Lord Chief Justice reading a lesson.

Approximately 600 guests attend both events, with a further 300 attending the breakfast. Guests include:

- *judges from England and Wales*

- *senior judicial officers*

- *the Law Officers of the Crown*

- *Queen's Counsel (QCs)*

- *overseas judges and lawyers*

- *members of the European Court, and Government ministers.*

Judges and QCs wear full court dress, while others wear morning dress.

Disruption of ceremonies

The ceremonies have been held continuously throughout the years but were cancelled during the First World War years (1915-18), and only held four times between 1931 and 1953.

During the Second World War, the service had to be cancelled due to bomb damage to Westminster Abbey and was not held again until 14 October 1946. In 1953 the ceremony took place in St. Margaret's Church because the structures and decorations erected in Westminster Abbey for the Queen's coronation had not yet been removed.

Lord Chancellor in the Commons

In June 2007, the Rt. Hon Jack Straw MP was appointed Lord Chancellor and Secretary of State for Justice - becoming the first Lord Chancellor in history who is a member of the House of Commons, rather than the House of Lords.

More on the Lord Chancellor
Lord Chancellor's breakfast: 1 October 2008

Timetable of events

- 10.30am - Guests start arriving at Westminster Abbey
- 11.30am - Procession into Westminster Abbey
- 12pm - Service begins
- 12.40pm - Leave Westminster Abbey for Westminster Hall

Lying-in-state

Lying-in-state describes the formal occasion in which a coffin is placed on view to allow the public to pay their respects to the deceased before the funeral ceremony.

Lying-in-state in the UK is given to the Sovereign, as Head of State, the current or past Queen Consort and sometimes former Prime Ministers.

Many notable occasions of lying-in-state have taken place in Westminster Hall at the Houses of Parliament, a few days before the funeral ceremony, including:

- 1898 - William Ewart Gladstone

- 1910 - King Edward VII

- 1936 - King George V

- 1952 - King George VI

- 1953 - Queen Mary

- 1965 - Sir Winston Churchill

- 2002 - Queen Elizabeth the Queen Mother.

The ceremony

During the lying-in-state period, the coffin rests on a raised platform in the middle of Westminster Hall. Each corner of the platform is guarded around the clock by units from the Sovereign's Bodyguard, Foot Guards or the Household Cavalry Mounted Regiment.

Members of the public are free to file past the platform and pay their respects.

Queen Mother

Queen Elizabeth, the Queen Mother, died on 30 March 2002. She lay in state for three days in Westminster Hall where people could visit before her funeral in Westminster Abbey on 9 April 2002.

An estimated 200,000 people paid their respects to the Queen Mother.

Vigil of the Princes

On some occasions (including the funerals of King George V and Queen Elizabeth, the Queen Mother), male members of the Royal family have mounted the lying-in-state guard, in what is known as the Vigil of the Princes.

For George V, his four sons stood guard. For the Queen Mother's lying-in-state her four grandsons held post.

Westminster Hall

Westminster Hall is the oldest part of Parliament. The walls were built in 1097 and the hall is one of Europe's largest medieval halls with an unsupported roof. It was extensively rebuilt during the 14th century.

Once used as a law court, the hall has held several notable trials, including that of Sir William Wallace (1305), the Gunpowder Plot conspirators (1606) and King Charles I (1649).

Today the hall is used for important occasions, including lying-in-state.

Publications

Business papers

The current and future business of Parliament is set out in a collection of daily documents. In the House of Commons, the hardcopy collection of these papers is called the 'Vote Bundle'. In the House of Lords the business papers are collectively known as 'House of Lords Business'.

Yesterday's business

In the House of Commons a publication called Votes and Proceedings formally records what the House did the previous day. It includes decisions, amendments to bills, and a list of publications and other documents laid before the House. It does not include what is said in the House, this is recorded in Hansard.

In the House of Lords the previous day's business, including judicial decisions, is formally recorded in the Minutes of Proceedings publication. It does not include what is said in the House, this is recorded in Hansard.

Today's business

A brief overview of the coming day's business in the Commons is set out in the Summary Agenda. A more detailed agenda is contained in the Order of Business. This includes questions for oral answer, subjects for debate, committee meetings and written ministerial statements to be laid before the House (presented). Together the Summary Agenda and Order of Business are often referred to as the Order Paper.

Questions to be answered in writing in the Commons today are contained in Part 1 of Questions for Oral or Written Answer (also know as the Questions Book).

The agenda for the coming day's business in the House of Lords is set out in Notices and Orders of the Day (also known as the Order Paper). This includes motions for debate and questions for answer.

Tomorrow and future business

Future business in the House of Commons is set out in the Future Business papers, made up of eight parts:

The provisional business for the following week

Backbench business
Remaining Orders and Notices (formally set down for today but not expected to be taken today)
Business for Westminster Hall
Other future business (usually Ten Minute Rule Bills and Private Members' Bills)
Business to be taken in European Committees
Notices of Public Petitions
Notices of written ministerial statements
Future Business in the Commons

Questions to be answered in the Commons on future days are contained in Part 2 of Questions for Oral or Written Answer (also known as the Questions Book). See also the Business Statement, produced weekly by the Office of the Leader of the House of Commons.

In the House of Lords, future business is set out in Notices and Orders of the Day, along with questions for written answer, forthcoming committee meetings and Bills in progress.
See also Forthcoming Business, produced weekly by the Government Whips Office.

Other Commons Business Papers

A number of other documents are included with the business papers described here, including material relating to private business, statutory instruments, amendment papers for Bills, divisions and early day motions.

Laid before Parliament: Published and presented to Parliament, sometimes as required by law.

Historical records

The Parliamentary Archives hold millions of historical records relating to both Houses of Parliament dating from 1497.

What's in the Archives?

The Archives' holdings include:

Official records of both Houses of Parliament, including Acts, Journals, Hansard, deposited plans and appeal cases.

Other collections relating to Parliament, including the papers of the Lord Great Chamberlain and the Lord President of the Council.

Collections of private political papers and records of political bodies and pressure groups.
Records about the Palace of Westminster, including the papers of architect Charles Barry.
Surviving the 1834 fire

A fire in 1834 destroyed most of the records of the House of Commons, so the bulk of records held on the Commons date from after 1834 (apart from a series of manuscript Journals and minutes that survived). Records of the House of Lords were undamaged and date back to 1497.

Government and Crown records

The Archives do not hold records of government departments or the Crown. These are held by the National Archives.

Contacting and visiting the Archives

Archive Enquiry Services

They can answer simple enquiries over the telephone, but most enquiries should be sent to us by post, fax or e-mail.

If you are telephoning to make a searchroom booking, please also give us your e-mail address if you have one, so we can confirm your appointment by e-mail.

We cannot undertake detailed research for users but we can provide advice about the scope of the records for particular topics. Our Reprographic Service can also supply copies of readily identifiable material, by post or e-mail. We aim to answer all enquiries within 10 working days.

Please ensure you have consulted the following before you send your enquiry:

Frequently Asked Questions
Planning Your Visit
Catalogue
E-mail archives@parliament.uk
Phone +44 (0)20 7219 3074
Fax +44 (0)20 7219 2570
Post Parliamentary Archives, Houses of Parliament, London, SW1A 0PW, United Kingdom

The Archives is open to all members of the UK public and overseas visitors from Monday to Friday, 9.30-5pm.

Planning your visit to the Archives
Planning Your Visit to the Parliamentary Archives
You may wish to print this page and bring it with you for reference.

Admission

Our service is open to everyone. No special letters of introduction are required and no readers' tickets are issued, but we do require photographic proof of identity. We don't charge fees to consult the records.

Visits are by appointment only and you will not be admitted without one. Please contact us in advance of your visit to make an appointment, and give at least two working days' notice. We have a limited number of seats in our searchroom, and are sometimes booked out. Also a few off-site records require ordering with two working days' notice. If we have not confirmed your booking, please do not turn up or you will be turned away.

Please note that all visitors to the Parliamentary Archives searchroom are required to produce photographic identification on request.

Location and Access

Our search room is inside the Palace of Westminster (the Houses of Parliament). The nearest Underground station is Westminster, on the District, Circle and Jubilee Lines. Buses stop near Parliament Square in Victoria Street and in Whitehall. Bus and Underground services provide good connections to the nearest main line railway stations at Victoria, Waterloo and Charing Cross.

There is no parking available at the Houses of Parliament, but there is a public underground car park at Abingdon Green, less than a minute's walk away. The Houses of Parliament are inside the London congestion charging zone.

Access to the Archives is via Black Rod's Garden Entrance, the public entrance nearest to the Victoria Tower on the west front of the Houses of Parliament. The searchroom can be accessed by wheelchair users, but please contact us in advance if you have any specific requirements. You will be security searched on entry to the building.

Opening Hours and Closure Dates

The search room is generally open to members of the public Monday to Friday (Public Holidays excepted) from 9.30 am to 5.00 p.m. We occasionally close for reasons including staff training and media use, so please contact us in advance of your visit to reserve a seat, giving at least two working days' notice.

From 20 May until the 12 July our searchroom hours will be 10am to 4pm. We apologise for any inconvenience this may cause.

Please search our online catalogue Portcullis in advance of your visit if possible, and email us a list of the records you wish to see. We can then fetch them out in advance of your arrival and save you waiting time once you are here. A maximum of twelve items will be produced in advance at one time, at the discretion of the searchroom supervisor. Once you are here, documents can normally be retrieved on request, except between 12.30 pm and 2.00 pm and after 4 pm.

Documents marked as 'Closed' on our online catalogue Portcullis should be requested in advance by email; for further advice on this, please see I want... a file marked on your catalogue as 'Closed'. It is not possible to retrieve closed material on request on the day of a visit.

The Archives search room closes for annual stocktaking in the last two weeks of November (exact dates are advertised near the time). No search room visits are possible during this period. We apologise for the inconvenience.

Facilities at the Archives

The search room supervisor will advise about use of the records and explain the range of catalogues and other finding aids which are available together with works of biographical and parliamentary reference.

Searchers are requested to help safeguard our documentary heritage for the use of future generations by observing the search room regulations for the handling of records. These are set out on the search room table placemats.

Searchers are welcome to use laptop computers (for which there are plug sockets). The use of dictaphones is at the discretion of the supervisor.

There are four PCs for public use in the search room with Internet access available for research purposes (checking of personal email is not allowed). Ethernet connections are not available. However, free wireless internet is available for searchers to use on their own laptops or mobile computers. Ask the search room supervisor for a login and password on your arrival.

Digital cameras are permitted but no flash may be used. There is a fee for use of digital cameras in the searchroom of £5 per day. See our statement on Use of personal technology devices for copying records in the Parliamentary Archives.

Onsite Reprographic services are available for copying and scanning records up to AO size.

Toilets (including one suitable for wheelchair users) and a first aid point are in the vicinity of the search room.

There is a small kitchen area where users may eat their own food. Tea, coffee and drinking water are available, plus a fridge and microwave. Refreshment facilities in the Palace of Westminster are not open to the public but there are various sandwich bars, pubs and restaurants nearby. No food or drink is permitted in the searchroom.

The nearest cash machines are at Westminster tube station, or on Victoria Street. Please be aware that only cash or cheques can be accepted in the search room for copying payments, not credit cards.

Mobile phones should be turned off or switched to silent mode in the searchroom. There is storage for bags and coats but not for large suitcases.

Interested parties can search the Archives' online catalogue, Portcullis, in advance to check a record exists. View Portcullis, the online catalogue

Parliamentary papers

The term parliamentary papers includes:

The working papers of Parliament (many of which are explained in other pages of About Parliament, such as Bills, Hansard, business papers and judgments).

Other papers produced by Parliament and its committees.

Papers presented to Parliament by outside bodies.

Papers produced by Parliament and its committees

Both Houses of Parliament publish documents that result from their work and that of their committees, such as:

- Votes and Proceedings (Commons) and the Minute (Lords) - the formal, authoritative record of the decisions taken by each House.
- Select Committee reports and evidence.
- Register of Members' interests.
- Standing Orders - the rules for conducting business in both Houses.
- Sessional Returns - which includes statistics on the work of the Commons for each parliamentary year.

These papers are published as House of Commons or House of Lords Papers.

Papers presented to Parliament

Many different types of papers are presented to Parliament by bodies outside Parliament - some are then published under Parliament's authority.

Most are presented because the bodies are required to do so either by law or by a decision of Parliament. Others are presented because the government has decided or has previously undertaken to provide the information to Parliament (these papers are called 'Command Papers').

The following are some of the categories of papers that must be presented to Parliament:

- Annual reports of government departments or other bodies and agencies.

- Periodic reports of certain activities or programmes (e.g., Reports of Her Majesty's Inspector of Prisons).
- Reports by the National Audit Office.
- Estimates, accounts and other government financial papers such as the Budget.
- Reports of inquiries into particular events (e.g., the Hutton Inquiry, the Home Office report on the 7/7 London bombings).

Many, but not all, of these papers are published as House of Commons Papers.

Numbering

House of Commons Papers and House of Lords Papers have separate numbering sequences, starting at one in every session. Therefore, papers are referred to in the format: 'HC 507 2000-01' or 'HL Paper 17 2004-05'. Numbers are allocated to HC papers by the Journal Office and to HL papers by the Table Office.

Access to parliamentary papers

Papers directly related to the work of Parliament, including committee publications, standing orders, sessional returns, registers of interests, and some financial publications, are available through the Publications and Records area of the Parliament website.

Publications and Records

The Official Documents website makes available the full texts of House of Commons Papers, which originate in government departments.

Deposited papers

Deposited papers are placed in the Commons or Lords libraries by a government minister, the Speaker of the Commons or the Lord Speaker.

Deposited papers are not presented or laid formally before Parliament. Members of the public can view deposited papers online or receive copies of the papers by writing to the House of Commons Information Office.

Why are deposited papers needed?

A minister will deposit material in both libraries in response to requests for information by MPs or Members of the Lords in the form of parliamentary questions or requests during debates. This means specific information can be made available to Parliament without the need to publish it formally.

What kind of information is deposited?

The type of information in deposited papers can include:

- tables of data

- research reports not intended for formal publication

- diagrams or maps

- exchanges of correspondence.

Deposited papers are held in a joint series by the libraries of both Houses as a set and are numbered chronologically within each calendar year.

Backbench MPs may not deposit items in this series; apart from government ministers, only the Speaker of the House of Commons, the Lord Speaker and MPs acting on behalf of bodies such as the Church Commissioners or the Speaker's Committee on the Electoral Commission, may do so.

How can I view deposited papers?

Deposited papers are public documents. Papers deposited from November 2007 are available to download:

From the Deposited papers database

If a particular deposit is not available electronically, you should write to the House of Commons Information Office, who will make a hard copy available.

How does an MP or Member of the Lords get a deposited paper?

Library staff can email copies of deposited papers on request. MPs and Lords (or their staff) can also ask for a printed copy to be made available in the Libraries. Deposited papers are all indexed on an internal database used by the libraries, which includes links to the full text of the document.

Is there an archive of deposited papers?

The series of deposited papers began in 1832. Older items from the set can be viewed by contacting the Parliamentary Archives.

Government publications (Command Papers)

Government publications presented to Parliament are known as Command Papers. Most but not all Command Papers are published in a numbered series.

Different types of publications

The Command Papers series includes the following types of government publication:

- State Papers - including treaties and international agreements.
- White Papers - government policy initiatives and proposals for legislation.
- Green Papers - government consultation documents.
- Some government responses to Select Committee reports.
- Reports of Royal Commissions and some other Committees of Inquiry.
- Statistics and annual reports of some government bodies.
- Unnumbered Command Papers include statements about gifts or guarantees made by government departments.

Presentation and numbering

Command Papers are government papers. They are presented to Parliament as conveying information or decisions that the government thinks should be drawn to the attention of one or both Houses of Parliament.

The term 'Command' is in the formula carried on the papers: "Presented to Parliament by the Secretary of State for ...by Command of Her Majesty".

The first numbered series of Command Papers was introduced in 1833. The current series is the sixth and began with 'Cm 1' in November 1986. The prefix changes with each series.

Access to government publications

Command Papers are government publications. The Stationery Office (TSO) Official Documents website hosts the full texts of many Command Papers. You can also view Command Papers in person at the Parliamentary Archives.

Official Documents website

Contact the Parliamentary Archives
Other government publications can be found on the websites of individual government departments.

Departments of State and Ministers

Government responses to Select Committee reports are available through the committee pages, either as links to government department websites or as special reports of the committee.

Committee publications
More details about Command papers can be found through the following publications:

Guidance and requirements for laying papers before the House of Commons and their publication
Information about papers ordered to be printed by the House of Commons

Hansard

Hansard is an edited record of what was said in Parliament. It also includes votes, written ministerial statements and written answers to parliamentary questions. The report is published daily covering the preceding day, and is followed by weekly and final versions.

Transcribing and publishing

Members' words are recorded by Hansard reporters and then edited to remove repetitions and obvious mistakes but without taking away from the meaning. Reports of the latest proceedings are published online and updated during the day. The Commons and Lords have separate reports.

The text of Daily Debates in the Commons and Lords are published online the following morning by 6am and is also available in hard copy. Weekly and bound final versions follow, proof-read to eliminate any errors that may have occurred in the original.

Today in the Commons and Lords

When the Commons and Lords are sitting, the reports of the latest proceedings are published about three hours after the live event and updated during the sitting. The following day this becomes the Official Report (Hansard).

Commons debates can be read back until November 1988 and Lords debates until 1995-96 on the Parliament website. Hansard debates from both the Commons and Lords from 1803-2005 can be read on the Historic Hansard website.

Bills v Acts

A Bill is not an Act of Parliament. A Bill becomes an Act if it is approved by the House of Commons and the House of Lords, and is formally agreed to by the reigning monarch (known as the Royal Assent). An Act of Parliament is a law, enforced in all areas of the UK where it is applicable.

Once a Bill becomes an Act of Parliament, it is the responsibility of the appropriate government department to implement it. For example, the Department for Transport would enforce a new law concerning speeding.

Access to current Bills and Acts

Texts of Bills are available on the Bills pages of the Parliament website.
Bills before Parliament

Texts of Acts of Parliament going back to 1988 are hosted on Legislation.gov.uk (National Archives) website. legislation.gov.uk

Access to earlier Bills and Acts

Earlier Bills and Acts that are not available on the Parliament or Legislation.gov.uk website are held in hardcopy by the Parliamentary Archives.

Parliamentary Archives

The Parliamentary Archives provides access to the archives of the House of Lords, the House of Commons and to other records relating to Parliament. We also provide a records management service for both Houses of Parliament.

The Archives is usually open to the public all year round, Monday to Friday, 9.30am to 5.00pm (apart from public holidays).

Judgments: archive

The House of Lords was the UK's highest court of appeal until 30 July 2009. From 1 October 2009, the Supreme Court of the United Kingdom assumed jurisdiction on points of law for all civil law cases in the UK and all criminal cases in England and Wales and Northern Ireland.

Access to judgments since 1996

All House of Lords judgments from 14 November 1996 to 30 July 2009 are available on the Parliament website. They are available in browsable html and print-friendly PDF formats.
House of Lords judgments: archive

Access to judgments prior to 1996

Access to judgments prior to 1996 can be arranged through the Parliamentary Archives. The Archives holds appeal cases and other records of the House of Lords acting in its judicial capacity, dating from 1621.
Parliamentary Archives

Other judgments

The archived House of Lords judgments are the only case law that Parliament holds. For any other court decision you will need to use a legal information service such as the British and Irish Legal Information Institute (BAILII), which is free to access. British and Irish Legal Information Institute (BAILII)

Research material

Parliamentary staff produces research publications to assist members of both Houses in understanding legislation, policy and topical issues.

All parliamentary research aims to be politically impartial and contain factual information. Where opinion is given it is presented as part of a range of opinions to ensure balance.

House of Commons Library Research Papers

House of Commons Library staff compiles these papers for the benefit of Members of Parliament. They are an occasional series of papers, numbered by year and sequence of publication. They usually deal with topics of current interest, science and technology, statistics or the background and potential effect of Bills before Parliament.

Parliamentary and constitutional research

The House of Commons Library organises its research material in this area into the following subjects: central government, constitution, Crown, devolution, elections, Parliament, and political parties.
Read Parliament and constitution research

Parliamentary Office of Science and Technology (POST)

The Parliamentary Office of Science and Technology (POST) is an in-house source of independent and balanced analysis of public policy issues related to science and technology. They publish POST notes (short briefing notes) and longer reports on biological sciences and health, physical sciences and IT, environment and energy, and science policy. (Read POST publications)

House of Lords Library Notes

The House of Lords Library produces briefing papers for the benefit of Members and their personal staff. They are an occasional series of papers covering parliamentary and constitutional issues and Bills before Parliament.

House of Commons

The UK public elects 650 Members of Parliament (MPs) to represent their interests and concerns in the House of Commons. MPs consider and propose new laws, and can scrutinise government policies by asking ministers questions about current issues either in the Commons Chamber or in Committees.

History of government

Why is history important?

Governments are remembered for their leaders and the course they set for their country. The British government has a long and fascinating history, and exploring its past can help us understand how it is run today.

The information here provides a starting point for research. It includes objective factual content and research carried out by independent and civil service historians.

Notable people

52 Past Prime Ministers

Gordon Brown
Tony Blair
Sir John Major
Baroness Margaret Thatcher
James Callaghan
Harold Wilson
Sir Edward Heath
Sir Alec Douglas-Home
Harold Macmillan
Sir Anthony Eden
Sir Winston Churchill
Clement Attlee
Neville Chamberlain
Stanley Baldwin
James Ramsay MacDonald
Andrew Bonar Law
David Lloyd George
Herbert Henry Asquith
Sir Henry Campbell-Bannerman
Arthur James Balfour
Robert Gascoyne-Cecil 3rd Marquess of Salisbury
Archibald Primrose 5th Earl of Rosebery
William Ewart Gladstone
Benjamin Disraeli The Earl of Beaconsfield
Edward Smith Stanley 14th Earl of Derby
Lord John Russell 1st Earl Russell
Henry John Temple 3rd Viscount Palmerston
George Hamilton Gordon Earl of Aberdeen
Sir Robert Peel 2nd Baronet
William Lamb 2nd Viscount Melbourne
Arthur Wellesley 1st Duke of Wellington
Charles Grey 2nd Earl Grey
Frederick Robinson Viscount Goderich
George Canning
Robert Banks Jenkinson Earl of Liverpool
Spencer Perceval
William Bentinck Duke of Portland
William Wyndham Grenville 1st Baron Grenville
William Pitt 'The Younger'
Henry Addington 1st Viscount Sidmouth
William Petty 2nd Earl of Shelburne
Lord Frederick North
Augustus Henry Fitzroy 3rd Duke of Grafton
William Pitt 'The Elder' 1st Earl of Chatham
Charles Watson-Wentworth 2nd Marquess of Rockingham
George Grenville
John Stuart 3rd Earl of Bute

Thomas Pelham-Holles 1st Duke of Newcastle
William Cavendish Duke of Devonshire
Henry Pelham
Spencer Compton 1st Earl of Wilmington
Sir Robert Walpole

Past Chancellors of the Exchequer
20th & 21st centuries

Alistair Darling 2007 to 2010
Gordon Brown 1997 to 2007
Kenneth Clarke 1993 to 1997
Norman Lamont 1990 to 1993
John Major 1989 to 1990
Nigel Lawson 1983 to 1989
Sir Geoffrey Howe 1979 to 1983
Denis Healey 1974 to 1979
Anthony Barber 1970 to 1974
Ian Macleod 1970
Roy Jenkins 1967 to 1970
James Callaghan 1964 to 1967
Reginald Maudling 1962 to 1964
Selwyn Lloyd 1960 to 1962
Derick Heathcoat-Amory 1958 to 1960
Peter Thorneycroft 1957 to 1958
Harold Macmillan 1955 to 1957
Rab Butler 1951 to 1955
Hugh Gaitskell 1950 to 1951
Sir Stafford Cripps 1947 to 1950
Hugh Dalton 1945 to 1947
Sir John Anderson 1943 to 1945
Sir Kingsley Wood 1940 to 1943
Sir John Simon 1937 to 1940
Neville Chamberlain 1931 to 1937
Philip Snowden 1929 to 1931
Winston Churchill 1924 to 1929
Philip Snowden 1924
Neville Chamberlain 1923 to 1924
Stanley Baldwin 1922 to 1923
Sir Robert Horne 1921 to 1922
Austen Chamberlain 1919 to 1922
Bonar Law 1916 to 1919
Reginald McKenna 1915 to 1916
David Lloyd George 1908 to 1915
H. H. Asquith 1905 to 1908
Austen Chamberlain 1903 to 1905
Charles Ritchie 1902 to 1903

19th century

Sir Michael Hicks Beach, Bt 1895 to 1902
Sir William Vernon Harcourt 1892 to 1895
George Goschen 1887 to 1892
Lord Randolph Churchill 1886
Sir William Vernon Harcourt 1886
Sir Michael Hicks Beach, Bt 1885 to 1886
Hugh Childers 1882 to 1885
William Gladstone 1880 to 1882
Sir Stafford Henry Northcote, Bt 1874 to 1880
William Gladstone 1873 to 1874
Robert Lowe 1868 to 1873
George Ward Hunt 1868
Benjamin Disraeli 1866 to 1868

William Gladstone 1859 to 1866
Benjamin Disraeli 1858 to 1859
Sir George Cornewall Lewis, Bt 1855 to 1858
William Gladstone 1852 to 1855
Benjamin Disraeli 1852
Sir Charles Wood 1846 to 1852
Henry Goulburn 1841 to 1846
Francis Baring 1839 to 1841
Thomas Spring Rice 1835 to 1839
Sir Robert Peel, Bt 1834 to 1835
Viscount Althorp 1830 to 1834
Henry Goulburn 1828 to 1830
John Charles Herries 1827 to 1828
The Lord Tenterden 1827
George Canning 1827
Hon. Frederick John Robinson 1823 to 1827
Nicholas Vansittart 1812 to 1823
Spender Perceval 1807 to 1812
Lord Henry Petty 1806 to 1807
William Pitt the Younger 1804 to 1806
Henry Addington 1801 to 1804

18th century
William Pitt the Younger 1783 to 1801
Lord John Cavendish 1783
William Pitt the Younger 1782 to 1783
Lord North 1767 to 1782
Charles Townshend 1766 to 1767
William Dowdeswell 1765 to 1766
George Grenville 1763 to 1765
Sir Francis Dashwood 1762 to 1763
Viscount Barrington 1761 to 1762
Henry Bilson Legge 1757 to 1761
Lord Mansfield 1757
Henry Bilson Legge 1756 to 1757
Sir George Lyttleton 1755 to 1756
Henry Bilson Legge 1754 to 1755
Sir William Lee 1754
Henry Pelham 1743 to 1754
Samuel Sandys 1742 to 1743
Sir Robert Walpole 1721 to 1742
Sir John Pratt 1721
John Aislabie 1718 to 1721
Viscount Stanhope 1717 to 1718
Robert Walpole 1715 to 1717
Sir Richard Onslow 1714 to 1715
Sir William Wyndhan 1713 to 1714
Robert Benson 1711 to 1713
Robert Harley 1710 to 1711
Sir John Smith 1708 to 1710
Henry Boyle 1701 to 1708

16th & 17th centuries
Sir John Smith
1699 to 1701
Charles Montagu
1694 to 1699
Richard Hampden
1690 to 1694
Henry Booth
1689 to 1690
Sir John Ernle
1676 to 1689

Sir John Duncombe
1672 to 1676
Lord Ashley
1661 to 1672
Sir Edward Hyde
1642 to 1646
Sir John Colepepper
1642 to 1643
Lord Cottington
1629 to 1642
Lord Barrett
1628 to 1629
Sir Richard Weston
1621 to 1628
Sir Fulke Greville
1614 to 1621
Sir Julius Caesar
1604 to 1614
Earl of Dunbar
1603 to 1606
Sir John Fortescue
1589 to 1603
Sir Walter Mildmay
1566 to 1589
Sir Richard Sackville
1559 to 1566

Foreign Secretaries
1782 to present
William Hague
2010 to present
David Miliband
2007 to 2010
Margaret Beckett
2006 to 2007
Jack Straw
2001 to 2006
Robin Cook
1997 to 2001
Sir Malcolm Rifkind
1995 to 1997
Douglas Hurd, Lord Hurd of Westwell
1989 to 1995
Sir John Major
1989
Sir Geoffrey Howe, Lord Howe of Aberavon
1983 to 1989
Francis Pym, Lord Pym of Sandy
1982 to 1983
Lord Peter Carrington, Baron Carrington
1979 to 1982
Dr David Owen, Lord Owen of the City of Plymouth
1977 to 1979
Anthony Crosland
1976 to 1977
James Callaghan, Lord Callaghan of Cardiff
1974 to 1976
Sir Alec Douglas-Home, Lord Home of the Hirsel
1970 to 1974
Michael Stewart, Lord Stewart of Fulham
1968 to 1970
George Brown, Lord George-Brown of Jevington
1966 to 1968

Michael Stewart, Lord Stewart of Fulham
1965 to 1966
Patrick Gordon-Walker, Lord Gordon-Walker of Leyton
1964 to 1965
Richard Austen Butler, Lord Butler of Saffron Walden
1963 to 1964
Sir Alec Douglas-Home, Lord Home of the Hirsel
1960 to 1963
John Selwyn Brooke Lloyd, Lord Selwyn-Lloyd
1955 to 1960
Harold Macmillan, Earl of Stockton
1955
Sir Anthony Eden, Earl of Avon
1951 to 1955
Herbert Morrison, Lord Morrison of Lambeth
1951
Ernest Bevin
1945 to 1951
Sir Anthony Eden, Earl of Avon
1940 to 1945
Edward Frederick Lindley Wood, Viscount Halifax
1938 to 1940
Sir Anthony Eden, Earl of Avon
1935 to 1938
Sir Samuel Hoare, Viscount Templewood
1935
Sir John Simon, Viscount Simon
1931 to 1935
Rufus Isaacs, Marquess of Reading
1931
Arthur Henderson
1929 to 1931
Sir Austen Chamberlain
1924 to 1929
James Ramsay MacDonald
1924
George Nathaniel Curzon, Marquess of Kedleston
1919 to 1924
Arthur James Balfour, Earl of Balfour
1916 to 1919
Sir Edward Grey, Viscount Grey of Fallodon
1905 to 1916
Henry Petty-Fitzmaurice, Marquess of Lansdowne
1900 to 1905
Robert Cecil, Marquess of Salisbury
1895 to 1900
John Wodehouse, Earl of Kimberley
1894 to 1895
Archibald Primrose, Earl of Rosebery
1892 to 1894
Robert Cecil, Marquess of Salisbury
1897 to 1892
Stafford Northcote, Earl of Iddesleigh
1886 to 1887
Archibald Primrose, Earl of Rosebery
1886
Robert Cecil, Marquess of Salisbury
1885 to 1886
George Leveson Gower, Earl Granville
1880 to 1885
Robert Cecil, Marquess of Salisbury
1878 to 1880
Lord Edward Stanley, Earl of Derby

1874 to 1878
George Leveson Gower, Earl Granville
1870 to 1874
George Villiers, Earl of Clarendon
1868 to 1870
Lord Edward Stanley, Earl of Derby
1866 to 1868
George Villiers, Earl of Clarendon
1865 to 1866
Lord John Russell, Earl Russell
1859 to 1865
James Harris, Earl of Malmesbury
1858 to 1859
George Villiers, Earl of Clarendon
1853 to 1858
Lord John Russell, Earl Russell
1852 to 1853
James Harris, Earl of Malmesbury
1852
George Leveson Gower, Earl Granville
1851 to 1852
Henry John Temple, Viscount Palmerston
1846 to 1851
George Hamilton Gordon, Earl of Aberdeen
1841 to 1846
Henry John Temple, Viscount Palmerston
1835 to 1841
Arthur Wellesley, Duke of Wellington
1834 to 1835
Henry John Temple, Viscount Palmerston
1830 to 1834
George Hamilton Gordon, Earl of Aberdeen
1828 to 1830
John William Ward, Viscount Dudley and Ward
1827 to 1828
George Canning
1822 to 1827
Robert Stewart, Viscount Castlereagh
1812 to 1822
Richard Wellesley, Marquess Wellesley
1809 to 1812
Henry Bathurst, Earl Bathurst
1809
George Canning
1807 to 1809
Charles Grey, Lord Howick
1806 to 1807
Charles James Fox
1806
Henry Phipps, Lord Mulgrave
1805 to 1806
Dudley Ryder, Lord Harrowby
1804
Robert Banks Jenkinson, Lord Hawkesbury
1801 to 1804
William Wyndham Grenville, Lord Grenville
1791 to 1801
Francis Godolphin Osborne, Marquess of Carmarthen
1783 to 1791
George Nugent Temple Grenville, Earl Temple
1783
Charles James Fox
1783

Thomas Robinson, Lord Grantham
1782 to 1783
Charles James Fox
1782

Government buildings

Number 10 Downing Street is the best known government building, but there are others that play a role in the day-to-day business of government and have had a significant role in our history.

11 Downing Street

Roots of the Treasury

Today's Treasury dates from around the Norman Conquest. Even before 1066, the Anglo-Saxon Treasury collected taxes (including the danegeld, first levied as a tribute to the Vikings to persuade them – sometimes unsuccessfully – to stay away) and controlled expenditure.

The first 'Treasurer' was probably 'Henry the Treasurer', who owned land around Winchester, the site of most royal treasure of both the Anglo-Saxons and the Normans. Henry is referred to in the Domesday Book (a systematic tax assessment of the whole country undertaken by the Treasury) and is believed to have served William the Conqueror as his Treasurer.

The rise of Downing Street

The has been prestigious for centuries, as even before modern government the site was close to Westminster Abbey and later Whitehall Palace. But it was Sir George Downing who made the most of its potential and built the street of houses that bears his name.

In his later career as a property speculator and developer, Downing sought – and won – the permission of King Charles II to name his prestigious new development at St James's Park 'Downing Street'. He died in 1684, 2 years before the houses were completed.

But not all Chancellors have chosen to live in Number 11 Downing Street, just as not all Prime Ministers have chosen to live in Number 10. Although Number 11 was not to become the Chancellor's official residence until 1828, Lord Henry Petty was the first to live there during his few months in office in 1806 and 1807. Those Chancellors who have chosen to live 'above the shop' have enjoyed a house, which is not only part of the nation's history, but also a comfortable and very distinctive home.

Hallway

The hallway is a modest introduction to the style of Number 11. The 18th century lantern illuminating the small room, the characteristic 19th century Vuilliamy grandfather clock and the unassuming marble fireplace reflect the influence of centuries of history on this house. Its status at the centre of the political world is announced by 2 portraits of the 19th century's great political adversaries, Gladstone and Disraeli, on opposite walls.

Sitting room and study

Past the hallway, and across the corridor, which connects the 3 official residences, is a sitting room where the Chancellor holds occasional informal meetings. In the recent past it has also been the location for a Budget tradition – the broadcast that is the Chancellor's direct address to the nation on the evening of the Budget Day. Nowadays the broadcasts are likely to be recorded in other parts of the house and have even, on good days, been filmed in the gardens.

The adjoining study is where the Chancellor of the Exchequer works on the contents of its ministerial boxes, amid further reminders of the building's political heritage. Disraeli and Gladstone feature again, although this time as porcelain caricatures.

State dining room

The ground floor sitting room also connects to perhaps the most architecturally significant room in Number 11 – the dining room, a long oak-panelled room designed by the renowned 18th century architect Sir John

Soane. Best known for his designs for the Bank of England, Soane created a bold and imaginative room with a spectacular vaulted ceiling, decorated with elegant mouldings.

He also devised an imaginative method of illuminating the long room, making as much use as possible of natural light by designing long, narrow skylights to run the length of the room between the ceiling and walls. The ceiling therefore remains an impressive and uninterrupted span, but daylight can still pour down the walls thanks to the innovative light-wells.

The Soane Dining Room is used nowadays for meetings such as business breakfasts with heads of industry and finance. As with the other rooms used for official entertaining, the walls are decorated with selections from the government art collection, which are changed regularly.

State drawing room

The room most regularly used for formal occasions is the State Room, which runs the entire width of Number 11, illuminated by a wall of high windows which look out over the shared gardens of the Downing Street houses and beyond into St James's Park.

The State Room has been recently refurbished following an earlier restoration in the 1960s, restoring the hardwood floor, removing wall lights and replacing faded wall coverings to create a bright, airy and adaptable space. The room can now be used as readily for conference-style meetings as it can for official receptions and parties.

Each end of the room features a grand 18th century marble fireplace flanked by 2 ornate mirrors. The westernmost wall also features 2 of Number 11's finest treasures – 2 antique black and gold lacquered Chinese cabinets.

The walls are covered with warm and creamy cotton damask, as are the curtains on the long wall overlooking the gardens.

Staircase

The staircase leading to the first floor landing is an ascent through the history of British politics. The walls of the staircase are covered with political cartoons, caricatures and engravings of past Chancellors of the Exchequer. It is a tradition that each Chancellor gets to choose the cartoon he wants to represent him.

Not all Chancellors have chosen to live in Number 11, just as some Prime Ministers have chosen not to live in Number 10, but all of the memorable holders of the office are represented here.

Budget box

The front door of Number 11 will always be associated with the countless Budget Day photocalls when the Chancellor holds up the red Budget box containing his speech before he makes his way to the House of Commons.

Since the 1860s, the Budget box has almost invariably been the one known as the Gladstone box, now displayed in the lobby of HM Treasury. The use of the Gladstone box became one of several Budget Day traditions (another is that only the Chancellor is allowed to drink alcohol in the House of Commons – and only during his Budget speech).

James Callaghan used a new box during his time as Chancellor in the 1970s, but the frail Gladstone box was later restored to duty once more. In 1997, Gordon Brown marked his first Budget by breaking from tradition – using a new box made by 4 young apprentices from his Dunfermline constituency and bringing the 4 to the steps of Number 11 to share his photocall.

Sir John Soane

One of the most revered architects Britain has ever produced, Sir John Soane (1753 to 1837) was the perfect choice to design what is arguably Number 11's finest room: the dining room which now bears his name.

Soane's reputation in his own lifetime was based largely on his designs for grand country houses, where he brought together the popular taste for classical design with a more modern feel for light and space.

Shallow domes, clean ornamentation and ingenious lighting effects, often from above, characterised his work. His greatest work was on a much larger scale – the design of the Bank of England. It was this formidable reputation as designer of some of Britain's grandest homes and also the heart of its financial community, which made Soane the obvious choice to design the dining room of 11 Downing Street in 1825.

Soane was at the same time also responsible for the state dining room of 10 Downing Street, and although Number 11's is much smaller, it is no less impressive for that. The light-wells, which allow daylight to fall on the long panelled walls of the dining room, are a characteristically imaginative solution to the problem of getting natural light into a deep room.

King Charles Street

A brief history of the FCO

The main Foreign Office building is in King Charles Street, London. It was built by George Gilbert Scott in partnership with Matthew Digby Wyatt.

The first Secretary of State for Foreign Affairs was appointed in March 1782, but the first purpose-built Foreign Office was not begun until 1861. It was completed in 1868 as part of the new block of government offices which included the India Office and later (1875) the Colonial and Home Offices.

George Gilbert Scott was responsible for the overall classical design of these offices but he had an amicable partnership with Matthew Digby Wyatt, the India Office's Surveyor, who designed and built the interior of the India Office.

Scott designed the new Foreign Office as 'a kind of national palace or drawing room for the nation' with the use of rich decoration to impress foreign visitors. The same was true of Wyatt's India Office. The Colonial and Home Offices, however, were seen purely as working buildings and their interior decoration, by contrast, was 'as plain as was compatible with a major department of state'.

During the twentieth century, the impact of 2 world wars and the growing complexity of public business and international affairs led to severe overcrowding within the buildings. Lack of money during post 1945 austerity Britain and distaste for anything Victorian helped to reduce grandeur to squalor, and many of the fine areas were lost from sight behind false ceilings and plasterboard partitions.

In the 1960s, as part of the grandiose plans for a new Whitehall, it was decided to demolish Scott's buildings and to erect completely new offices on the same site.

Lack of money and a public outcry, which led to the offices being designated as a Grade 1 Listed Building eventually resulted in the rejection of demolition in favour of restoration.

The rolling programme of restoration and refurbishment carried out between 1984 and 1997 not only brought the Fine Rooms and other public areas back to life but produced 25% extra usable space for far less than the cost of demolition and rebuilding.

Fine Rooms

Durbar Court

Durbar Court, at the heart of the India Office, is the masterpiece of Matthew Digby Wyatt.

Originally open to the sky, the 4 sides of the court are surrounded by 3 storeys of columns and piers supporting arches. The ground floor doric and first floor ionic columns are of polished red Peterhead granite, while the top floor Corinthian columns are of grey Aberdeen granite. The pavement is of Greek, Sicilian and Belgian marble.

The court was first used in 1867 for a reception for the Sultan of Turkey. The name 'Durbar Court' dates only from 1902 when some of the coronation celebrations of King Edward VII were held there.

India Office Council Chamber

The India Office Council Chamber is the work of the architect Matthew Digby Wyatt, who was responsible for designing and decorating the interior of the new India Office building from 1861 to 1868.

The Secretary of State for India and his council met in this chamber to discuss policy affecting the subcontinent, and many important decisions were taken here between 1868 and 1947. The significance of this room is emphasised by its height and size. There is also lavish use of gilding, and Wyatt linked old with new by transferring to it the great doors and doorcases, the furniture and the great marble chimneypiece from the former Director's Court Room in East India House at Leadenhall Street in the City.

The chimneypiece and overmantel were commissioned from the Flemish sculptor Michael Rysbrack and date from 1730. The centre panel represents Britannia, seated by the sea, receiving the riches of the East Indies. Behind stand 2 female figures symbolising Asia and Africa, the former leading a camel, the latter a lion. On the right, a river god represents the Thames, while in the background ships are going off to sea.

The splendidly carved and ornamented chairs and tables which used to furnish the chamber are too precious for everyday use in the present office, and have been transferred to the India Office Library (now part of the British Library) at St Pancras. Original furnishings which still remain in the chamber are the early 19th century mahogany chairs, newspaper stand and the chairman's seat bearing the East India Company's crest of a rampant lion within a medallion.

In 1867, before the new India Office was completed, a magnificent reception was held in its courtyard (now known as Durbar Court) for the Sultan of Turkey, who was in Britain for a state visit. The Council Chamber, decorated with silken draperies and regimental standards, was transformed into a dining room for the Sultan, the Prince of Wales and the most important guests, and it was reported that every item on the tables was made of gold.

When the India Office ceased to exist as a separate department of state in 1947, its building was taken over by the Foreign Office, which was in need of extra accommodation. The Council Chamber and its environs became the home of the greatly enlarged German Department, and 1948 it was the venue for the 1948 Three-Power Conference on Germany. In 1950 some preliminary discussions relating to the first meeting of the NATO deputies were held in the India Office Council Chamber and the archives of the secretariat were kept nearby.

The Council Chamber, together with Durbar Court, was one of the earliest fine areas to be restored in the course of the first phase (1984 to 1987) of the FCO's rolling programme of refurbishment.

Grand reception room of the Locarno suite

The Locarno Suite consists of 3 rooms originally designed by Scott for diplomatic dinners, conferences and receptions. The largest room, looking out on to the Main Quadrangle, was originally designated the Cabinet Room, but seems never to have been used as such in the 19th century. The adjacent Dining Room was also used for meetings but is best remembered as the room used by Lord Salisbury in preference to the Secretary of State's room. Beyond is the Conference Room with its gilded ceiling supported by metal beams covered by majolica decorations.

During the First World War an acute shortage of space within the Foreign Office led to the occupation of the suite by the Contraband Department. This was not a success. The original decoration by Clayton and Bell had become very shabby, and the rooms were too dark and draughty for daily use. It was impossible to clean the original stencilling, and the rooms needed redecoration.

Before any decision was made, the Locarno Treaties, designed to reduce strife and tension in Europe, were initialled at Locarno in Switzerland in October 1925. The delegates agreed to come to London for the formal signature of the treaties and the only possible venue for the ceremony was Scott's Reception Suite in the Foreign Office. The Reception and Dining Rooms were cleared of their occupants, and the walls adorned with royal portraits to hide the shabby decorations. The formal signing of the accords on 1 December 1925 was an impressive occasion, recorded, according to The Times, by journalists from half the world 'wedged in tiers' behind a barrier half-way down the room, and by 'photographers and cinematographers…perched high up in nooks above the windows'.

Following Chamberlain's instructions that the suite should be redecorated after the ceremony, the Royal Fine Art Commission was asked to advise. A subcommittee headed by Sir Reginald Blomfield recommended that the original Victorian stencilling should be removed from the 2 largest rooms in favour of repainting in shades of parchment colour. The walls of the middle room were covered in crimson silk stretched on battens, and were hung with portraits of famous Foreign Secretaries. The 3 rooms were then renamed the 'Locarno Suite', as a memorial to a supposed diplomatic triumph promising an era of international co-operation. Many conferences and diplomatic functions took place there until the outbreak of the Second World War.

Thereafter, however, the chandeliers were shrouded and the Locarno Suite became the home of the cyphering branch of Communications Department. Renewed lack of office space after 1945 led to the division of these rooms into cubicles under false ceilings, and in these makeshift plasterboard hutches, the legal advisers and others worked.

All this changed in the late 1980s, when the FCO's rolling programme of restoration and refurbishment reached the area surrounding the suite. The plasterboard shroud was stripped from the second largest room of the suite to reveal once more the coffered ceiling, pilasters crowned with Corinthian capitals, and quadrants supporting gilded iron beams. Circular majolica plaques bearing the national arms or emblems of 20 countries further ornament these quadrants, and the original stencilled design has been reinstated on the walls. The Locarno Conference Room reverted to its original purpose in summer 1990, while the restoration of the Reception and Dining Rooms proceeded between 1990 and 1992.

In the Dining Room, the removal of the plasterboard and the very dirty red silk hangings uncovered the original stencilled decoration in olive and gold, with red and gold borders. Although faded and damaged, its survival ensured that an exact copy could be superimposed on the walls, restoring the room's authentic Victorian splendour. Two new doors, matching exactly Scott's originals, give direct access into the adjacent former India Office.

The restoration of the Reception Room involved much painstaking detective work. The great barrel-vaulted ceiling was known to have borne an elaborately detailed design of classical figures and signs of the zodiac, but it was feared that the decorators in the 1920s had removed every last scrap of colour and gilding using pumice stone. Close examination nevertheless revealed that one section had simply been painted over, and scientific analysis of the remains below enabled the ceiling to be reinstated according to Clayton and Bell's original design. The marble fireplaces throughout the suite, like those in the Secretary of State's Room, date from the 18th century and were transferred from the old Foreign Office.

Following the restoration, the entire Locarno Suite is once more available for conferences and ministerial and government functions.

Lancaster House

Introduction

The Foreign & Commonwealth Office manage Lancaster House. Situated close to Buckingham Palace, this historic house offers a magnificent setting, a prestigious central location and first-class facilities for all types of events and hospitality.

Steeped in political history and magnificently preserved, Lancaster House has a wide range of rooms and a large garden – the ideal place in central London for meetings, conferences and entertaining.

It is the perfect backdrop for any occasion from an intimate dinner to an international summit. The house also has a glamorous side. It has been used for receptions and shows during London Fashion Week, and in 2007 various rooms were used in the filming of The Young Victoria, Disney's National Treasure Book of Secrets, and BBC/HBO's production of Churchill at War.

History

Commissioned in 1825 by the 'grand old' Duke of York, York House – as it was then known – was a hub of social and political life throughout the 19th century.

When the Duke died, the lease was purchased by the then Marquess of Stafford (later the first Duke of Sutherland) whose family occupied the house from 1829 until 1913. The Sutherlands' liberal politics and love of the arts attracted many distinguished guests, including factory reformer Lord Shaftesbury, anti-slavery author Harriet Beecher Stowe and Italian nationalist leader Garibaldi.

Almost as influential as the visitors were the décor, which was to set the fashion for London reception rooms for nearly a century. The mainly Louis XIV interiors created a stunning backdrop for the Sutherlands' impressive collection of paintings and objets d'art, many of which can still be seen in the house today.

In 1913, Lord Leverhulme, a Lancastrian, bought the lease for the nation and Stafford House became Lancaster House. At one time home to the London Museum, the house has been an important centre for government hospitality ever since.

Location

Lancaster House is 5 minutes walk from Green Park underground station.

Lancaster House,
Stable Yard,
St James's,
London SW1A 1BB

Ministry of Defence, Whitehall

MOD Main building

By the turn of the twentieth century some government offices were already established in several old Georgian houses in the area of Whitehall Gardens on the east side of Whitehall.

In 1909 it was decided to erect a new building primarily for the Department of Trade. The site was to extend over other parts of Whitehall Gardens and also on ground running down to the Embankment, but opposition to this plan led to the agreement that the southern building line should be that of Whitehall Court and the National Liberal Club, thus conceding some 10,000 square feet.

The architect selected was Mr E Vincent Harris, who won a national competition to design a new building for occupation by a number of Government departments. Planned as a single block faced in Portland stone, some 128 feet high and 570 feet long with a depth of 205 feet widening to 300 feet, it had four internal blocks with ten storeys and three large internal courts; the two main facades faced Whitehall and the Victoria Embankment. The estimated cost was some £5 million.

However, construction was delayed by the First World War and then by the inter-war depression, so that it was not until 1938 that the demolition of the houses in Whitehall Gardens began. Major building operations were then halted during the Second World War, except for work on two underground citadels which continued until 1942, albeit with a reduced labour force.
Although the Georgian houses in Whitehall Gardens were to be demolished, five rooms from 'Pembroke House', 'Cromwell House' and 'Cadogan House' were to be dismantled and incorporated as Conference Rooms (known today as 'Historic Rooms') on the third and fourth floors of the new building.

In addition, following a request from Queen Mary in 1938 and a promise in Parliament, provision was made for the preservation of the Wine Cellar, the only substantial part of the old 'Whitehall Palace' that remained after the disastrous fire of 1698 and a fine example of a Tudor brick-vaulted roof some 70 feet long and 30 feet wide. However the existing position of the Cellar, used in the years immediately prior to the demolition of 'Cadogan House' which surrounded it, as a luncheon club for Ministry of Transport staff, was found to interfere not just with the plan for the new building but also with the proposed route for Horse Guards Avenue. Accordingly, once building was resumed after the war, work was set in hand to relocate the whole Cellar into the new building itself, moving it both some nine feet to the west and nearly nineteen feet deeper. This major operation was carried out without significant damage to the structure and it now rests safe within the basement of the new building.

In this immediate post-war period, work recommenced in earnest and by 1951 the north part of the building (known as the New Government Offices) was ready for the Board of Trade. Statues of 'Earth' and 'Water' sculpted by Sir Charles Wheeler were placed over the main north door. These were meant to be complemented by similar figures to represent 'Air' and 'Fire' at the south end, but in the event these were not incorporated when this part of the building was handed over to the Air Ministry in 1958/59.

Although the building's appearance was praised in the Building Magazine in its September 1951 issue, the architectural historian Nicholas Pevsner was less complimentary: he called it a 'monument of tiredness'. (5)

In 1964, a requirement for a single, large building was created by the merger of the three Service Ministries and the formation of the unified Ministry of Defence. The new Government Building in Whitehall was considered most suitable; with the move of the Board of Trade to Victoria, the Building was free for sole occupancy by the new Ministry of Defence (MOD) and became thereby the 'Main Building'.

After 50 years, the Building was refurbished to provide modern, fit for purpose, office accommodation for MOD staff in London and has been occupied since the end of 2004.

1 Horse Guards

Introduction

New office accommodation for the Treasury at 1 Horse Guards Road (1HGR), Whitehall, was opened by Alan Greenspan, former Chairman of the United States Federal Reserve Board on 25 September 2002. The increased space available in the new building enabled all Treasury staff to work in the same building for the first time in over 50 years.

This major step forward in working conditions and working methods for Treasury staff was achieved through a complete refurbishment of the western end of the building known as Government Offices Great George St (GOGGS).

Government Offices Great George Street (GOGGS): a history

The Treasury has been based at GOGGS in Whitehall since 1940.

The royal treasure was originally located in Winchester, and was moved to the Whitehall area following the Norman Conquest. The Treasury then operated from the Exchequer Receipt Office in Westminster Cloisters until the Restoration in 1660.

On ascending to the throne Charles II, perhaps wanting to keep a close eye on his finances, allocated it rooms in Whitehall Palace. This consisted of a number of timber-framed buildings grouped around formal gardens, originally built in 1529 by Henry VIII.

In 1698 a huge blaze, caused by a servant airing some linen too close to the fire, destroyed all but the Banqueting House (built by Inigo Jones for Charles I) which still stands on Whitehall today, and Cardinal Wolsey's wine cellar which is now under the Ministry of Defence building.

Following the fire, the homeless Treasury moved to Henry VIII's Cockpit (near today's Horse Guards Parade). Cock fighting had ceased there under the Tudors but the building was used as a theatre and as chambers for members of the Royal Household.

In 1734 a new Treasury was built by William Kent, which still stands on Horse Guards today. The Treasury continued to occupy this building, and expanded into a new Treasury building designed by John Soane, until both buildings were severely damaged by bombs in 1940.

Since then, GOGGS has been the department's headquarters, housing staff and ministers, including the Chancellor of the Exchequer.

The building of GOGGS

GOGGS was designed and built between 1898 and 1917. It stands on the site of a number of narrow old streets cleared to make way for the building. Construction was in 2 phases. The Parliament Street (Whitehall) end was built first, completed in 1908. The aim was to build light, open-plan offices so offices were built around the perimeter walls of the building and around three large courtyards, while corridors were placed beside light-wells. An entrance on to the park was added in the second building phase, the St James' Park end, between 1910 and 1917. In order to maximise floor space, offices were arranged either side of dark internal corridors – the opposite of what had been intended.

The building is an island site bounded by Parliament Street, Great George Street, Horse Guards Road and King Charles Street. The principal architect was John Brydon, who was selected by the Minister of Works after a competition. Brydon's early works include the Elizabeth Garrett Anderson Memorial Hospital, Chelsea Town Hall, and the Victoria Art Gallery in Bath and an extension to the Bath Pump Room. In Bath, Brydon made use of the local stone – a feature he repeated in GOGGS, cladding it in Portland stone.

The large circular court in the middle of the building is derived from Inigo Jones' design for a new Whitehall Palace (never built), and is a very distinctive piece of architecture. Brydon died before completion of the project and Sir Henry Tanner, the government's Chief Architect of Works, took over. The architectural merit of the building was compromised by this change: in 1910 the Architectural Review said: "the intrusion of another hand less inspired than the original designer is plainly evident." But the building has some architectural merit – it's now Grade II* listed.

Other notable features of the building are the central courtyard, the main conference room overlooking Whitehall and the Chancellor's old office.

GOGGS was originally called the New Public Offices, as opposed to the Old Public Offices – now the Foreign Office – next door. It was home to the Board of Education, the Local Government Board and the local Ministry of Works Office.

Local people queued along the ground floor corridor for inoculations at the Public Health Office. The building has housed a number of departments besides the Treasury, including parts of the Foreign Office, the Northern Ireland Office, the National Investment and Loans Office and the Ministry of Housing and Local Government.

The Cabinet War Rooms

In the build–up to the Second World War, the government began looking for a strong basement in which a map room and a Cabinet Room could be constructed without major alterations.

The basement of GOGGS was chosen, not only because it was convenient for Downing Street, but because the concrete frame used in phase 2 would help prevent the collapse of the building should it receive a direct hit from a bomb. Initially, only a few rooms were commandeered but when Horse Guards was bombed on October 14, 1940, wrecking parts of 10 Downing Street, all Churchill's staff moved into GOGGS.

Within months, the departments moved to the basement included the Air Ministry and their main War Room. The Joint Intelligence Chiefs also occupied basement rooms, as did the people responsible for the D-Day Landings and associated deception plans and the Air Ministry Photographic Department.

To protect the basement, a thick bombproof concrete slab was constructed within the rooms at sub-ground floor level, and a large torpedo net was slung across the western courtyard to catch falling bombs. Air was filtered through a series of vents and ducts to guard against poisonous gases.

Hillsborough Castle

Hillsborough Castle is the official residence of Her Majesty the Queen in Northern Ireland, and also the residence of the Secretary of State for Northern Ireland.

Hillsborough Castle is a golden-orange ashlar, 18th century mansion house built in the 1770s by Wills Hill, first Marquis of Downshire. The building was remodelled in the mid-19th century and early 20th century to its present form. The present state entrance is formed by a single storey shallow portico of 4 pairs of coupled ionic columns.

The castle was the principle seat of the Marquis of Downshire for over 200 years before passing into public ownership in 1922 when it became home to the governors of Northern Ireland. Now the residence for the Secretary of State for Northern Ireland, it is a 'working' building, serving as the venue for official royal and state functions.

The castle is set in 96 acres of ornamental grounds, much of which was developed from the 1760s onwards. The different styles and eras of development are still distinguishable and although not large, the grounds offer significant contrasts of woodland, waterways, and formal and informal gardens with trimmed lawns and meadows as well as specimen trees and rare plants.

Hillsborough Castle is open to the public each Saturday and Sunday from early April until late September, offering guided tours of the house and gardens. Group tours of the house and gardens can be arranged during the week, throughout the year, subject to the castle diary.

Rooms in Hillsborough Castle

State Entrance
The state entrance is formed by a single storey shallow portico of 4 pairs of coupled ionic columns. The double doors lead into a grand hall, the focal point of which is the newly re-instated fireplace with a marble

chimneypiece designed by the architect James Wyatt (1746 to 1813). Sitting either side of the fireplace are the 2 silver plated spades used by members of the royal family when planting ceremonial trees.

Mounted on the wall above the doors are the antlers of an Irish elk, discovered by a peat cutter around Peatlands Park outside Portadown. On the wall, either side of the doors leading to the Candlestick Hall are two paintings of the castle and surrounding village by the artist Marcus May. These were presented to the people of Northern Ireland by Lord Ballyedmond to celebrate Her Majesty the Queen's Diamond Jubilee.

Candlestick Hall
The Candlestick Hall was the point in the house where candles were collected before retiring for the night in the 18th century. Today this is where members of the royal family and visiting dignitaries sign the visitor's book. The panels around the walls of this room are made from hand painted wallpaper by Joseph Dufour, and depict scenes from Cervantes' Don Quixote and date from the early 19th century.

Dufour started making wallpaper in Macon, France before moving to Paris in the early 1800s. The Cervantes wallpaper may have been made towards the end of his life as he died in 1827. The wallpaper is grisaille (tones of grey) and by Dufour standards very plain. These were bought in Paris by Major Charles Dunlop in 1820 and brought to Edenderry House, Ballylesson, County Down until acquired for Hillsborough Castle from his great granddaughter Sheila Denton in 1989.

The mid 20th century Italian crystal chandelier was originally in the Old Speaker's House in Stormont and was installed in Hillsborough Castle in 2008.

Small dining room (Red Room)
This room is called the Red Room as the walls are lined with a red damask fabric. This room looks out onto the Granville garden and the largest Rhododendron in Europe (a title held in the Guinness Book of Records). In this room are various pieces of furniture and objets d'art, such as the late George III mahogany and chequer-lined bow-fronted sideboard with brass railed superstructure which was left behind by one of the Governors of Northern Ireland, the Duke of Abercorn.

Over the fireplace is a carved gilt wood over mantel of Chinese, Chippendale design, which would have been fashionable in the late 18th century. Between the windows is a Regency kingwood commode with cast ormolu feet in the style of Louis XV with a moulded red and white marble top. The dining table is mahogany topped with an ebony inlay with a suite of Chippendale style seats with red fabric, which matches the walls.

The floor is covered by an Indian carpet of Ziegler design, a pattern of trelliswork with flower heads. The cut glass chandelier is George III style, the faceted baluster stem with moulded corona has two tiers of scrolled branches suspended with pear shaped lustre pendants. Also in this room is a section of underground pipe used for distributing water in Belfast from 1682 to 1837. This was presented to another of the Governors of Northern Ireland, Lord Erskine, by the water commissioners in 1966.

State Dining Room
As with the state entrance the fireplace in this room has been re-instated. A marble chimney-piece by the architect James Payne (1717 to 1789) was installed in August 2012 and the room redecorated in various shades of slate. The dining table is George IV Honduras mahogany with reeded end sections and can seat 32 when fully extended, the accompanying chairs are George III style mahogany with pierced vase-shaped splats.

Between the windows is a pair of gilt wood and gesso console tables with marble bow front tops and hoofed pad feet above which hang a pair of gilt wood pier mirrors with stylised shells and scrolled surmounts. Above the George III mahogany barrel fronted sideboard is a portrait of Lord Arthur Hill in military uniform (artist unknown), second son of the 2nd marquis who became Baron Sandys on the death of his mother in 1846.

During official dinners crystal from Tyrone Crystal is used. This is based on the 'Hillsborough' design based on the style of 18th century glass from Edward's factory in Belfast. The place card holders used are sterling silver representations of the Giant's Causeway. The pantry and serving doors are shielded by mid 18th century Spanish leather four-fold screens.

Throne Room
This room has various uses from citizenship ceremonies to charity musical evenings. The walls are adorned with a green damask fabric with various works of art on loan from the Schorr Collection on show.

On the walls between the windows are George III style gilt wood oval mirrors with carved gilt wood demi-une side tables with marble tops beneath. A pair of carved gilt wood 'throne' chairs made for Hillsborough Castle in the 1920s sit on a dais. These chairs are based on a design of chair made for George IV's visit to Ireland (presently in Malahide Castle).

Behind the throne is gilt thread and silk armorial worked with Royal Arms made by the Belfast College of Needlework in 1937. A Bechstein of Berlin rosewood grand piano with gilt wood piano stool (dating from George II) sits to the side of the dais. The carpet in this room was made in Egypt to a Persian hand-woven design of stylised flowers.

Staircase Hall
This room, like the State Entrance, is painted with a trompe l'oeil effect bringing the sandstone from the outside in. Against one wall is a Regency rosewood and gilt metal mounted console table, the rectangular top above a frieze mounted with floral wreaths and anthemions on gilt wood lotus carved scrolled supports. Against another stands a George III mahogany coffer with hinged domed top and brass bailed handles on ogee bracket feet.

As you proceed up the staircase 3 armorials painted on silk are hanging. They are from 3 of George III's 15 children:

Duke of Kent (died 1820) - the father of Queen Victoria
Princess Augusta (died 1840)
King George IV (died 1830)
These were draped on their coffins while lying in state in the Chapel Royal at Windsor and were acquired from the Hobart family, the Earls of Buckinghamshire. The carpets in this hall and staircase were made at the Ulster Carpet Mills.

State Drawing Room
In the State Drawing Room the fireplace has been re-instated, enabling the burning of logs from the estate. This chimneypiece dates from the second half of the 18th century and was brought from a house in Mountjoy Square, Dublin and installed in the castle during the late 1980s. The French windows overlook the Jubilee garden and to the left along the south terrace to the Greek temple.

The State Drawing Room has a very intimate feel with photographs of Her Majesty Queen Elizabeth II and other members of the royal family during the many visits to the province.

Among the many photographs there are pictures of visiting dignitaries such as Hilary Rodham Clinton (visiting with the then Secretary of State Mo Mowlam) and President of Ireland, Mary McAleese (8 December 2005 during the first meeting between Heads of State for the United Kingdom and Ireland to take place on Irish soil).

The room is furnished with many George III and Regency pieces in Honduras mahogany and rosewood. The curtains are gold silk damask with pelmet and tie backdating from around 1830. The gilt brass chandelier which hangs in the centre of the room in Louis XVI style from the early 20th century – this was originally hung in the Russian Embassy, London.

There is also a silver christening cup and spoon given to the castle by Rose Granville Carson in 2008. During the winter of 1946 to 1947 while the Earl and Countess of Granville were journeying to America, Mr Carson, the chief engineer of the ship, received a cablegram informing him of the birth of his daughter. On hearing this Countess asked that she be called Rose Granville after her and said she would come and act as godmother at the baptism which was held in Kells Presbyterian church.

Exiting the Drawing Room into Lady Grey's Sitting Room there is a mahogany cased grand piano by Danemann, coupled with an early Victorian gilt wood duet stool of Italian design with a tapestry rectangular top.

Lady Grey's Sitting Room
The mahogany secretaire with associated bookcase top (situated facing the window) is reputed to have been made for the Britannic (the sister ship of the Titanic) which sank in the Aegean in 1915.

The Britannic never sailed as a passenger ship, she was stripped out and went to sea as a hospital ship during the First World War. The George III mahogany bookcase with moulded cornice and glazed doors opposite were originally made for the castle but went by marriage to the Montgomery family.

The Montgomery family was from Rosemount House in Greyabbey – the bookcase was purchased for the castle in the late 1980s.

Hillsborough Castle gardens
The small park was created by the Hill family, laid out in an informal style. The house was built on the highest ground and looks over lawns with scattered planting of trees and shrubs while in the distance is a more thickly planted area bordering a stream which runs through the grounds. Formal elements were introduced by 1856 and today the terraces are embellished with mixed borders, planted with herbaceous perennials and shrubs. Throughout the grounds are exotic plants, mature specimens and modern commemorative trees.

Richhill Gates
For Her Majesty the Queen's Diamond Jubilee, work was carried out at the Richhill Gates and completed for Her Majesty's visit to Northern Ireland in June 2012. This means that any subsequent royal visitors to the castle can enter via the gates to the State Entrance of the castle.

Ossian
The rotunda in front of the State Entrance is grassed with a sandstone plinth as its centrepiece supporting a heroic-scale bust of Scotto-Irish bard Ossian, son of Fingal. Ossian is seen directing his blind gaze northwards to the high Ulster headlands, the sea beyond and the Scottish Highlands further still. He looks across waters that do not divide, but unite people, just as he surveys a span of time in which various traditions and styles, ancient and modern are seen to meld.

Yew Tree Walk
By 1895 the old line of the Moira Road had been transformed into a dramatic yew walk.

Lady Alice Temple
A domed temple constructed in 1880 and containing a circular seat behind a screen of Ionic columns. This temple was named after Lady Alice Maria Hill, Countess of Bective.

Ice House
The entrance to the Ice House is a large rustic arch of rounded sandstone giving way to a vaulted tunnel and brick lined coned store. A fernery has been established around it, which includes several thriving tree ferns.

Pinetum
Amongst some excellent specimens of pines, spruces and firs is a commemorative Pinus radiata, planted in 1872.

Cromlyn Ruin
This late 18th century sham ruin of standing stones and lintel is intended to represent the earlier Christian Church of Cromlyn. The original chapel dates to 7th century.

Lime Tree Walk
This walk is approximately 150 years old. It has a moss path that is soft in contrast to the crisp gravel of the Yew Tree Walk. During early spring this walk is a multitude of primroses, bluebells and wood anemone.

Quaker Burial Ground
The Quaker Burial Ground is what remains of a former Quaker Meeting House and today it is marked by a hedged enclosure planted with rows of Irish yew.

Jubilee Garden
The Jubilee Garden, previously named the 'Sundial Garden' and laid out in rose beds to the south façade of the castle, was re-designed to celebrate Her Majesty's Diamond Jubilee in 2012. A new sandstone plinth was erected for the sundial commemorating John Lewis-Crosbie, first Chairman of the Hillsborough Castle Advisory Committee and the beds were planted with geometric topiary in an Italian style.

Documents and records

The National Archives is preserving UK government information from letters and treaties to web pages Cabinet papers. You can search the archive, or browse the themed collections.

You can also explore the Government Art Collection online, which contains over 13,500 works of art, mainly from British artists.

http://www.nationalarchives.gov.uk/webarchive/

Printed in Great Britain
by Amazon.co.uk, Ltd.,
Marston Gate.